Metropolitan College of NY
Library - 7th Floor
60 West Street
New York, NY 10006

Rhetorical Healing

SUNY series in Feminist Criticism and Theory
Michelle A. Massé, editor

Rhetorical Healing
The Reeducation of Contemporary Black Womanhood

Tamika L. Carey

Cover image: "The Better Half" by Kevin Okeith, oil on canvas. © Okeith Design.

Published by State University of New York Press, Albany

© 2016 State University of New York

All rights reserved

Printed in the United States of America

No part of this book may be used or reproduced in any manner whatsoever without written permission. No part of this book may be stored in a retrieval system or transmitted in any form or by any means including electronic, electrostatic, magnetic tape, mechanical, photocopying, recording, or otherwise without the prior permission in writing of the publisher.

For information, contact State University of New York Press, Albany, NY
www.sunypress.edu

Production, Jenn Bennett
Marketing, Fran Keneston

Library of Congress Cataloging-in-Publication Data

Names: Carey, Tamika L., 1978– author.
Title: Rhetorical healing : the reeducation of contemporary Black womanhood / Tamika L. Carey.
Description: Albany, NY : State University of New York Press, [2016] | Series: SUNY series in feminist criticism and theory | Includes bibliographical references and index.
Identifiers: LCCN 2016007284 (print) | LCCN 2016014136 (ebook) | ISBN 9781438462431 (hardcover : alk. paper) | ISBN 9781438462448 (e-book)
Subjects: LCSH: African American women—Intellectual life. | African American women—Psychology. | African American women in literature. | Psychic trauma in literature. | Healing. | Self-help techniques—United States. | Psychological literature—United States. | Spiritual life in literature. | American literature—African American authors—History and criticism. | American literature—Women authors—History and criticism.
Classification: LCC E185.86 .C298 2016 (print) | LCC E185.86 (ebook) | DDC 305.48/896073—dc23
LC record available at http://lccn.loc.gov/2016007284

10 9 8 7 6 5 4 3 2 1

Contents

List of Illustrations	vii
Acknowledgments	ix
Life Class: An Introduction	1
1. Are You Sure You Want to Be Well?: Healing and the Situation of Black Women's Pain	15
2. I Need You to Survive: Theorizing Rhetorical Healing	31
3. I'll Teach You to See Again: The Rhetoric of Revision in Iyanla Vanzant's Self-Help Franchise	48
4. Come Ye Disconsolate: The Rhetoric of Transformation in T.D. Jakes's Women's Ministry	78
5. Take Your Place: The Rhetoric of Return in Tyler Perry's Films	112
6. With Vision and Voice: Black Women's Rhetorical Healing in Everyday Use	143
Reverberations	165
Notes	169
Bibliography	183

Illustrations

Figures

I.1 Oprah Winfrey and Iyanla Vanzant on the set of the second-season premier of *Oprah's Lifeclass*—The Tour, in March 2012. Fair use. — 3

3.1 Iyanla Vanzant counsels Evelyn Lozada on the OWN series *Iyanla*: *Fix My Life,* in 2012. Fair use. — 71

4.1 Kimberly Elise portrays Michelle, the battered protagonist who retaliates against her abuser in the 2004 Magnolia Pictures film *Woman Thou Art Loosed*. Fair use. — 80

5.1 Madea counsels her granddaughters in the sport of "gritball" in the 2006 film *Madea's Family Reunion*. Fair use. — 135

6.1 Steve Harvey answers questions from an all-female audience on *The Oprah Winfrey Show*. Fair use. — 145

Acknowledgments

There have been so many acts of kindness and encouragement that do not show up on the pages of this book but have shaped it nonetheless. I give thanks to God for the vision of this project, the resources to complete it, and the gift of great examples—women such as my late grandmother, Virginia Carey—who let me see wisdom at work. My parents, Orlando and Evelyn Carey, deserve so much of my gratitude. As my earliest teachers, they taught me to trust what and whom I know, and they expressed the kind of unflinching confidence in me that makes my moments of self-doubt seem illogical. I can only strive to reciprocate their love. I am indebted to the aunts and cousins who always "kept it one hundred" with me and the chosen sisters—Carlisse, Kia, Shawntee, Sherri, Ebony, Melissa, Shawnita, and Rhonda—who were an inspiration for this book. I am grateful for them. My late partner, Chris, also deserves much of my thanks. He was there at the start and close of this book; and even though I did not always understand his sacrifices, I do now, and all is well. *Thank you, babe.*

Beyond this circle, this book is a reflection of a number of professional relationships that I deeply cherish. Gwendolyn Pough modeled the kind of question asking and inquiry that gave me the courage to do this project and changed the course of my academic career. Adam Banks continues to live a set of commitments that remind me of what the best outcomes of scholarly work can be. Lois Agnew, Vivian May, Beverly Moss, Tricia Serviss, Denise Valdes, Polina Chemishanova, Jamie Martinez, Anita Guynn, Carmen Kynard, Elaine Richardson, Shirley Wilson Logan, Cheryl Glenn, Keith Gilyard, Eric Darnell Pritchard, Rhea Estelle Lathan, Aja Martinez, David Green, Gabriela Rios, Steven Alvarez, Bill Endres, Roxanne Mountford, Candace Epps Robertson, Laura Davies, and LaToya Sawyer all gave formal and informal feedback on this project that pushed my thinking and inspired me. And because they deserve special acknowledgements, I thank Denise, Tricia, Melissa, Gwen, Eric, Rhea, Polina, and LaToya for the gifts of stimulating conversations, laughter, and friendship.

The University at Albany, SUNY, has provided me with the kind of nurturing and supportive working environment necessary to bring this project to fruition. As department chairs, Randy Craig and Glyne Griffith have both been wonderful sources of sound advice and guidance. Steve North, Laura Wilder, and Janell Hobson have never denied me the luxury of their attention, mentoring, and thoughtful feedback. I consider it an honor to be a part of the English Department faculty and I am particularly grateful for the camaraderie and care of Sami Schalk, Bret Benjamin, jil hanifan, Pat Chu, Derik Jalal Smith, Martha Rozett, Helene Scheck, Ineke Murakami, Ed Schwartzchild, Jen Greiman, Eric Keenaghan, Tomas Noel, Paul Stasi, Bob Yagelski, Jeff Berman, and Mary Valentis. For their guidance in navigating the ins and outs of the university, I thank Liz Lauenstein and Lynn Bearup. I also thank Robert W. Miller, Jr., Lani Jones, Tamra Minor, and Rafael Gomez for various acts of kindness and support throughout this project. Lastly, for letting me learn with them and clarify my ideas, I thank the students in my Fall 2013 Women Writers class, my Spring 2013 Black Women's Writing and Rhetoric course, and my Fall 2014 African American Rhetorical Traditions graduate seminar.

I have received generous portions of support and instruction throughout the course of this book project. I remain grateful for the American Association of University Women Dissertation Fellowship that gave me an opportunity to dive into this work; the University of North Carolina at Pembroke, which provided me with a Summer Research grant that allowed me to continue this work; the Dr. Nuala McGann Drescher Writing leave; and the University at Albany English Department Writing leave for the time to complete this work. The mentoring of the National Center for Faculty Development & Diversity Faculty Success Program also gave me an additional boost needed to complete this project. And to Beth Bouloukos, Jenn Bennett, Rafael Chaiken, and the staff at SUNY Press who exercised patience with me, I offer my sincere thanks. This book is better because of their work.

An earlier version of chapter 3 entitled, "I'll Teach You to See Again: Rhetorical Healing as Reeducation in Iyanla Vanzant's Self-Help Books" appears in *Enculturation 15* (January 2013). It is reprinted here by permission of *Enculturation* (http://enculturation.net/rhetorical-healing-as

-reeducation). Additionally, an early version of chapter 5 entitled, "Take Your Place: Rhetorical Healing and Black Womanhood in Tyler Perry's Films" is published in *Signs: Journal of Women in Culture and Society* 39, no. 4 (2014): 999–1021. The copyright is 2014 by the University of Chicago. It is reprinted with permission. Finally, I thank Kevin Okeith for allowing me to reprint his beautiful painting *The Other Half* as the cover of this book.

In closing, I thank all the women who openly shared their stories with me and the wise people who reminded me that iron can sharpen iron. I dedicate this book to them and, of course, to wisdom.

Life Class
An Introduction

> I look on the show as my own ministry. I want it to free people from their fears and constraints. I want it to teach them.
>
> –Oprah Winfrey

Before a live audience of 9,000 attendees at St. Louis's Peabody Opera House, the second-season premier of *Oprah's Lifeclass* debuted on March 26, 2012. *Lifeclass* was one of the first original content offerings Winfrey and her production company developed to launch her then newly self-named television network (Oprah Winfrey Network or OWN) as her talk show's historic twenty-five-season run was ending. The series was an apparent homage to the teaching career she has professed she would have gone into had she not chosen broadcast journalism. *Lifeclass,* with its new, interactive format featuring Skype interviews and streaming Facebook and Twitter commentary, was supposed to showcase "Oprah's lessons, revelations, and aha moments" from the last twenty-five years in an accessible format that would make viewers' lives "better happier, bigger, richer" and "more fulfilling."[1] To encourage participation, the OWN staff launched an email campaign. Replete with an offer of customized leather journals, the emails extolled the virtues of writing as a way "enrolled students" could process their thoughts on such class topics as "being true to yourself" and the dangers of "straying from your center." The journals did not arrive in time for the first season and ratings suggested that fans were somewhat lukewarm to watching in-studio coverage of Winfrey discussing video footage of her previous interviews with such guests as Maya Angelou, Joel Osteen, Tony Robins, Terry McMillan, and Deepak Chopra. Ultimately *Lifeclas*s survived the first season with solid enough ratings, but the most popular episodes from the first season were those featuring guest teachers.

1

The Series's second-season premier showed intentional attempts at improvement. To capitalize on the appeal of face-to-face interaction, the OWN production team launched a six-week, cross-country *Lifeclass* tour and even brought in fan-favorite Iyanla Vanzant as the guest teacher for the season premier. Nearly a decade and a half earlier, the Yoruban priestess-turned-lawyer-turned-*New-York-Times*-best-selling-author and life coach became a regular guest during the "Change Your Life Television" phase of Winfrey's talk show in the late nineties. In an effort to shift the talk show's focus from what the host had once called "dysfunctional whining and complaining and blaming" to generative endeavors such as working on one's individual issues, Winfrey and her producers developed a series of regular segments containing two-minute spots called "Remembering Your Spirit," featuring testimonies from celebrities about how they learned to live more spiritual lives. "I'm talking about each individual having his or her own revolution," Winfrey once remarked about her talk show's new focus:

> I am talking about each individual coming to the awareness that I am Creation's son. I am Creation's daughter. I am more than my physical self. I am more than this job that I do. I am more than the external definitions I have given myself. . . . those roles are extensions of who I define myself to be, but ultimately I am Spirit come from the greatest Spirit. I am Spirit.[2]

Still largely unknown to mainstream American audiences, Vanzant regaled Winfrey's viewers with a combination of personal wisdom and accessible teaching, often imparting to audiences the insights she shared with her own readers in such books as *One Day My Soul Just Opened Up: 40 Days and 40 Nights Towards Spiritual Strength and Personal Growth*.

The topic "Stopping the Pain" that Winfrey and her producers selected for the *Lifeclass* second-season premier was inspired by a comment Vanzant had made on an appearance during the show's first season (see figure 1.1). On the first season's episode, Vanzant had remarked that "until you heal the wounds of your past you will continue to bleed." During the second season's premier, Winfrey asked Vanzant to discuss pain, and her guest offered an alternative definition: "Pain is meant to get your attention," Vanzant explained. "It's beyond your physicality." Winfrey responded in amazement and affirmation. As the host scribbled down her own personal notes, Vanzant explained that when sensations such as hunger, frustration, and even "horniness" arise, the discomfort they

Oprah Winfrey and Iyanla Vanzant on the set of the second-season premier of *Oprah's Lifeclass*—The Tour, in March 2012. Fair use.

produce are a signal that individuals are supposed to retreat into themselves for introspection. "When we feel pain, it's a sign to 'pay attention inward now,'" Vanzant continued. Fans seemed to embrace the acronym PAIN. Throughout the remainder of the segment, the images of viewers' tweets containing the message "Pay Attention Inward Now" flashed on monitors behind the stage. Ratings for the premier episode were among the highest of the entire season.

Critics who might attribute this episode's high ratings to the psychotherapeutic "gospel" some scholars and journalists consider central to the talk show host's brand certainly have a point. With the mandate to think positively, *Lifeclass* promotes the notion that viewers can achieve a "mind cure" that literary and religion scholars such as Janice Peck and Kathryn Lofton identify as a current throughout Winfrey's early shows.[3] Additionally, on *Lifeclass*, Winfrey advances the same assumption that forms of internal and situated dialogues and public confession are means for wellness—which psychoanalysts refer to as the "talking cure." Finally, by bringing back some of her favorite authors as *Lifeclass* instructors, Winfrey endorses the virtues of bibliotherapy, or the practice of reading for self-improvement, which Rebecca Wanzo calls a "reading cure" in her research on the host's popular book club. Indeed, any one of these explanations is a plausible way to understand why this episode might resonate with fans. With her new series, Winfrey resumes her role as one of the most influential producers in an industry of "spiritual capitalism," as Lofton terms it, to emerge throughout the twentieth and twenty-first centuries.[4] She makes resources available to people who may not even recognize that they are being conditioned to need them.

It is precisely because any one of these cures—mind, talking, or reading—can explain why this episode of *Lifeclass* might resonate with viewers that this book takes up a different set of questions. According to Eva Illouz in *Oprah Winfrey and the Glamour of Misery*, Winfrey's appeal and popularity are due, in part, to an African American[5] habitus, or a set of styles, skills, repeated practices, and intentions that allow agents to continually produce actions that are meaningful to people around them.[6] The claim is valid. Winfrey's communicative style, at times, has shown the influence of African American preaching cadences and techniques. Additionally, during her talk show's run, she and her staff devoted numerous episodes to addressing the topics of marital, sibling, or parental discord among African Americans. Moreover, Winfrey's decision to build a school for African girls and her efforts to address matters concerning Black women indicate that she has not waivered from the life motivation she expressed in a 1995 interview when she said, "The fact that I was created a Black woman in this lifetime, everything in my life is built around honoring that. I feel a sense of reverence to that. I hold it sacred. And I am always asking myself the question, 'What do I owe in service of having been created a Black woman?'"[7] Illouz suggests that the "spectacle" of individual change Winfrey demonstrates and sponsors on her shows and in her magazine bears "an affinity with ritual systems of healing." Since these systems seem to have also influenced the host's sense of identity, language practices, and social commitments, I see cause for deeper investigation.[8] What does the alternative definition of pain that Winfrey makes available to viewers on *Lifeclass* mean for Black women, a group for whom matters of wellness have always informed the theories, rhetorics, and literacies they have used to engage their respective communities? What impact does Winfrey's professed goal of teaching and ministering have on the distribution of these alternative definitions? And, how should we understand the forms of spiritual capitalism in which so many Black women are engaging?

The short answer to these questions is that instructional messages such as "pay attention inward now" on this episode of *Lifeclass* require us to reconsider how writers have wielded and continue to wield African American rhetorical traditions as forms of social praxis in light of the development of Black feminism as a social theory. The concept of habitus Illouz draws on to acknowledge Winfrey's socialization as a Black woman and cultural upbringing as influences on her career draws upon Pierre Bourdieu's use of the term which, among other things, signifies how institutions shape identity. When individuals or groups engage an institution, they often embrace the institution's values, or they adopt particular communication practices, styles, and modes of social engagement. That engagement, in turn, reconstitutes the need for that institution as a vital component of everyday life. Given the focus on style, values and intentions, and repeated practices and skills inherent in the concept of habitus, Thomas Miller's discussion of literacy campaigns offers a useful way to understand how a show such as *Lifeclass* can become a site and a commodity within this process. According to Miller, literacy campaigns enable us to understand how rhetoric functions as a form of social praxis through education by revealing which urgencies a community, an institution, or a person invested in an institution may try to remediate through instruction. When groups experience the types of cultural changes that may "destabilize" how they teach members and pass on "values and privileged modes" of transmitting them, literacy campaigns become restorative efforts that enable the dominant group to draw back in those individuals who may have rejected or doubted their values.[9] In these moments, defining relevant issues and framing learning agendas become imperative steps to creating a discourse community and engaging in a rhetorical education project that instructs individuals how to understand and perform their social roles. Identifying these campaigns, then, enables us to trace the discursive choices a culture undertakes to explain themselves "in new ways or lose authority to a competing paradigm."[10]

Miller's concept offers one way to understand the proliferation of projects responding to issues impacting Black women's quality of life throughout the last two decades. Since the end of the period scholars call the Black Women's Literary Renaissance—a moment that happens to parallel the ascent of *The Oprah Winfrey Show*—a lucrative market of African American self-help books, inspirational literature, and film has emerged. In a significant number of these texts, writers take up the issues that Alice Walker, Ntozake Shange, and other Black women authors and theorists Winfrey cites as influences on her journey in spirit discussed decades earlier. Directed predominantly towards women in states of disease over past emotional, physical, or mental traumas and to women in states of discontent over the status of their spiritual, romantic, and professional lives, these texts contain *rhetorics of healing*, or a set of persuasive discourses and performances writers wield to convince their readers that redressing or preventing a crisis requires them to follow the steps to ideological, communicative, or behavioral transformation the writer considers essential to wellness. As arguments about individual processes such as revision, transformation, or return, and corresponding curricula, these rhetorics transcribe problems into lessons by invoking messages of personal affirmation, notions of familial belonging, institutional responsibility, or broader racial uplift. More often than not, the effects of these discourses are potent. Readers feel that they have taken away valuable coping strategies, while the most popular proponents of these projects feel that writing texts that pursue a goal of healing is something of an activist endeavor. Teaching individuals the ways of knowing, being, and acting that enable them to reread their pasts, revise their sense of self, and resume progress towards their life goals becomes a way to help ensure individual and community survival. Ideally, reeducation becomes a learning cure.

The strategy is not entirely novel. In *African American Literacies*, Elaine Richardson explains that self-education and pedagogical activism has always been a means of subverting and resisting the forms of dehumanization and disenfranchisement that result from a "Black Rhetorical Condition" where African Americans' lives have historically been "desired and devalued."[11] Shirley Wilson Logan's discussion of free-floating literacies in *Liberating Language: Sites of Rhetorical Education in Nineteenth Century Black America* also indicates the importance of reeducation. As she notes, African Americans have invested in self-improvement and uplift efforts to enhance all terrains of their personal and civic lives.[12] For them, self-education was a means of moral improvement and a strategy for attaining the social, economic, and political status to promote racial uplift and social activity. Black women, more specifically, have had a particularly profound investment in these projects. Becoming literate, as Jacqueline Jones Royster explains in *Traces of a Stream: Literacy as Social Change Among African American Women*, was a way to make "whirlpools in the pond of public discourse."[13] To borrow the words of the old gospel tune, "We've Come This Far by Faith," it appears that some African Americans and Black women believe they've come this far by literacy.

Given this tradition, *Rhetorical Healing: The Reeducation of Contemporary Black Womanhood* takes a pragmatic approach to understanding how writers compose texts and wellness campaigns that resonate with readers and why these texts and campaigns retain their appeal. Throughout this book, I examine the processes of rhetorical healing within three of the most popular wellness campaigns for Black women that Winfrey has sponsored. As a procedural extension of rhetorics of healing, rhetorical healing is both an analytical and conceptual framework for identifying the innovation and implications in how writers construct and instruct Black female audiences. On the analytical end, rhetorical healing identifies the persuasive choices and performances African Americans make when using discourse as a means of sociopolitical or pedagogical action. It also makes clear which ways of reading, knowing, and being—or literacies—writers expect individuals to recognize and demonstrate or acquire as a means for healing. As a conceptual framework, rhetorical healing pulls into our purview the controlling ideologies, logics, and motives embedded in the writer's conception of wellness. In this way, rhetorical healing enables us to account for how easily a message or a genre and its conventions can be appropriated. This insight is the broader argument of this book. The call to "pay attention inward now," which Vanzant makes on *Lifeclass* and Winfrey's fans embrace, is not a passive or apolitical statement for Black women because they have not suddenly become more invested in matters of wellness. Instead, this message and others like it reflect the complexity in how writers are employing African American rhetorical traditions as action-taking, knowledge-making, and community-sustaining resources towards Black female audiences and how elements of Black feminism and womanist thought have been coopted and decontextualized through some of the very same discussions of healing and wellness where these philosophies and theories emerged.

In Plain Sight: Why Healing? Why Rhetoric? Why Now?

Scholarship on the social function of wellness is not new. To date, feminist scholars have interrogated the gender dynamics embedded in wellness and self-empowerment projects with such books as *The Mismeasure of Woman* by Carol Tavris and *Sisters of the Yam: Black Women and Self-Recovery* by bell hooks. Dana L. Cloud's *Control and Consolation in American Culture and Politics: Rhetorics of Therapy* remains one of the most incisive and important treatments of discursive nature of wellness to date. In her study of therapeutic discourses, or messages that apply such psychotherapy terms as "adaptation" and "coping" to social issues, such as unemployment, that emerge in times of social upheaval or conflict,

Cloud reveals how rhetoric can dissuade individuals from joining and organizing to pursue social change. Often, these discourses work to preserve systems of power by asserting the benefits of normalcy.[14] The intervention Cloud makes by theorizing rhetorics of therapy is still timely as scholars have continued to explore the relationship between wellness and social pressure within discussions of neoliberalism. Recently, Sara Ahmed has explored this pressure and coined the term "promise of happiness" to describes as a cultural imperative to transform one's attitude to reflect and perform positive goals and outcomes. At this moment and in such cultures, the impact of these therapeutic messages can be difficult to see and ascertain.

Since the idea of normalcy suggests a particular kind of wellness goal that can obscure the racial-, gender-, and class-based assumptions embedded in how groups of people understand themselves in relation to others or how they mobilize around issues that wound its members, I see the therapy culture Winfrey has participated in with her shows as an important launching point for considering how wellness can extend our understandings of the relationship between language, literacy, race, gender, and identity through rhetoric. For example, the idea of the "mind cure" that Janice Peck uses as a frame for understanding Winfrey's ability to persuade her viewers to follow such new-age religious practices as Rhonda Byrne's *The Secret* in "The Secret of Her Success: Oprah Winfrey and the Seductions of Self-Transformation" is a concept that invites us to consider its implications for Black women and their communities. Rooted in nineteenth-century religious and spiritual movements renouncing negative thinking and extolling transcendence as a mental and emotional practice, these "theologies" as Peck refers to them, are thought to have resonated most with a rising American middle class that was "comfortably removed" from economic and material struggle but also cautious about preserving their social class during moments of social upheaval. Among this group, "mind cures" cemented the benefits of hard work and meritocracy while obscuring the function of white privilege and its economic benefits. The outcome was a set of religious beliefs that foreshadowed neoliberal ideology by promoting the idea that individuals with good fortune had achieved such good fortune as a result of self-change and transformation. Peck and others suggest that this ideology hit home with the primary audience demographic of white middle-class women who watched and supported *The Oprah Winfrey Show*. But what about Black women? We still have not interrogated in depth how these arguments and lines of thought appear in the literatures and discourses specifically targeting them and what effect these arguments have had.

What psychoanalysts call the "talking cure," or the idea that communication and confession can be cathartic, is another concept that challenges us to think about matters of race, gender, access, and privilege. As the "queen of daytime talk," Winfrey makes obvious her prowess as a savvy rhetor. During the course of her talk show, she routinely divulged her own painful, personal experiences as a confessional mechanism at key moments and, in doing so, endeared herself to her viewers and other fans. The host has always been a work-in-progress. While Eva Illouz credits Winfrey with creating a "self-help ethos" and cultivating "virtual communities of suffering and sufferers" through these narratives and with her forms of "therapeutic interviewing," the question of where she has drawn these strategies from and how they resonate with Black women remains, particularly given the fact that Winfrey has expressed her goals of teaching and commitments to Black women.[15] How, specifically, does the idea of a talking cure work within broader rhetorical education norms Black women have adopted?

Similarly, the idea of the "reading cure" that seems like one of the most obvious ways Winfrey participates in therapy culture can be expanded when we consider it in relation to contemporary Black women. In "The Oprahfication of Literacy," Mark Hall contextualizes Winfrey's endorsement of reading as a means for self-improvement and her enthusiasm for sharing these insights with others through Deborah Brandt's well-known concept of literacy sponsors, or those individuals or entities that "assume responsibility for another person or group during a period of instruction, apprenticeship, or probation." Because Winfrey sponsors these authors throughout their careers and has enacted what Hall describes as a "teacherly" ethos when trying to emphasize the entertainment and educational value of participating in her club or engaging her protégés' works, she has shaped the national discourse about books and brought unknown figures to mainstream attention. While we know that taste is subjective and it can often reflect assumptions about social class, we must also consider what Winfrey's sponsorship means for the messages she hopes to share with Black women and the mainstream representation of the people she deems as worthy influences. As both Nan Johnson's research on post-civil-war-conduct books illustrates and Shirley Wilson Logan's analysis of the self-education projects African Americans undertook after slavery reveals, participating in lyceums, book clubs, and other activities centered on interpreting and discussing texts has always been a means for elite individuals to prepare for civic participation through reading.[16] Does the idea of bibliotherapy as a strategy for reaching wellness still carry these class-based customs and aspirations among Black women? Also, what do the multiple channels of media that Winfrey has developed mean for the spread of these messages?

Exploring any of these concepts gives us an avenue for responding to some of the gaps in how we understand cultural rhetorics as everyday, critical practice and how Black women are recognized as literate media consumers or audiences. There is an existing body of rhetorical, linguistic, and literacy scholarship on the shared epistemologies, language and speech acts, literacy practices and technologies African American men and women use to assert, preserve, and transform themselves, their communities, and their sociopolitical conditions (Asante, 1970; Smitherman, 1977; Gilyard, 1991; Logan, 1999; Royster, 2000; Moss, 2002; Richardson, 2003; Pough, 2004; Nunley, 2004 and 2011; Banks, 2005 and 2011; Holmes 2006; Kynard 2007 and 2013; Lathan 2007; Perryman-Clark, 2012; Prichard, 2014; Browne, 2013). Yet, as observed in the forward to Elaine Richardson and Ronald Jackson's 2004 edited collection, *African American Rhetorics: Interdisciplinary Perspectives,* there remains a call to "pull forth for contemporary critical inquiry" the practices and performances that constitute the contours of a rhetorical landscape that remains relatively unknown in mainstream scholarly discourses.[17]

The call for "critical inquiry" into overlooked rhetorical landscapes is not limited to those of us who theorize African American rhetorics. In her research on the rhetorics of survivance Native Americans employ in their writings, Malea Powell called for composition and rhetoric scholars to consider writings from other cultures "critically important rather than mere anomalies."[18] Although similar sentiments are echoed in scholarship on Latino/a and Chicano/a rhetorics (Villanueva, 2009), Asian American rhetorics (Young, 2004; Mao, 2008), Queer rhetorics (Goltz, 2013; Rand, 2014) and other communities, Powell's articulation of this call provides a broader yet more nuanced exigency. In using the term "anomaly" to describe how the field of rhetoric and composition has historically conceptualized of cultural rhetoric practices, she describes the dominant ways of seeing that lead to objectification and subjugation. Powell is right. It is difficult to see a cultural system when its practices are reduced to isolated feats of exceptionalism.

Kent Ono and John Sloop offer a different reason for the attitudes and orientation that position what I see as landscapes of cultural rhetoric practice beyond the purview of rhetoric and composition studies in "The Critique of Vernacular Discourse." Calling for a critical framework to discuss vernacular discourse rather than the "recuperative" or "descriptive" nature found in current studies that have brought attention to basic trends and new audiences and practitioners of rhetoric, Ono and Sloop argue that rhetorical critics have been preoccupied with the discourse of the powerful and the (seemingly) socially significant. Rhetorical studies, they argue, is "missing out on, and writing out of history, important texts that gird and influence local cultures."[19] There have certainly been insightful and critical examinations of the practice and function of vernacular discourses since Ono and Sloop's 1995 essay, but their emphasis on critique in this piece is important because respectability, which broadly refers to the desire to present one's best image in the face of a dominant group, can be dangerous. It prioritizes exceptionalism over efficiency. At worst, this type of orientation can leave us underprepared to talk about and talk back to the discourses in and around our homes that can affect our quality of life.

In *Rhetorical Healing: The Reeducation of Contemporary Black Womanhood*, I explore the project of Black women's wellness to consider how African American rhetorical traditions work efficiently within Black communities and what happens when these efforts and practices move beyond our spaces into the mainstream. Prevalent yet unassuming, wellness campaigns for Black women are landscapes of rhetorical action that impact numerous individuals while appearing to hide in plain sight. Multi-genre in nature and ongoing throughout extended periods of time, these campaigns showcase various examples of the application of African American rhetorical traditions and sense-making processes. Because some measure of normalcy appears to be their goal, these campaigns generally go overlooked. In other words, wellness campaigns can give off an appearance of people doing what they should already be doing to protect and care for their communities.

Although my aim throughout this book is to consider the implications of these traditions in practice, I have decided to take a pragmatic approach to recognize the agency Black women demonstrate in respect to these campaigns and their own, as well as my own, goals for collective community wellness. No campaign can achieve success as a form of social action, praxis, or otherwise without a community that agrees to act and move together towards a particular end. This premise means that if we are to understand the social and political significance of such books as Riva Tims's *When It All Falls Apart: Finding Healing, Joy, and*

Victory through the Pain, Hill Harper's *Letters to a Young Sister: DeFINE Your Destiny,* or Rev Run and Tyrese Gibson's *Manology: Secrets of Your Man's Mind Revealed,* and films such as David Talbert's *Baggage Claim,* which have all been published recently and all offer to teach or illustrate presumably heterosexual female audiences how to repair themselves, we must ask pragmatic questions of how and to what extent these works function. For example, how is pain defined and made to seem urgent enough that contemporary Black women feel compelled to act? Where do these contemporary efforts fit in relation to earlier discussions of wellness among Black women? Among African Americans? What are the solutions and processes writers find useful in addressing these matters as forms of healing? What are the implications when one site becomes a repeated source for these projects and, as has been the case, these projects are absorbed into other self-help and commercialized commodities? And, how might we seize the possibilities of these projects since masses of Black women remain fans of these works? Our focus must examine the techniques, incentives, and consequences. To be sure, some healing discourses function in ways similar to therapeutic discourses. My focus on healing is an effort to address concerns regarding Black women in relation to African American communities because healing carries a focus on the body as an entire collective unit.

With this approach in mind, I begin by recognizing the existing traditions we must consider to understand these campaigns. Chapter 1, "Are You Sure You Want to Be Well? Healing and the Situation of Black Women's Pain," explores Black women's literary writing, essay writing, and memoir writing. In it, I offer a context for recent discussions of wellness and healing. As I show, in such books as Ntozake Shange's *For Colored Girls Who Have Considered Suicide When the Rainbow is Enuf,* Black women readers have been able to find clear discussions on matters of wounding and strategies for healing. While this literary renaissance is a specific hypervisible moment, it exists within a continuum of intellectual resistance and creativity that Black women have used to move themselves closer to peace and wellness.

Recognizing this continuum, chapter 2, "I Need You to Survive: Theorizing Rhetorical Healing," develops an analytical framework for understanding these discussions. As Keith Gilyard explains in "A Legacy of Healing," African Americans have always remained critical of schooling processes even as they have pursued reeducation with the belief that "knowledge is power." To understand how Black women have been persuaded to undertake these processes of healing, I situate these discourses within rhetorical studies, literacy studies scholarship, African American vernacular culture, and Black feminist thought to develop a procedural and critical approach to identifying and understanding the choices these writers make when attempting to construct a text that can move a reader to a state of healing.

Chapter 3, "I'll Teach You to See Again: The Rhetoric of Revision in Iyanla Vanzant's Self-Help Franchise," focuses on the wellness campaign of one of Winfrey's top protégées. What viewers of the current series *Iyanla*: *Fix My Life* observe as strategies to "do the work" of healing originated in *Tapping the Power Within: A Path to Self-Empowerment for Women, Interiors: A Black Woman's Healing in Progress*, and *The Value in the Valley: A Black Woman's Guide Through Life's Dilemmas*, three of the self-help writer's earliest books. Engaging and endearing, Vanzant is a persuasive teacher with an important testimony. In analyzing the process of rhetorical healing in her early works as a type of explicit teaching action and the ways her arguments and pedagogies have manifested in her more current projects, I unearth the complex discourse on revision she uses to persuade women to follow her approach to empowerment and recovery, and I provide an example of how African American women craft self-help books to address crises in their communities.

Even though Bishop T.D. Jakes has an extensive body of writing, I look at editions of his best selling *Woman, Thou Art Loosed!: Healing the Wounds of the Past*, his workbook and film bearing variations of his name, and his book *Daddy Loves His Girls* as the sites of analysis in chapter 4, "Come Ye Disconsolate: The Rhetoric of Transformation in T.D. Jakes's Women's Ministry." Jakes is one of the first and most visible Black preachers in the last three decades to make the healing and restoration of his female congregants a visible focus of his ministry. His work does not directly identify Black women as the audience for his books but, given the makeup of his early congregation, this demographic has always been his primary audience. By reading his work as attempts at rhetorical healing through modified sermons and teachings, I uncover the discourse on transformation circulating within his women's ministry and offer a contemporary account of how ministers are modifying Black preaching traditions for the sake of intervening into the lives of Black women.

The fifth chapter, "Take Your Place: The Rhetoric of Return in Tyler Perry's Films," is an examination of the narratives of Black women's empowerment that seem to draw female viewers to playwright/screenwriter's plays and films. The popularity of Perry's portrayals of women journeying from heartbreak to redemption in such films as *Diary of a*

Mad Black Woman and *Madea's Family Reunion* have helped him become the most lucrative African American filmmaker in the last three decades and though he has appeared to transition to television by producing most of the original content of the *Oprah Winfrey Network's* scripted television offerings, to date he still holds one of the largest bodies of work featuring Black women. Analyzing his films as a visual and narrative process of rhetorical healing reveals the discourse on return that he uses to instruct women how to reach the state of wellness that enables them to take their places within their families.

In the conclusion, I discuss the implications of these wellness campaigns. Specifically, I outline the research avenues these efforts illuminate for us because, as this book shows, rhetorics of healing tap into some of the deepest and most longstanding arguments African Americans make about the lives they believe they deserve. Ultimately, *Rhetorical Healing* illustrates how Black women's specific wellness efforts have become commodified and depoliticized in the name of commercialized instructional activism. Yet, as I show through a reflection from my own efforts to teach a recent course on women writers, there is still much to reclaim from discussion of Black women's wellness, healing, and reeducation, however complex they continue to be.

CHAPTER 1

Are You Sure You Want to Be Well?
Healing and the Situation of Black Women's Pain

> Are you sure, sweetheart, that you want to be well? . . . I like to caution folks, that's all. . . . No sense us wasting each other's time, sweetheart. A lot of weight when you're well.
> –Minnie Ransom in Toni Cade Bambara's *The Salt Eaters*

Unfortunately, we cannot know exactly how the late Toni Cade Bambara would respond to the messages about Black women's pain and wellness appearing on shows such as *Lifeclass* over three decades after publishing *The Salt Eaters*. Her 1980 novel extended a conversation she launched a decade earlier about the importance of Black women's self-care. In her 1970 edited collection, *The Black Woman: An Anthology*, Bambara told women who were fed up with the racism of the women's liberation movement and tired of the forms of sexism she and other women had encountered in Black liberation movements to turn their attentions inward. Her reasoning was simple: "Revolution begins with the self, in the self" because "the individual . . . must be purged of poison and lies that assault the ego and threaten the heart, that hazard the next larger unit . . . that put the entire movement in peril."[1] For Bambara, an inward turn was crucial. Only by focusing on themselves could her readers begin to develop an "Afrafemme worldview," or a standpoint situated in the experiences of Black womanhood.[2] This was a worldview that situated "first the interiority of an in-the-head, in-the-heart, in-the-gut region of discovery called the *self*" and tested "the desires, the longing, the aspirations of this discovered self with and against its possibilities for respect, growth, fulfillment, and accomplishment."[3]

With the cautionary tale of Velma Henry in *The Salt Eaters*, Bambara illustrated what could happen if Black women fail to make this inward shift and invest in this process of self-discovery in time. The novel opens with a disheveled Henry meeting Minnie Ransom, a "fabled" healer in Bambara's fictional Clayborn, Georgia town. Ransom questions whether Velma actually "want[s] to be well" and do the work to get there given the responsibilities a healthier version of the protagonist would face. What seems like an unnecessary question makes sense as the novel progresses. In subsequent chapters, readers discover that Ransom's concern about "wasting each other's time" is not only an indicator of how extensive her spiritual healing ritual is, but it is also an indication of the investment Henry's community has in her wholeness, an investment best exemplified by the twelve-member group referred to as the "Master Mind" that assembles to participate in the healing. The pathway to wellness Ransom unfolds is as multi-faceted as the forms of disillusion, mounting work pressures, threats of nuclear destruction, and emotional betrayal at the hands of the man with whom she's been having an extramarital affair that precipitates Henry's nervous breakdown and suicide attempt. But this is the point of Bambara's novel. Acquiring the types of revolutionary self-knowledge that enables African Americans to address what Kimberly Nichele Brown describes as "the American diseases of 'disconnectedness' and double-consciousness" that likely inspired Bambara's novel is a process.[4] Healing takes time, community, and work.

Since we can only speculate if Minnie Ransom would ever be invited to participate on *Lifeclass* as a teacher, this chapter explores discussions of pain within Black women's literature as a context for understanding the rhetorics of healing that have emerged in the last three decades. In *Sisters of the Yam: Black Women and Self-Recovery*, bell hooks explains how teaching *The Salt Eaters* to a group of young Black women illuminated conditions that wound members of this group and revealed how their writings sometimes contain imaginative "maps to healing."[5] The number of her female students to identify with Velma Henry's suicide attempt validated the work of "progressive" Black women writers in such texts as Ntozake Shange's *Sassafrass, Cypress and Indigo*, Toni Morrison's *The Bluest Eye*, and Paule Marshall's *Praisesong for the Widow*. In these works and others, Black women writers make legible "the deep, often unnamed psychic wounding" and help readers name these forms of pain.[6]

What hooks describes as the transformative aspects of books such as *The Salt Eaters*, Patricia Hill Collins identifies as part of the consciousness-raising processes and forms of empowerment Black women have developed over time as a social theory for surviving and subverting dehumanizing contexts. In *Black Feminist Thought: Knowledge, Consciousness, and the Politics of Empowerment,* Collins outlines a variety of landscapes where Black women have developed unique epistemological standpoints, oppositional knowledges, and discursive practices for understanding, protecting, and, when necessary, healing themselves. Historically, literature and essay writing have been some of the most potent textual spaces for Black women's self-empowerment because, as Collins explains, readers can observe women moving from states of "internalized oppression to the 'free mind' of self-defined, womanist consciousness."[7] These moves have not come without consequences or backlash though. Therefore, to understand how writers launch discussions of wellness that feel urgent and relevant to Black women, it is necessary to start here.

The Balm of Memory: Literature and Language as a Domain for Healing

The esteemed roles of healers within African and African American cultures and the efforts of Black women writers to recover their traditions through literature offer a fertile starting point for understanding rhetorics of healing. Historically, healers held the dual position of being their tribe's priest and physician. Through their spiritual authority and their training in the "arts of magic" and the "science of medicine," healers were responsible for offering religious rituals and ministering to the body and soul of the sick. According to Athena Vrettos in "Curative Domains: Women, Healing, and History in Black Women's Narratives," these acts helped ensure their "tribe's coherence and communality" against outside threats.[8] Unsurprisingly, the healer's authoritative role evolved once the transatlantic slave trade brought Africans to the Americas. In this context, intentional threats to the Black family through separation and other means made tribal reformation relatively impossible. In turn, healers reinvented themselves as conjurers. Assuming the role of medicine men and medicine women, conjurers held roles of social reverence on plantations and beyond.[9] When necessary, they dispensed traditional African medicines as cures for new-world ailments and as antidotes to the forms of neglect and malnutrition slaves would incur at the hands of their masters. Healers and conjurers helped preserve African Americans' physical lives within dehumanizing conditions.

Conjurers did not work just to ensure the survival of African Americans during slavery. Occasionally, they put into practice spiritual methods such as voodoo to inflict pain on oppressive slave masters or evil individuals. Zora Neale Hurston's discussion of Madame Marie Laveau in *Mules and Men* illustrates how the healing conjurer posed a direct threat to oppressive power throughout history.[10] In an interview with a Louisiana native about the famed New Orleans voodoo priestess, Hurston describes the way Laveau came to study the religion, her appeal among local and visiting whites who were in awe of her power, and the fear she invoked when she reportedly walked on the waters of Lake Pontchartrain during one of her annual feasts to celebrate Midsummer's Eve.[11] This fear has obviously held its historical currency. Writers of the FX Network series *American Horror Story: Coven* featured Laveau as a character during the show's 2013–2014 season. In the storyline, a set of modern-day witches cross paths with an immortalized Laveau who spends the majority of the season wreaking havoc on the witches while running her braiding shop, Cornrow City, as a front.

Hurston offers a better indicator of the healing conjurer's day-to-day role within her respective communities through the account of a woman who approached Laveau seeking help with an "enemy" who had "tried [her]" and convinced her "loved ones" to leave her. According to Hurston's interviewee, by the time the woman finished her plea for help, Laveau had transformed herself and was "no longer" a woman "but a god."[12] Much to the woman's relief, Laveau responded, "Oh, my daughter, I have heard your woes and your pains and tribulations, and in the depth of the wisdom of the gods I will help you find peace and happiness."[13] Part spiritual conduit, part social worker of sorts, Laveau exemplifies one of the appeals of the healing conjurer among African Americans in this example. With their ability to tap into otherworldly resources, healers held the capacity to challenge forms of systemic authority and remedy cultural as well as material wounds. In this respect, healing conjurers posed a threat to the institution of slavery in antebellum America by offering African Americans another measure of agency in their social lives; and they provided a measure of balance within the interior lives of Black communities. In doing so, these healers resisted and repaired what Gay Wilentz calls the cultural forms of "dis-ease," or deep emotional and sometimes physical trauma and illness that result from oppressive social conditions.[14]

Early- and mid-twentieth century Black women novelists seemed to pay homage to this tradition in their fiction. In such books as Gloria Naylor's *Mama Day*, healers are women who hold integral functions within their communities. With their knowledge of medicinal treatments and spiritual remedies as well as their understanding of the relationships African Americans hold with the land even as their people have been transported to American soil, fictional healers were vehicles for the enacting and preservation of cultural traditions. In the characterization of female healers such as Bambara's Minnie Ransom and Naylor's Mama Day, Black women writers turned African and African American healing traditions into what Vrettos calls a "metaphor for spiritual power" by illustrating a current of resistive and restorative agency.[15] The choice to adopt the genre of the novel as the venue for these stories enabled these writers to "emphasize the restorative potential" of Black women's "own narrative acts" in "reclaiming a tradition."[16] As a result, Black women writers of this period have made historical memory a balm, seizing "the inspiration and authority to heal" their readers by "locating in language a new curative domain" of experiences, memories, and possibilities.[17]

The narrative landscape Vrettos identifies in Black women's writing about healers and healing is one we must also understand as a domain of linguistic and rhetorical practice. In addition to using religious and medicinal remedies, African Americans have continually used language as a form of preventative and restorative agency. As Keith Gilyard explains in "A Legacy of Healing: Words, African Americans, and Power," African Americans historically developed subversive counterlinguistic strategies as adaptive responses to cultures of victimization and wounding.[18]

Toni Morrison's *Beloved* is an example of the ways Black women writers portray this practice. The novel vividly depicts the dialectic between the forms of repression African Americans have had to navigate to preserve their sanity, life, and wellness and the means of expression they used in doing so. For example, as a child, Sethe, Morrison's protagonist, suffers the unthinkable trauma of witnessing slaveholders hang her mother. The experience is made more traumatic because young Sethe had barely had time to know her mother or learn any of her mother's traditional African language and had been taught to recognize her only by a mark on her body.[19] Morrison also shows the influence of language in the experiences of those around Sethe. Fellow Sweet Home slave and love interest Paul D suffers because of the fear of African Americans' communication and language. He is forced to wear bits that render him silent as punishment for trying to escape. Even after Sixo, another Sweet Home plantation slave, defends his act of stealing a pig with the argument that he was actually improving the owner's property, logic and verbal skill offer him no long-term protection. Schoolteacher, the sadistic plantation overseer, still beats Sixo to teach him the lesson that "definitions belonged to the definers—not the defined."[20]

Through these stories, Morrison's novel gives a historical account of the ways oppression has been linked directly to the suppression and denial of language and the consequences of African Americans' subversive use of it. The character Sixo is brutally whipped, burned, and shot later in the novel but, in a final act of defiance, he yells out "Seven-O" to symbolize that a part of him will live on in the life of his unborn child. The act is one of several illustrations of resistance throughout the novel. Baby Suggs and Stamp Paid, two former slaves, both reject imposed names later in their lives, choosing, in the case of Baby Suggs, to retain the name that would allow her husband to find her and opting, in the case of Stamp Paid, to proclaim himself free from all debts to this world. The gestures allow them to seize a small type of salve for their wounded spirits.

These literary representations of healers offer two precedents for what Black women's wellness should involve. As cultural histories, the depictions of conjurers and medicine women by writers such as Hurston remind readers of a tradition linking healing to spiritual practices and acts of resistance. In illuminating these additional domains of agency that readers can tap into to repair and enhance their quality of life, these Black women writers suggest that Black women's healing and—in this instance, the healing of African Americans collectively—has to champion alternative means of empowerment and expansive visions of individual agency. Further, as writers such as Morrison portray their characters using their expressive agency and language rhetorically to move themselves closer to healing, they offer what Gilyard calls a "counterstory" to dominant and pejorative narratives about the inferiority of African Americans' language traditions. As characters such as Sixo subvert or, as Gilyard would proclaim, "flip the script[s]" of linguistic hegemony, they expose the flawed logics upholding their condition and push those logics back in the face of their oppressors. Healing can involve verbal warfare and should result in a woman's rhetorical agency. Among Black women writers of this period, acquiring knowledge of cultural memory and developing a command of language are steps to reclaiming and restoring the self.[21]

Talking and Reading Cures: Renaissance and the Situation of Black Women's Pain

Through works such as Ntozake Shange's *For Colored Girls Who Have Considered Suicide When the Rainbow is Enuf,* critics have come to interpret Black women's attempts at self-healing as a rhetorical situation.[22] When Shange began to write and perform the poetry that would become her famous choreopoem in the mid-seventies and called for somebody, "anybody"—to "sing a Black girl's song" and help them to discover the "sound of [their] own voice[s]," she joined a community of Black women writers and intellectuals producing art, literature, and theory from Black women's experiences. Consciously transgressing unspoken codes on gender, respectability, and privacy in Black communities, Shange and her peers went public with accounts of rape, physical abuse, emotional trauma, and mental illness to show how Black women survive the sexism in their communities that complicates the existing racism and classism many of them endure. They wrote about the ways of knowing that some Black women have chosen to practice as a radical form self-love while living in environments and participating in families and communities that did not always love them back. Through their characterization of Black women moving from states of being wounded to wellness, their insight into the specific sources of these traumas, and their critiques of the institutional and individual complicity in their hurt, these writers called out the contradictions in their relationships with themselves and others. Their writings mobilized an audience, many of whom were Black women who wanted to hear a Black girl's song in a Black girl's voice, while providing narratives to support public conversations about the sexism and racism, which feminist scholars such as Michele Wallace were raising at that time in books such as *Black Macho and the Myth of Superwoman.*

The criticism was intense. Some Black scholars, journalists, and literary critics tore into the work of Shange and her contemporaries, arguing that the stories of empowerment were sensational and promoted anti-Black-male and anti-Black-family sentiments. Vernon Jarrett of the *Chicago Defender* compared Shange's choreopoem to the pro-KKK film *Birth of a Nation*, calling it a "degrading treatment of the Black male" and a "mockery of the Black family."[23] Slightly less incendiary was Mel Watkins's charge. For Watkins, Shange and other women writers of that period had breached the "unspoken but almost universally accepted covenant" among Black writers "to always present positive images of Blacks," and they did so by portraying men as "thieves, sadists, rapists, and ne'er-do-wells."[24] Similarly, in his 1986 parody *Reckless Eyeballing*, Ishmael Reed's depiction of emasculating female characters makes a subtle, but no less pointed suggestion that second-wave Black feminism was oppressive to Black men. Shange, Alice Walker, and a cadre of other writers and intellectuals such as June Jordan and Angela Davis brought to the public's attention a different conversation about the fracturing and wounding women were incurring behind the doors of Black homes at a time when most discourses about Black power were masculinist. By the end of the eighties, the conversations these works generated had galvanized a substantially large publishing market for writing for, by, and about Black women. Scholars coined the moment a "renaissance," but it was a period that would never fully escape controversy because of the attitudes expressed by such Black male literary critics as Darryl Pinckney who described the moment with the claim that "Black woman writers seemed to find their voices and audiences," while "Black men seemed to lose theirs."[25]

The increased period of publishing by Black women at this time was a literary renaissance, but the term "renaissance" is something of a misnomer given the ongoing discussions of pain Shange and her contemporaries engaged in during this moment. Literary critics tend to agree that depictions of physical suffering can achieve levels of aesthetic pathos where civil discussions and oratory fail because, as Elaine Scarry explains, pain is "unsayable."[26] When it comes to Black bodies and forms of African American subjectivity, this pain has registered somewhat differently. In *African Americans and the Culture of Pain*, Debra Walker King suggests that depictions of pain can function as arguments among African Americans. When invoking images of wounded African American bodies, writers employ what she calls "Black pain," or the visual and verbal representation of pained bodies, as a symbolic device. In this metonymic function, "Black pain" stands in as a sign of social, economic, and cultural woundedness that, at best, makes legible the sources of oppression and lack. Other times, Black pain is synecdochical through disidentification. By invoking images of the pained and wounded Black body, a writer—African American or otherwise—can establish distance between idealistic conceptions of America and realistic ones. They can define what America should not be.[27]

Mid-twentieth-century Black women writers practiced similar forms of definition in their novels. With depictions of characters such as Lutie Johnson, the protagonist in Ann Petry's 1946 novel *The Street*, novelists cultivated notions of Black pain to illustrate what Black womanhood as a state of being could entail. Despite Lutie Johnson's social and economic position as a Black domestic who commutes to work for a white family in Connecticut, she is optimistic about her future at the start of the novel. Visions of affluence make her aspire to a notion of the American dream that would help her elevate herself and her family. The first crisis occurs when she discovers that her husband, who still resides in Harlem, has been unfaithful and her son needs full-time care. Despair sets in as Johnson returns, searches for suitable work in the city, and eventually discovers that she cannot rely on her extended family to help with childcare and financial obligations. As the single, poor, urban Black mother struggles to feed her young son and to raise the money to get him out of juvenile detention later in the novel when he is tricked into stealing mail and seized by authorities, the systematic obstacles that prevent her from achieving a measure of the American dream or maintaining faith in meritocracy become apparent. Johnson is not a victim of poor decision-making. Rather, she is positioned within a system of socioeconomic, gendered, and racialized oppression. Consequently, when a colleague attempts to rape her and she kills him in self-defense, Lutie's rage seems plausible. She does not feel as if she has any choices. Her final request for a one-way ticket to Chicago—as she flees Harlem with the resolve that her son is better off in the system than having her attempt to intervene—ultimately becomes a metaphor. Her plight and flight represent the converging issues that can make Black women feel they have no agency against oppression. Petry's novel illustrates how Black women writers use what King describes as a characters' "silent mobility" and "bold and, sometimes, violent screams" to give voice to the communal crises shaping their experiences. No, Lutie Johnson does not channel her frustrations into vocal screams. Strangely enough though, her final train ride is a literal form of "silent mobility."[28]

By the 1950s, novelists were not only defining states of Black womanhood, but also illustrating their female protagonists achieving forms of self-definition. The dialogue in Shange's "Latent Rapists" poem in *For Colored Girls* reflects this shift as it shows female characters acquiring the self-knowledge as a way of identifying, resisting, and overcoming assaults on Black womanhood. In the scene, the lady in blue, lady in red, and lady in purple articulate common reactions to rape: "A friend is hard to press charges against," one says. "A rapist is always to be a stranger to be legitimate / someone you never saw / a man with obvious problems." They determine that when rape occurs, it can be dismissed as a "misunderstanding" or something "women must have known."[29] Although the dialogue seems to serve a clarifying function within the scene, it is also instructive. Through their dialogue, the women identify forms of internalized and community-based shame that can prevent some Black women from reporting these acts. When the lady in red finally surmises that "it turns out the nature of rape has changed . . ." because "we cd even have em over for dinner / & get raped in our own houses / by invitation, / a friend," she brings into focus some of the ideologies that sustain rape culture.[30] Unlike Petry's portrayal of Lutie Johnson who never fully conceptualizes the intersecting forces at work against her, Shange's female characters voice their pain, identify their sources, and name them. Eventually, they take charge of their own wellness by performing a "laying on of hands" ritual where they administer healing to themselves and each other. It is a powerful moment. Together they enact a collective-knowledge-making experience as Shange's characters ultimately determine that "finding God" in themselves and "loving her fiercely" is one way to resolve the "metaphysical dilemma" of "bein alive & bein a woman & bein colored."[31]

The significance of Shange's choice to make pain a site of interrogation cannot be overstated. In her analysis of this closing scene from *For Colored Girls,* Patricia Hill Collins identifies the importance of choice in Black women's healing. In the "laying on of hands" scene, it is the lady in brown's choice to move forward in pursuit of healing while grieving the murder of her child that illustrates for Collins the importance of self-definition. Even when Black women are in painful circumstances where they must remain "motionless on the outside," they can still develop changed consciousness "inside" by moving towards sites and rituals that produce self-knowledge and aid in recovery.[32] In these moments, Black women cultivate what Collins calls "oppositional knowledges," or a type of knowledge developed to defend and benefit the oppressed.[33] When the lady in brown and her sisters begin to find "God" in themselves, they embark on a willful, intentional "journey toward finding the voice of empowerment." Although Shange wisely ends *For Colored Girls* without delineating exactly what lady in brown's vocal state of empowerment might involve, we can assume she has acquired the resources and self-knowledge to act in her own agency and change the conditions that diminish her quality of life.

In Alice Walker's 1981 epistolary novel *The Color Purple*, the coming-to-voice process that Celie, the protagonist, experiences while working through the pain of sexual, physical, and emotional abuse is partially textual. The epistolary form of Walker's novel serves a dual purpose. In one regard, Celie's letters form a narrative arc that enables readers to understand how she, as a poor and uneducated Southern Black woman, exists in both a material condition as well as social condition. Writing is a way for her to negotiate the exploitation of her labor and, at times, the denial of her personhood. In other respects, the developing legibility of Celie's letters documents her emotional development and transition to wellness. In what begins as brief prayers of desperation, Celie's letters reflect her growing awareness of her plight as a poor, uneducated, Southern Black woman. As the sophistication of the letters evolves, so does the protagonist's sense of self-awareness and engagement with her family members. Celie's voice moves from a tone of desperation to analysis, and ultimately argument as she shifts from addressing her letters to God to addressing her sister. These acts of self-composing and self-composure illustrate a transformation process. Celie literally writes her way from a state of silence about the forms of abuse she had encountered to, ultimately, a vocal and legible state of self-empowerment and economic independence. Literacy is freedom and empowerment. Moreover, it is a vehicle for emotional stability. As Celie explains how she came to terms with the limits of her on-and-off-again relationship with her female lover, Shug, in one of her final letters to her sister, her changed consciousness is clear: "*I be so calm*. If she come, I be happy. If she don't, I be content. And then I figure this the lesson I was supposed to learn."[34] As Celie rereads her past, rewrites her sense of self, reimagines sources of love, and revises her relationships, she experiences a form of healing.

Given the forms of autonomy, voice, and agency Celie develops throughout *The Color Purple* and the vision of Black women's wellness Walker portrays, the rhetoric of threat literary critics such as Darryl Pinckney used to characterize this literary renaissance is ironic. As Duchess Harris notes in *Black Feminist Politics from Kennedy to Obama*, the female characters Black women create continually profess their desire for healthy relationships with Black men and families, even when they are not in romantic in nature.[35] Although Celie ultimately chooses to embrace a romantic and sexual relationship with her female lover, Shug, and retain a friendly relationship with Albert, she retains a steady commitment to her family and an insistence on healthy relationships with members of the opposite sex. The suggestion from Walker's text, then, is that healing need not uphold heteronormative standards of desire and traditional family formations. To be "womanish" or grown, as Walker would later define the term, is a broad conception of wellness that enables Black women to love without restraint and stay committed to their own wellbeing and the "survival and wholeness" of their respective communities.[36]

The irony of the anti-Black-male and anti-Black-family discourses surrounding the publication of *For Colored Girls* and *The Color Purple*, then, reflects how matters of healing became urgent and discursive during the Black Women's Literary Renaissance. As many of the vocal critics of this literary moment missed the opportunity to collectively theorize Black lives through the experiences of women, the fear of these texts as teaching tools and mirrors into Black communities and the potency of Black women's agency as readers and as a rhetorical community remained. Coupled with the apprehension that these books would perpetuate historical images of the fictional brutish and villainous Black male character, these fears reflect what Kimberly Nichele Brown describes as the deep concerns about the "dirty laundry" of their "interior lives" and questions about the impact of Black spectatorship at this moment.[37] This type of fear is a thief that can make wellness contentious and healing a means of social redemption. The suggestion is that if women were to become well at a time when African American communities were still claiming a more visible place within the broader American mainstream, it could not be at the expense of their family or community's reputation.

Independent Study: Reeducation as Remedy

Beyond poetic and fictional illustrations of empowerment, Black women writers during this literary renaissance also revived a rich tradition of essay writing as a means for working through painful situations. Cheryl Clarke's "Lesbianism as an Act of Resistance" offers one example of the joint function of personalized theorizing Black women writers carried out through the genre by the mid-eighties. With an acknowledgement of the "white male-supremacist, capitalist, misogynist, racist, homophobic, imperialist culture" wherein most Black lesbians live, Clarke unpacks the ways this culture teaches them to despise themselves before concluding with a call for readers to stop "hating ourselves" and start to practice self-love.[38] Though the essay is brief, her deft movement between acknowledging macroscopic issues and calling for personal action illustrates what Jacqueline Jones Royster considers one of the appeals of the essay for Black women. Unlike poetry, drama, and fiction wherein writers construct "imaginatively rendered worlds" and rely on the mediation of their characters, the essay, Royster argues, is a forum to address personal and social issues and their consequences and to call for action. Essay writing both reflects and fosters Black women's intellectualism by providing them access to public discourse as pedagogues and theorists. When rhetorically sound, an essay can become an "instrument for healing," Royster writes, or a means for Black women to enact their agency in resisting or repairing the conditions that wound them.[39]

Audre Lorde exemplifies this tradition in the essay "Eye to Eye: Black Women, Hatred, and Anger" from her 1984 collection *Sister Outsider* by outlining a pathway to healing that is procedural. Lorde opens with the question, "Where does the pain go when it goes away?"[40] The question is an inspiration for her to interrogate the "wide curve of ancient and unexpressed anger" that chips away at the positive forms of self-esteem Black women must develop to survive the "deathwish" of being born Black and female in America. Not unlike Shange's "metaphysical dilemma," the "deathwish" complicates their development of positive self-esteem and corrodes the most intimate parental, familial, social, and romantic relationships they may desire to form with other Black women. "We do not love ourselves. . . . Therefore we cannot love each other," she surmises. "We see in each other's face our own face, the face we never stopped wanting" and "we try to obliterate it."[41] Given the self-loathing and self-destruction this situation perpetuates, Lorde declares the "task" of training that "anger with accuracy" as one of the major works she has had to undertake in her life.[42]

With her focus on clarification and relearning, Lorde's essay "Eye to Eye" is one of the most effective examples of Black women's writing where healing is not only a pedagogical act but it is a curricular process. As Royster explains, the appeal of the essay among Black women is that it offers them a means to communicate directly with audiences and demonstrate their intellect in practice. Lorde lays bare for readers a set of challenges to wellness and solutions specific to the experience of Black women—a group that has "had to build the knowledge of so much hatred into her survival and keep going," while frequently lacking the "tools" to dissect it "or language to name it."[43] In relaying her own process for acquiring these tools, Lorde directly instructs readers on a process for radical self-care that involves debunking the myths about Black women's presumed inferiority, destabilizing the flow of hatred against them, and "reclaim[ing] the weapons" Black mothers give their daughters to survive.

Elaine Richardson makes a similar argument about the necessity of Black women applying the generational wisdom they receive from their mothers in *PHD to Ph.D.: How Education Saved My Life* where she cites her Jamaican mother's personal proverb "shame chree dead" to emphasize the importance of protecting one's self-worth.[44] Throughout Richardson's memoir, the shame chree becomes a motif in her journey to overcome the internal shame and low self-esteem that made her prey for human traffickers and predators and vulnerable to the lure of drugs as a teenager.

In her memoir, Richardson does not name steps readers must follow. A memoir does not have to. On the other hand, Lorde's "Eye to Eye" can be read as a process for radical self-care that almost formalizes a map for developing oppositional knowledge. As Lorde explains,

> Learning to love ourselves as Black women goes beyond a simplistic insistence that "Black is beautiful." It goes beyond and deeper than a surface appreciation of Black beauty, although that is certainly a good beginning. But if the quest to reclaim ourselves and each other remains there, then we risk another superficial measurement of self, one superimposed upon the old one and almost as damaging, since it pauses at the superficial. Certainly it is no more empowering. And it is empowerment—our strengthening in the service of ourselves and each other, in the service of our work and future—that will be the result of this pursuit.[45]

Lorde does not go so far as to place the process of empowerment back into domains of epistemology and language, but her essay is a gesture towards the development of a situated literacy through forms of rhetorical instruction. Because reaching wellness is a process that requires Black women to decipher dehumanizing messages and images, navigate hostile situations and traumatic events, invest in more liberating language, and draw upon the survival strategies of their foremothers, the task of ridding oneself of pain can also be a way of cultivating forms of feminist epistemologies and discursive strategies. Healing, in this sense, becomes a learning cure.

Black Women's Discourses as a Learning Cure

This genealogy is an overview of the evolving ways Black women writers have understood the role of the healer, the narrative function of pain, the constitution of healing, and procedures for these processes. Although it is partial, it suggests that the Black Women's Literary Renaissance—and the subsequent ways theorists have articulated Black feminist and womanist thought in response—were literacy events that inspired wellness campaigns. Consider once again the indignation in Darryl Pinkney's response about Black men losing their voice. If there was a concern that Black women would no longer listen to Black men or invest in maintaining social institutions, then Thomas Miller's theory about the motives of a literacy campaign holds weight. When the oppositional knowledges and epistemologies that Black women began to articulate from their own standpoints and use towards liberation are viewed as literacies—and I very much hold that they are—the perception that Black feminism or womanist thought poses a threat makes healing an endeavor that can be appropriated. A wellness campaign can become a way to restore order, and the idea of Black women's pain can become an easily exploited crisis that recurs with increasing vagueness.

Regardless of how much we debate this theory about the relationship between the Black Women's Literary Renaissance and the rise of wellness campaigns, it does not negate that Black women do have agency and an investment in collective progress and wellness. Another point this genealogy drives home is that Black women have always been talking about matters of pain and wellness. Moreover, even if writers of this moment did foster among Black women rhetorical communities that invite people to respond to these matters with solutions, these writers have consistently inscribed the value of acquiring wisdom and choice. *The Salt Eaters* exists within this tradition because Bambara does not offer her readers specific or formulaic strategies for wellness. Instead, she seems to trust that her readers are literate and discerning enough to embrace what Kimberly Nichele Brown describes as an "epistemological challenge to recognize alternative ways of thinking and being in the world."[46]

Many have accepted the challenge that writers such as Bambara pose in their books. In Beth Daniell's *A Communion of Friendship: Literacy, Spiritual Practice, and Women in Recovery,* for instance, she describes how reading books such as *The Color Purple* was formative for the presumably white female Al-Anon members of her study. For Tommie, one of the participants, reading Celie's letters was evidence that she could also write herself free. "To me, my journal is writing to God. If Celie could do it, I could do it."[47] Oprah Winfrey's experience reading Walker's book and purchasing copies to share with her friends also attests to this community-forming function of these works. In one interview she confesses, "I remember getting out of bed and buying every single copy that they had in stock. I read it that day. I was devastated, overwhelmed, empowered. All of that. I gave the book to everybody I knew. I couldn't have conversations with women who hadn't read *The Color Purple*."[48] An evangelist indeed.

Winfrey's response to these books is a reminder of the social impact of these texts. In her need to talk about *The Color Purple* with other women discerning enough to understand its value, she highlights how these healing efforts foster discourse communities around the importance of learning as a step towards a better and more fulfilling life. Furthermore, through the strategies and customs for addressing pain and wellness I show in this chapter, Black women have established a set of conventions for writers who feel compelled to respond to matters of pain. Yet, because of the images they have invoked, the forms of knowledge-making these writers privilege, and the capacity of these books to resonate among and beyond communities of Black women, even the most well-intentioned individuals hoping to address the situations these writers illustrate or to market the processes for healing in Walker's and Shange's works would have to navigate these conventions and constraints as well. Given these communities and the conventions and constraints within Black women's writing, interrogating the processes of invention writers have adopted to launch healing must be the paradigm for understanding these campaigns and who may be served by Black women becoming well.

CHAPTER 2

I Need You to Survive
Theorizing Rhetorical Healing

In the opening of *The Spirituals and the Blues,* James Cone describes one of the misconceptions about the function of Black music traditions in relation to the African American experience. According to the theologian, early collectors of Black music such as William Francis Allen, publisher of the 1867 collection *Slave Songs of the United States,* were surprised that there had been no concerted efforts to preserve or study these traditions despite the clear consistency in the way these songs appeared on plantations across the country. Cone does not suggest that Allen might have been even the slightest bit self-congratulatory over his feat of documenting a tradition that had been occurring in plain sight, but the idea is not beyond the realm of imagination. Allen was a part of a generation of music researchers who acknowledged the tonal and harmonic creativity of expression in African American spirituals yet also marveled that "half-barbarous people" had developed such a vibrant and creative form.[1] "It never occurred to him," Cone states, that "art and thought cannot be separated" or that there were subversive political critiques, social messages, and forms of instruction within the songs. Black music was functional and evolving "unity music." Through sacred and secular forms, Black music was a means of structuring and, when necessary, restructuring African Americans' understanding of their collective existence and a way to inspire the acts of resistance, reform, and renewal that might advance the whole. Over these melodies and chord configurations were textual scripts reminding African Americans that the work of establishing Black identity and making group progress is only achievable in a "communal context" of collaborative work.[2] Survival is a group project.

In chapter 1, I concluded that invention must be a focus when attempting to understand Black women's wellness campaigns. This contention acknowledges the insights of Rhetorical Genre Studies scholars such as Anis Bawarshi who explains that the beginnings of conversations are rarely discreet, temporal moments. Invention is not as much an indicator of a writer's originality as it is a reflection of their orientation. "Writers invent within genres and are themselves invented by genres," Bawarshi explains.[3] This paradox means that an individual cannot precede existing works or disregard the characteristics and customs of the sites where they write and the communities they may attempt to address because there is always a precedent. At best, writers are joining conversations and, ideally, shifting them by choosing to follow or depart from the conversation's conventions. Subsequently, the genres writers gravitate to and transform become indicators of the logics and forms of cognition that guide successful communicative exchanges between a writer and an audience. Genres influence which strategies, resources, and techniques "users generally imagine as possible within a given situation" and how they "come to know and respond to certain situations."[4] In this way, genres are places of cultural and community articulation.

The most prevalent logic undergirding rhetorics of healing is the need for collective survival, but the complexity of this set of thought patterns can go understated in analytical models of African American rhetorical praxis. The assumption that learning can be a form of liberation from pain, which inform the writings I analyze in the previous chapter, is central in both broad African American freedom efforts and the specific women's rights endeavors in which Black women have participated and continue to participate. Liberation, however, requires consistency because a person, group, or community cannot reach this state if it has succumbed to external forces or adverse systems and circumstances. Similarly, reaching a state of wellness cannot happen if a person, group, or community succumbs to wounding or oppression. Surviving is the vehicle for this continuous movement. It is an ongoing form of striving and overcoming and, where Black women are concerned, it is often constructed as a social one. Recognizing this tradition, I trace themes of survival through discussions of African American vernacular culture and rhetorical space, literacy studies, and Black feminism in the remainder of this chapter; and I outline a set of steps and criteria for determining how these discourses can work as well as who pays and who profits from these wellness campaigns.

Consider the Call: On Worldview and Interpretation

Most frameworks for analyzing forms of social action rightly begin with a consideration of the historical or cultural context out of which a discourse seems to have emerged because the preliminary step to invention and, ultimately, action is always a process of interpretation. As Carolyn Miller explains in "Genre as Social Action," rhetorical situations can rarely be traced to isolated incidents. They are not so much material endeavors as they are social urgencies and motives that reflect the values and customs of a group. As such, it is more useful to consider the pattern of choices and the sites where groups deliberate in order to understand what might inspire collective action than to focus on an isolated event. By destabilizing cause-and-effect paradigms for understanding persuasion and movement, genre frameworks enable us to understand the ways collective conceptions of rhetorical action have functioned during any one period of history.[5]

Songs such as "I Need You to Survive" encode messages of affirmation messages that often circulate as rhetorics of healing. Within many of these messages is a focus on resistance that African American community leaders, thinkers, and activists have historically embraced as a social imperative that requires them to take group action. In *Let Nobody Turn Us Around: An African American Anthology,* Manning Marable and Leith Mullings explain that collective survival has historically depended on African Americans' ability to resist oppression, reform systems and structures, and renew their communities within aggressively racist environments.[6] Enslaved Africans were not tabula rasas, void of cultural memory when they were forcefully brought to America. They brought with them traditions, practices, and values with the intent of preserving connections to their home cultures and ways of life. To preserve those cultures and transmit them to new generations, African Americans undertook a process of re-creation. By cultivating customs and interior spaces, they carried out the project of "utilizing, transforming, and giving new meaning to cultural material from Africa and the Americas" that could aid them in withstanding daily forms of dehumanization or assault.

Refashioning cultural material for everyday use is a function of the African American vernacular culture in which many wellness efforts and campaigns take their historical roots. Through song, story, folk sayings, and rich verbal interplay, African Americans have transmitted underlying thought patterns, belief sets, values, and ways of looking at the world that make up a traditional African worldview. As Geneva Smitherman explains in *Talkin and Testifyin: The Language of Black America*, traditional African worldview asserts that there is a "fundamental unity between the spiritual and material aspects of existence" that transcends imposed forms of segregation and disconnect.[7] Sacred spaces such as the traditional Black church and secular spaces such as the street, barbershop, beauty salon, or juke joint operate as a continuum by fostering the "coping strategies for this world" that are essential in "gittin' ovuh."[8] As Smitherman explains, the concept of 'gittin' ovuh,' in a religious sense, refers to "spiritual survival in a sinister world of sin." In a secular sense, the term "speaks to material survival in a white world of oppression. Since men and women live neither by bread nor spirit alone, both vitally necessary acts of gittin' ovuh challenge the human spirit to 'keep on pushin' toward higher ground.'" Both conceptions of the act foreground the kinds of psychic pain associated with second- and third-class citizenship and offer a response to systemic racism, economic injustice, and political oppression that can negatively influence an individual's self-esteem and sense of self-worth. Vernacular spaces and practices that affirm and reinforce one's sense of self-purpose foster the rhetorical acts of resistance necessary for an individual's survival in a hostile environment.

The idea of traditional African worldview undoubtedly influences how writers interpret the troubling issues and painful situations that healing efforts must address; however, healing can also reflect a writer's sense of subjectivity as a racialized or gendered "other." The concept of the "Black Rhetorical Condition" that I glean from Elaine Richardson's discussion of the relationship between vernacular culture, epistemology and ways of knowing, and rhetorical activity in *African American Literacies* brilliantly encapsulates the duality of consciousness that can also drive the impulse to heal and its implications. A state of being "desired and devalued," Richardson's term is a contextual and cognitive lens for understanding the same complex forms of identity W.E.B. Du Bois describes as "double consciousness," or a psychosocial condition of looking at oneself from the eyes of another, in *The Souls of Black Folk*.[9] Vernacular customs and discourse practices such as call and response originated because African Americans have needed ways of "self-identification" and communication that are apart from the dominant cultures that embrace their labor and reject their humanity.[10] Counterlinguistic practices and vernacular arts such as gospel music are the means African Americans have used to make their lives better.[11]

Richardson's definition of the vernacular is central to *Rhetorical Healing* because implicit in her description of the "Black Rhetorical Condition" is an acknowledgement of the disparaging narratives about and perceptions of African Americans circulating within dominant culture that uphold the need for vernacular culture. African Americans have not sought just to create these songs, messages, narratives, and separate spaces; at times, segregation, vilification, denial, and other oppressive practices have either pushed them into the spaces or made these cultures necessary. The vernacular offers individuals ways to resist and subvert the white gaze. And yet, the white gaze continues to hold an adverse affect on African Americans' relationships with each other because it promotes internal judgment and forms of behavior policing.

The same gaze that fosters a need for African American vernacular culture can manifest in the concerns for respectable representations that also make writers decide to address situations affecting Black women. As African Americans have taken on more visible roles within the mainstream public, so too have the corresponding forms of surveillance and monitoring. Vernacular practices and performances once considered valuable means of community building, expression, or innovation within hostile environments have come to be monitored by critics who fear such practices will be used to validate disparaging ways of viewing the Black community as a whole. A look at some of the reactions to Black women's participation in reality-television culture over the last decade shows this trend as deep and sometimes ugly forms of self-consciousness and nervousness are unearthed in the fear that all African Americans will be lumped together in the eyes of the other groups through the behavior of these small groups of women. Wellness campaigns can also stem from these forms of self-consciousness and the fear of how the body, or the collective, is perceived by the dominant other. To account for these discourses in action, it is always necessary to consider the conditions of the call a writer makes to gain the readers' participation. Healing can also be a way to ensure a community retains its respectable reputation.

Question the Crisis: On Invention and Institutional Politics

Rhetorics of healing also stem from complicated efforts to ensure collective group identity. To make group survival a renewable practice, African Americans transformed some of their vernacular spaces into socioeconomic and religious institutions that provided goods, services, and resources. During the enslavement era, these efforts involved free African Americans in the North establishing mutual benefit organizations to help Black families in need and free women of color actively organizing abolitionist activities and self-help efforts. These efforts led to the creation of such institutions as the Black press, schools and colleges, hospitals, insurance companies, banks, and commercial enterprises of various sorts. By constructing this interior Black world, African Americans became keepers of their own history and custodians of their educational practices. Maintaining this interior world has required that African American leaders, in particular, attempt to write and rewrite what Marable and Mullings call "boundaries of Blackness," or the "expectations that African Americans remain loyal to their race, support the goals and values generally accepted as cultural norm for their communities."[12]

Because "boundaries of Blackness" are unstable, the rhetorics of healing that writers deploy to take action against the social ills that wound members of their communities also have to be situated within the spatial and ideological histories of the writer and their intended audience's shared rhetorical community or institution. Many of the frameworks for understanding the rhetorical dynamics of space originate out of efforts to rework the concept of the public sphere (Arendt, 1958; Habermas, 1989), or a zone of social activity between civil society where private individuals with social capital use their intellectual reason to appropriate the state-governed public sphere, create a commonwealth and, ultimately, the rise of public opinion.[13] To date, Nancy Fraser, Michael Warner, and the Black Public Sphere Collective have all reworked Habermas's concept. While Fraser observed that the traditional conception of the public sphere ignores the presence of women, the presence of women, people of color, and the lower class,[14] Warner coined the concept of "counterpublics" to describe the spaces and spheres of activity marginalized groups have developed to negotiate limited participation and to resist hegemonic ways of thinking in *Publics and Counterpublics* (2005).[15] Warner argues that counterpublics are sometimes defined by their opposition to the larger public. Participants within these spaces are "marked off" from persons or citizens in general. The conversations that occur within these spaces are understood to conflict with the dominant rules upheld in the broader public at large because they are structured by alternative dispositions or protocols and different assumptions about what can be said or what goes without saying.[16] This kind of public constitutes a counterpublic because it maintains at some level, conscious or not, an awareness of its subordinate status. Correspondingly, many of the discourses circulating in these spaces reinforce what it means to be a part of these counterpublic groups.

These interventions into the concept of public space highlight the types of identity and institutional politics that inspire some rhetorics of healing. Both Vorris Nunley and Gwendolyn Pough have theorized how race and gender influence rhetorical space and praxis. With his discussion of the construction of Black audiences and subjectivities in hush harbor spaces and through hush harbor rhetoric, Nunley's concept suggests that the step of invention that may follow the act of interpretation within a healing process is often related to conceptions of spatiality. In *Keepin' It Hushed: The Barbershop and African American Hush Harbor Rhetoric,* Nunley illustrates how African American counterpublic spaces foster and preserve the types of epistemes, or worldviews, that signify an ethos of Blackness. Hush harbors are material goegraphies such as the "slave quarters, woods, and praise houses where Black folks could speak frankly in Black spaces in front of Black audiences" and where they can replenish themselves from the types of "social death" that occur when they must suppress their own ontologies and culturally situated ways of knowing in order to engage in the dominant public.[17] A facet of the interior Black world Marable and Mullings describe, hush harbors are the private spaces that cultivate nomoi, or social conventions and beliefs that constitute a worldview or knowledge and epistemology. In turn, hush harbor rhetorics are discursive resources that enable individuals to circulate these "hidden" ways of collective knowing and thought in the presence of dominant audiences.[18] Within spaces such as the Black theatre or targeted periodicals, writers have been able to invent and construct a "Black audience" to whom they can pass on instructions about survival and healing that enable its members to disrupt the collective assumptions, or *sensus communis*, that have operated against African Americans. In this way, Black women's magazines such as *Essence* and novels become the genres and strategic sites where a writer can invoke discourses that promote the goal of individual healing and community survival.

Of course, even African American counterpublic spaces that originate out of the goal of establishing "boundaries of Blackness," nationalist projects, or attempts to ensure the continuance of an interior world can replicate some of the same narrow ideologies and unwelcoming characteristics that make them necessary. The kinds of silencing and wounding that occur in these spaces is one catalyst behind Black women's use of "wreck," which Gwendolyn Pough theorizes as a disruptive communicative practice. In *Check It While I Wreck It: Black Women, Hip-Hop Culture, and the Public Sphere*, Pough advances the work of scholars such as The Black Public Sphere Collective who, in the nineties, defined the Black public sphere as a space of "critical practice and visionary politics" that includes magazines, salons, coffee shops, and highbrow tracts as well as vernacular practices such as street talk, new music, radio shows, and church voices where members deliberate to challenge the exclusionary violence occurring in much of the public space within the United States.[19] As Pough notes, Black public spheres have promoted resistance strategies such as the "politics of respectability," or a behavioral strategy advocated by Black clubwomen that emphasizes the "reform of individual behavior," moral living, and self-conduct that African Americans could employ to demonstrate to themselves and whites that they deserve respect.[20] Ironically, these practices have also fostered a culture of dissemblance, or a collective and often oppressive silencing regarding issues of Black women's sexuality, morality, and behavior. Marked by the same heightened sense of self-consciousness that creates controversies over vernacular practices and texts, the culture of dissemblance that Pough identifies accounts for the way these tensions converge with gender norms and result in Black women's oppression within vernacular culture and spaces. In this culture, spaces that seem to provide refuge and invite discussions on community building and knowledge making can become exclusive zones where Black women's behaviors are monitored through discourses, texts, and public opinion.

Given this history, questioning the nature of a crisis must also be a step when analyzing forms of rhetorical healing because institutional and ideological self-checks are necessary in these African American wellness projects. The traditional African American church has been one of the spaces where Blacks could gather away from the guise of surveillance, and spirituality and organized Christianity are worldview systems that have had the heaviest influence on the campaigns that I study in this book. By virtue of the church's institutional role, it is necessary to interrogate how writers affiliated with it and other religious organizations invent strategies in response to their interpretation of crises affecting the African American body. In *Digital Griots: African American Rhetorics in a Multimedia Age*, Adam Banks demonstrates why it is important to always consider the genres, discourses, and efforts that come from spaces such as the church. As he notes, the Black sermon is one of the most parodied yet influential genres because of the church's and the minister's deeply influential roles in these communities. As such, the propensity of this genre and these ministers to uphold cultures of dissemblance is high because even as the church has been integral in the freedom struggle, it has also demonstrated what Banks describes as a "conservative tolerance of and even participation in the oppression of African Americans."[21] Banks points to Black liberation theology, or an anti-oppression effort asserting that God is on the side of the distressed; and individuals need to provide immediate help rather than relying on "otherworldly" remedies as an ethical way to account for these tensions. Liberation may be a future goal but, ideally, some semblance of it should be visible within one's lifetime.[22]

The matter of ethics that Banks interrogates within the institution of the Black church raises one of the critical concerns that rhetorical healing must address. It has only been recently that prominent African American pastors have begun to discuss hypocrisies in the church's treatment towards LGBTQ individuals and even then the silence has remained strong and the vocabulary still remains tentative and politically ambiguous. These cultures of dissemblance and overall lukewarmness can have a high influence on the curricula writers generate and teach Black women audiences to adopt as means for obtaining wellness. It is always necessary to consider the motives and timing behind any healing effort particularly when institutions and institutional agents have their own agendas. Wellness should not be a "by and by" type of project.

Identify the Yield: On Intervention and Application

Rhetorics of healing also reflect an emphasis on literacy as a means of intervening in social problems as well as enacting and extending community. One of the more popular adages from *The Oprah Winfrey Show* to work its way into social media and general discourse is the late poet Maya Angelou's observation about the importance of continuous learning and forgiveness. During a November 2011 *Lifeclass* episode devoted to the eighth most important life lesson Winfrey had learned, the host reflected on her love of the late poet's books, the mentor relationship the two shared, and the advice Angelou had given her about a mistake Winfrey had made when she was younger. "That was when you were twenty," Angelou explained. "Once you know better, you do better."[23] Winfrey confessed that she had quoted Angelou's advice forty-three times during her talk show's run, interjecting the advice during moments when guests appeared to be consumed with personal guilt over their past mistakes.

Winfrey's ability to apply this adage demonstrates the emphasis on social and practical application that distinguishes how rhetorics of healing need to be conceptualized and assessed. To date, the concept of the 'social turn' remains the prevailing way that scholars have expanded the traditional conceptions of literacy. Through ethnographic studies of literacies found in working communities, churches, and Latino gangs, and explorations of the efficacy of multicultural approaches to language instruction, literacy studies scholars have challenged dichotomies between orality and literacy, mythologies asserting that literacy competence is innate in upper-class Western societies, and monolithic approaches that limit literacy to traditional forms of reading and writing (Heath, 1983; Brandt, 1990; Street, 1993; Gee, 1996; Cintron, 1998; Royster, 1999; Moss, 2003; Richardson, 2003). The body of scholarship categorized as a 'social turn' asserts that literacies are socially and culturally situated forms of reading and writing discursive and non-discursive scripts implicated in social processes and individual action.[24]

Since dominant cultures within the United States have traditionally used narrow conceptualizations of literacy to impede, regulate, and assess the interactions of African Americans in broader society, adopting the insights of this social turn as a framework for examining African American literacy practices requires an understanding of the inherently rhetorical nature of literacy within this community. As Royster points out in *Traces of a Stream: Literacy and Social Change Among African American Women*, the move to examine literate practices as behaviors or events within sociocultural contexts that is characteristic of the social turn frequently fails to observe or articulate the human aspect of engaging in literate practices. Accounting for this human aspect requires the type of conceptual frame that acknowledges how cultural mandates, or social imperatives as Royster describes them, make people in historically marginalized groups feel obligated to use their literacies for the protection, preservation, and improvement of themselves and their communities. Cultural mandates influence the styles and techniques writers use to engage in sociopolitical action and the ingenuity they demonstrate when undertaking long-term campaigns. As such, analyzing African Americans' literacy practices requires some attention to how acts of writing, reading, meaning-making and other interpretive and communicative processes can be undertaken as means of performance.

Rhetorics of healing build upon these literacies and knowledge systems because are the resources writers draw upon as forms of agency to intervene in crises affecting members of their communities. Moreover, they illustrate the types of agency readers and viewers are supposed to gain and demonstrate through a healing curriculum. With her discussions of sociocognitive ability and rhetorical competence, Royster introduces a theory of literacy as sociopolitical action, which provides the second major theoretical framework for my analysis of African American rhetorics of healing. For Royster, literacy is sociocognitive ability, or the ability to "gain access to information and to use this information variously to articulate lives and experiences and also to identify, think through, refine, and solve problems, complex problems, over time."[25] An objective resource, sociocognitive ability becomes a subjective form of literate agency for Black women when they identify hermeneutical problems, or the gaps in sense that produce crises that warrant action, and develop the tasks that enable them to solve them. Despite the renaissance I discussed in chapter 1, Black women have historically had their access to public and publishing platforms restricted or overtly blocked. The task for the Black woman writer, then, is to determine how to negotiate literacy challenges and to figure out how to perform in a way that yields changes in thinking, perception, attitudes, and behavior.

Royster's concept of rhetorical competence is one of the evaluative concepts I use throughout this book. An individual's rhetorical competence reflects the writer's orientation, as Bawarshi terms it, and his or her ability to apply literacies at the appropriate time and towards a specific goal. Although Royster's study focuses on African American female essayists who have influenced public opinion and social change by using their rhetorical competence for creating hermeneutical space to join with their audiences and solve problems, its implications for understanding rhetorical action holds. The writer who is invested in his or her audience's survival has to demonstrate awareness of the community's values and principles. Most often, these performances occur through literate acts of deciphering and analyzing existing scripts that have wounded African Americans or Black women as a body. These performances enable writers to create consubstantial space with audiences that do not necessarily share their interests and to offer these audiences incentives for adopting practices and processes the writers consider conducive to promoting social change.

The emphasis on change inherent in this literacy tradition means that analyzing rhetorical healing processes must identify the yield that writers and readers expect to gain from a wellness campaign. Along with Richardson's concept of the Black Rhetorical Condition, which helps us see how the impulse to "heal" individuals in crisis can be an act of resistance that aids in survival, Royster's theory of literacy as sociopolitical action highlights the human aspect of care and social relationship that inspires the forms of crisis intervention and problem solving writers aim to carry out by writing books, sermons, and films such as the ones I study. Both concepts show the pragmatic and utilitarian goals of healing. Since wellness requires sustainability, Richardson's definition of African American literacies articulates the kinds of day-to-day practices that are assumed to promote preservation. Like Royster's definition, Richardson's definition foregrounds the social, because literacy for people of African descent is

> the ability to accurately read their experiences being in the world with others and to act on this knowledge in a manner beneficial for self-preservation, economic, spiritual, and cultural uplift. African American literacies are ways of knowing and being in the world with others.[26]

African American literacies thereby include cultural practices of reading, writing, speaking, storytelling, listening, rhyming, rapping, dancing, computing, phoning, signifyin', and other "vehicles for deciphering and applying knowledge of public transcripts to one's environment or situation" in ways that allow them, and Black women in particular, to "advance or protect the self."[27] Through these literacy acts and practices, Richardson argues that African Americans activate their culturally situated knowledges in persuasive ways that enable them to resist and challenge negative images or discourses circulating within and around their communities and participate in the collective writing of community-based scripts that preserve their communities.

Richardson's conception of literacy among Black women means that any attractive wellness curriculum should offer incentives that position them to be vocal and socially active citizens. Because these resources and the arguments that writers invoke to essentially market them overlap with the goal of collective survival, identifying the yield can show who benefits from the work Black women undertake to protect themselves and others. Given the emotional, physical, and mental labor that Black women enact to promote overall wellness, identifying the yield of a wellness campaign enables us to determine if healing, like survival, is sustainable and liberating or if a wellness campaign is simply a gesture of repair.

Determine the Fit: On Consciousness and Quality of Life

Rhetorics of healing have also emerged out of the concerted efforts Black women have made to focus on their own self-preservation and survival. The discussions of pain and healing I trace in chapter 1 are the creative and narrative counterparts to the specific resistance, reform, and renewal efforts they have waged with and within broader liberation efforts pursuing the well-being of the collective race. From the stinging social and political critiques of figures such as Maria Stewart, Sojourner Truth, and Frances Ellen Watkins Harper, to Ida B. Wells's masterful anti-lynching analyses, Black women have often composed arguments that, out of necessity and social urgency, placed a precedent on the preservation of African American lives and matters of racial and social uplift. When most Black women activists and leaders of the nineteenth century did centralize issues specific to them and their needs in their speeches or writings, they did so to make bigger arguments about social inequity. Offering their experiences as proof of various types of oppression, Black women intellectuals frequently made the argument that if the Black woman was oppressed then all women were oppressed and all Blacks were oppressed. Addressing their needs and incorporating their perspectives was vital to the survival and progress of both groups.

The shift away from these synecdochical forms of thinking and argument ignited the individualized focus on wellness launching most contemporary rhetorics of healing. As mentioned in chapter 1, Toni Cade Bambara's groundbreaking collection *The Black Woman: An Anthology* was one of the first defined efforts to assemble Black women's critical perspectives on their struggles with and within African Black liberation efforts and feminist liberation efforts. With essays such as Kay Lindsey's "The Black Woman as Woman" wherein the author describes how the masculinist focus of Black liberation and the lack of race-based focus within feminist liberation efforts placed Black women "on the outside" of both political entities, the book was a critical stance against liberation efforts mired by false notions of universal womanhood and universal Black experiences.[28] Moreover, with Bambara's own move to outline an "Afrafemme" worldview that explored "first the interiority of an in-the-head, in-the-heart, in-the gut region of a discovery called the *self*," the anthology showed the kinds of spatial politics that second-wave Black feminists were exposing at that time.[29] Survival had to become a self-centered process because other liberation efforts were pushing Black women to the margins.

Whereas Bambara's call for self-examination gives historical and social context to the internal work Black women are often encouraged to do as part of the healing process, the Combahee River Collective's 1977 "A Black Feminist Statement" best articulates the paradigmatic shift and focus on autonomous consciousness that foregrounds one of the motives for addressing Black women's healing needs. Committed to combating racial, sexual, heterosexual, and class-based oppression, the Collective had a motive for developing an analysis of interlocking systems of oppression that stemmed from their recognition that liberating the Black women was a necessity "not as an adjunct to somebody else's but because of our need as human persons for autonomy."[30] In their recognition that society, even Black society, was constructed on the premise that "anyone is more worthy of liberation" than the Black woman, their desire "to be recognized as human, levelly human" is an epistemological shift that lays the groundwork for discourses on healing that pertain specifically to Black women.[31]

These two epistemological shifts offer historical markers for the focus on individual consciousness and gender foregrounded in rhetorics of healing. In *Black Feminist Thought: Knowledge, Consciousness, and the Politics of Empowerment*, Patricia Hill Collins argues that Black women's efforts to "expose and resist the exploitation of Black women's labor, to challenge the denial of Black women's political, social, and sexual liberties [and] to resist, challenge, and transform controlling ideologies and images regarding Black women," constitute a critical social theory.[32] Among this group, this type of critical social theory encompasses the "bodies of knowledge" and "institutional practices" that promote Black women's equitable participation in dealing with central questions facing them as collective; in this manner, Black feminist thought's identity as a "critical" social theory lies in its commitment to justice, both for Black women as a collectivity and for other oppressed groups.[33] Healing discourses are often framed as endeavors to right or prevent wrongs and ensure that justice is served for the individual in crisis and the community in which she exists. When healing projects make explicit the ways of knowing that enable Black women to combat injustice, they are an extension of these movements. Ideally, healing should transfer authority to the subjects and audiences of these discourses.

This focus on transferring authority means that the process of analyzing rhetorical healing has to test the fit of any curriculum purporting to guide Black women to wellness or to provide them with resources. The forms of intellectualism, mobility, and access that Black feminist thought works to promote make it easy to assume any healing discourse prioritizing learning offers the same measure of empowerment. This is not necessarily the case. As Joy James's research on liberal, radical, and revolutionary feminisms indicates, rhetorics of healing are vulnerable to the expectations of Black women's service that can lead to a depersonalization of these messages even as they seem specific and catered to this group's needs. In *Shadowboxing: Representations of Black Feminist Politics,* James traces the distinction among forms of Black feminism that have emerged in histories of Black women's intellectualism. To varying degrees, each form produces a type of change and reform. Liberal feminisms are political stances and efforts that reflect an acceptance of the political legitimacy of corporate-state, institutional, and police power while emphasizing the need for only humanistic reform.[34] Radical feminisms are different in that they view oppression as a lingering effect of capitalism, neocolonialism, and the corporate-state structure. Revolutionary Black feminisms are the most dynamic of the three. They are rooted in explicitly political practices relevant to existing material conditions and an understanding of Black women's social consciousness. Although these feminisms are episodic, they transgress "corporate culture by focusing on female independence; community building and caretaking, and resistance to state domination."[35]

By determining the fit of a wellness campaign, I am arguing that rhetorical healing processes must centralize Black women's quality of life. With the multiplicity of feminisms that James identifies, it is easy to lose sight of the distinctions between liberal, revolutionary, antirevolutionary, and counterrevolutionary politics and how they encode different conceptions of the worlds Black women will live in as citizens. When writers co-opt the arguments and styles of the discourses advancing these separate traditions, the result can be a form of blurring that makes feminism—much like forms of healing—normalized to the point where it loses its distinction and political drive. To test the fit, then, is to keep Black women at the center of these efforts, remember the personal and spatial politics that inspire these discourses, and consider what long-term effects healing projects have.

On Competence and Consequence: Assessing Rhetorical Healing

Like survival, the term 'healing' can be a subjective term. When cast as the goal of sociopolitical action or an educational endeavor, it can refer to a myriad of processes that include resolving crises, identifying social ills, redressing the results of individual trauma or violence, or covering up disparaging representations and images about Black communities. In this respect, healing can operate like the "slippery discourses" researchers and teachers employ in efforts to advance the "critical" literacy curricula or "emancipatory" pedagogy they offer as ways of promoting vaguely defined concepts of 'social change' or 'empowerment.' As Ellen Cushman explains, the slippery discourse instructors and researchers employ in these endeavors stems from a "slick assumption" that social change and empowerment lead to "collective action or resistance involving the masses of people we teach."[36] When the teacher or researcher is imbued with more institutional, financial, or social privilege than the individual or group she or he is trying to teach, the slippery discourse of intended outcomes such as 'social change' or 'empowerment' reflects not only the writer's worldview, loyalties, and sense of personal power, but also his or her attitudes towards the audience.

The assessment portion of rhetorical healing extends from these contexts and discussions. In addition to undertaking the steps of considering the call, questioning the crisis, identifying the yield, and determining the fit, I draw upon the heuristic for rhetorical decision-making Royster develops in *Traces of a Stream*. I use this approach to evaluate the particular choices writers make and discursive performances they undertake when identifying crises that warrant their response and inventing strategies to make healing feasible. She uses the concept of the "writer's task" to account for the particular imperative inspiring writers to take action through writing and the corresponding constraints they must navigate, and the "writer's choice," or the persuasive and textual resources at their disposal as a means for understanding writing as a form of rhetorical activity.[37] In taking these matters into account, I aim to identify the *rhetorical competence*, or innovation and savvy, writers demonstrate to carry out a sociopolitical agenda, such as healing, in ways that make readers or viewers feel compelled to act.

With the consistent message that African American communities need the Black woman to survive and be healed, the second aspect of this framework focuses on the *rhetorical consequences* of these campaigns.

Although Royster's theory identifies the forms of agency writers take in solving problems, it foregrounds Black women as the agents of these discourses. We still need to consider what happens when they are the subjects and students of these campaigns and when the curricula and actions they are persuaded to adopt emerge out of contexts and institutions that benefit from their participation and labor. We also need to understand how the recurrence and transfer of these messages throughout books, plays, films, television adaptations, spin-offs, and so forth, constrict, normalize, and obscure these messages in ways that make their political implications more difficult to see. To account for these outcomes, I rely on scholarship on each figure's social impact and Black feminism and womanist thought to consider the agency these healing efforts are supposed to promote since much of Black feminist thought has developed to guide women in navigating their social spaces and worlds. In this way, identifying the *rhetorical consequence* of a campaign enables us to determine the pedagogical techniques and discursive implications of these messages.

CHAPTER 3

I'll Teach You to See Again
The Rhetoric of Revision in Iyanla Vanzant's Self-Help Franchise

Amid speculations that OWN (the Oprah Winfrey Network) would not survive through its second season, Black women gave the fledgling network a ratings bump in fall 2012 by tweeting during the official series premier of *Iyanla: Fix My Life*. The highly promoted two-part episode featured *Basketball Wives*' star Evelyn Lozada. One of the most volatile figures within the wave of reality-based television series such as Bravo's *The Real Housewives of Atlanta* and VH1's *Love and Hip Hop*, Lozada seemed to revel in the role of antagonist until critics began to question what her drink-throwing tantrums and physical and verbal attacks meant for representations of women of color. Calls for viewer boycotts followed. Lozada responded in a June 2012 issue of the *Huffington Post* by penning an open letter addressed to her seven-year-old self wherein she vowed to "be better."[1] Her contrition and desire for self-improvement made her an ideal candidate for the new show. As if the idea that Lozada might reveal to a therapist why she lashed out at fellow guests on her show was not enough to draw reality television fans to the new show, the news (just weeks after her letter appeared in the *Huffington Post*) that the reality star had filed domestic violence charges against her then recently wed husband, football star Chad Ochocinco Johnson, made the season premier all the more salacious. Ratings for Vanzant's show were among the highest on Winfrey's network that month.

On both *Fix My Life* episodes, Vanzant counseled Lozada using techniques from books such as her 1996 best seller, *The Value in the Valley: A Black Woman's Guide Through Life's Dilemmas*. In the book, Vanzant likens "valleys" to schools that serve the purpose of teaching people where they should place their focus and channel their work. Valleys are important learning opportunities for Black women, Vanzant explains, because

> black women do not understand there is no wrong in being human, only lessons. . . . Self-knowledge is not about picking your scabs, beating up yourself, feeling bad about your wounds or weak spots. It means that you recognize you have them, make a commitment to nurture and strengthen them, and leave them alone to heal.[2]

By the end of the episode, Vanzant's compassion and challenging exercises seemed to endear the host to a new group of fans, some of whom had not read her books or known of the personal and financial struggles that prompted her to "do the work" of learning to be well again. The following week, viewers responded. During an episode of the TV One reality series *R&B Divas* featuring a discussion of domestic violence, fans tweeted that Vanzant needed to make an appearance so the "healing can begin." Another fan named Sojourner Ruth tweeted that the practice of "pouring out her feelings on paper" had been a means of healing from the pain of her father's death. Vanzant was back.

Criticisms of *Fix My Life* did not emerge until midseason. After a November 2012 episode entitled "Fix My Fallen Star," featuring former teen actress Maia Campbell, questions about the appropriateness and implications of Vanzant's strategies began to circulate online. Campbell, the daughter of the late fiction novelist Bebe Moore Campbell, first achieved fame as the teenage star of the NBC sitcom *In The House* and then appeared in a series of small movie roles and music videos. Later years were difficult for her. Cellphone video of her in an erratic state had gone viral, and then she had a series of arrests. With the subsequent reports of her bipolar disorder and her eventual residency in a mental-health facility, Campbell became one of the first *Fix My Life* guests with an actual, diagnosed medical condition.

Although Vanzant did open the show by acknowledging that her guest's condition was beyond the realm of her actual training, the host was not as careful during the acting simulation she and the producers staged to process Campbell's trauma. Assuming the role of the director, Vanzant guided Campbell, cast as a thespian, through a series of self-examination and relanguaging exercises while forcing her guest to confront enlarged images of herself at the height of one of her episodes.

Even though Campbell's discomfort was visible, Vanzant kept prodding her guest to take a hard look at herself, "do the work," and accept responsibility for her actions. The portions of their sessions that may remain on the cutting room floor are unknown to us, but the "work" segments that made the final cut were so troubling that Five East, a Black female blogger, penned an open letter to Vanzant: "There is a reason people have to become licensed to do the work that you haphazardly began to dismantle. . . . You tried to force her to bend her mind back into its darkest corners so that you could get the reaction you wanted, needed even, for ratings. Or maybe just for your own ego. Who the hell knows?"[3] For Five East, these healing efforts did not justify the means.

The rhetoric of revision throughout Vanzant's earliest books reveals the forms of redirection embedded in her concept of healing that enable us to see the implications of these instructional means. Since publishing her first essays in *Essence* in the late eighties, Vanzant has carved a sustaining space in a self-help market featuring writers such as Susan Taylor, the former editor-in-chief at *Essence* and author of the collections *In the Spirit* and *Lessons in Living*; and Eric V. Copage, author of *Black Pearls: Daily Meditations, Affirmations, and Inspirations for African-Americans*, credited with helping African Americans balance toxic messages and elevate their self-esteem. Her initial contribution was a series of books promising readers instructions on how they can acquire the "spiritual vision" necessary to unify the African American community. While she confessed that her initial choice to write books was a response to what she saw as fractures within African American communities stemming from strained financial, political, familial, and interpersonal relationships, Vanzant has directed much of her writing, teaching, and healing work toward Black women, a group whose wellness she considers a catalyst to resolving a myriad of broader social problems. As she explains in *Interiors: A Black Woman's Healing in Progress*, America is bound to remain in disrepair until Black women are well. "Slavery, racial violence, segregation, poverty, and contemptuous disregard for life" are all social issues that will persist. "Of children killing each other. Of men killing and abusing women and warring with one another," she notes. "Of starvation, homelessness, and disease, and despair in every corner of the world—not one of these wounds will be healed until the Black woman in the United States is healed, or rather, heals herself."[4]

Vanzant's arguments and methods position her near several resistance traditions. In its urgency, Vanzant's call for Black women's healing resembles the claims of Anna Julia Cooper, the late educator and activist, who argued in the late nineteenth-century that it is only the Black woman who can say "when and where I enter in the quiet, undisputed dignity of my womanhood, without violence and without suing or special patronage and then the whole Negro race enters with me"[5] In addition to situating Black women's wellness as leverage for social and political reform, her relanguaging strategies are similar to the counterlinguistic language practices Keith Gilyard identifies as subversive ways African Americans have confronted attacks and victimization. These are the strengths in her approach. Vanzant's process of revision seems to indicate how contemporary Black women undergo forms of reeducation to cultivate and understand their literacies in relation to individual and social crises.

Reading Revision: Narratives and Textbooks as a Form of Pedagogical Action

In *The Suffering Will Not Be Televised: African American Women and Sentimental Political Storytelling*, Rebecca Wanzo uses the term "homogenization" to define a practice where writers or speakers cast suffering as a universal experience.[6] Devoid of specific race, class, or gender inequities, homogenization invites wider identification among reading, viewing, or listening audiences. As mentioned in the introduction, Wanzo considers Oprah Winfrey one of the most visible proponents of this technique and points to the way the host facilitated discussions of Toni Morrison's *The Bluest Eye* on an episode of her show in 2000 as an example of what homogenization promotes. With the esteemed author and a group of book-club members at the host's home, Winfrey reduced discussions of Pecola Breedlove, Morrison's protagonist, to a conversation about the importance of self-determination. By homogenizing the obvious forms of racism and sexism this book illustrates in favor of discussing broader forms of universal discomfort or suffering, Winfrey promotes what Wanzo considers dangerous "sentimental reading practices" that acknowledge broad forms of social inequity all the while redirecting readers' attention away from them.

Homogenization is a useful concept when conceptualizing the challenge in analyzing the rhetoric of healing within Vanzant's work and its implications. As suggested in chapter 1, even if Black women writers may not set out to write fiction in instructional ways, readers are apt to look for themselves in these texts and glean forms of instruction and wisdom from them. The lived testimony is a very effective genre.

While Vanzant had already attained a loyal following among African American readers when she became a regular guest on Winfrey's show in the mid-to-late nineties, it is shortsighted to neglect editorial influence and make causal arguments regarding her appearances on Winfrey's talk show and the less-racially specific tone she employs to address audiences in books such as *In the Meantime: Finding Yourself and the Love You Want*. Still, when considering what these rhetorical choices may mean for the Black women who consistently read and support her work, recognizing homogenization is a step towards identifying the forms of appropriation writers undertake when crafting arguments or the implications when these efforts are enacted across different genres.

To gain a clearer view of Vanzant's process, I analyze the performances she stages to construct and instruct readers in three of her earliest books: *Tapping the Power Within: A Path to Self-Empowerment Among Black Women*, *Interiors: A Black Woman's Healing in Progress*, and *The Value in the Valley: A Black Woman's Guide Through Life's Dilemmas*. I draw upon scholarship in histories of African American education, self-help culture, literacy studies, therapeutic writing, and Black feminist thought as analytical and critical frameworks to contextualize the process of construction and instruction as a form of rhetorical healing. I begin by situating the genre of non-fiction, self-empowerment literature—of which Vanzant is a part—within the contexts of American self-help history, African American and African independent educational efforts, and Black women's intellectual traditions to illustrate why her arguments about healing might resonate among this group. Secondly, I analyze and critique the arguments and performances Vanzant uses to respond to and construct a mandate for healing to show where she exists within and departs from a tradition of Black women's writing. Finally, I combine the insights of scholars such as Elaine Richardson, Beth Daniell, Micki McGee, bell hooks, Patricia Hill Collins and others to determine the implications of her healing curricula on how we understand the role of literacy and empowerment through critical consciousness in these campaigns. The rhetoric of healing Vanzant employs to teach women how to see again or "do the work" of reversing miseducation suggests her books contain the forms of critical pedagogy that promote critical consciousness; but it also purports contradictory and distorted notions of Black women's personal and political agency. Ultimately, the state wellness her curricula promote falls short of cultivating in Black women the rich legacy of critical sociopolitical engagement with the public that the rhetorical themes she uses have symbolized.

Reinvention: Legacies of Self-Education and Intellectual Resistance

Self-help-literature scholars cite several reasons for the genre's popularity among American audiences. These reasons are useful in illuminating the legacies of educational resistance and Black women's intellectualism that Vanzant tapped into with her choice to write books as a tool for healing. In *Self-Help Inc.: Makeover Culture in America,* Micki McGee explains that books such as *You Don't Have to Be Thin to Win* or *Looking Out for Number One*, for instance, reveal how entrenched the concept of the "self-invention" remains in American culture. With roots in the notion of individual success epitomized by such "self-made men" as Benjamin Franklin, Andrew Carnegie, and, most recently, Bill Gates, the idea that an American—in this case, heterosexual, able-bodied, white male—could attain unlimited material, social, and personal success was an identifiable worldview in some of the earliest texts now classified as self-help.[7] Ironically, as exclusionary as the idea of the self-made, self-invented man is, McGee argues that this literary genre grew more culturally relevant with the advent of the civil rights and women's liberation movements. As individuals who had not historically been granted access to spheres and resources of power sought insight on how to obtain their versions of an "American dream," the growing field of individuals competing for status in the workplace and other social arenas led to an increased value for books promising to teach readers strategies and processes for advancement. Conversely, individuals who desire to protect their economic capital and social privilege also turn to these books for strategies on how to stay in power.

McGee does not acknowledge in detail the systemic inequities that have oppressed historically marginalized groups here. Still, her suggestion that self-help books focusing on invention and reinvention appeal to individuals seeking to resist or maintain forms of power holds some weight given African Americans' longstanding perspectives on the value of literacy education. In *The Education of Blacks in the South, 1860–1935*, James Anderson observes that slaves considered access to traditional literacy training a step towards individual and community autonomy because, as Louisa Gause, a former slave, explained, "White people never teach colored people nothing, but to be good to dey massa en mittie."[8] As an explanation, Gause's discussion of one-sided teaching illustrates the means some whites employed to combat what Heather Andrea Williams calls the "threat of literacy" to a system of slavery upheld through the "lie" of Blacks' inferiority and insubordination.[9] Similarly, Gause's statement reflects the awareness many slaves had of the efforts white slave masters used to indoctrinate them into thinking their forced servitude was natural and appropriate and that the world was too dangerous a place for escaping slaves or newly freedmen. Becoming literate meant more to slaves than obtaining the skills to decipher the bible and political texts in relation to such "lies" of their presumed inferiority. It also meant that they could imagine a world beyond their captivity, compose, if necessary, written passes enabling them to travel, and acquire the critical vocabulary to participate in political and broader civic discourse.

As a critique, Gause's statement also indicates some of the values within the self-education efforts developed in the night, Sabbath, and freedmen's schools African Americans and their supporters formed during and after slavery. According to Williams, self-help often appeared at the forefront when African American leaders attended postemancipation educational conventions. "Fully cognizant of the history of white suppression of Black education and aware of continuing white hostility," she notes, "delegates urged Black people to establish their own schools and to take full advantages of educational opportunities provided by other Blacks or by northern associations."[10] The now popular adage that "knowledge is power" that Reverend John Turner stressed during an 1863 delegation meeting to encourage attendees to invest in education exemplifies the early rhetorics of self-resilience, accountability, and determination African Americans invoked to shape and sustain these early, independent, schooling efforts. He implored attendees to "get education for ourselves and our children. Each of us ought to consider the character and elevation of the colored people of Kansas as in his own keeping and labor with that view."[11]

Although Turner's concerns rested with the uplift of his community, many of the qualities of character development, continuous improvement, and work that he considered necessary reflect the tenets of the "social" self that Sandra Dolby describes in *Self-Help Books: Why Americans Keep Reading Them*. At the root of self-help culture, she argues, is a notion of individuality that privileges the concept of self within community that is emblematic of an American worldview. Writers appealing to the "social self" recognize the individual as a person who is accountable to society, and they balance the dichotomy of rugged individualism and community membership by emphasizing that people will feel greater personal contentment if they use their lives to respond to societal needs.[12] Because achieving this balance requires that individuals learn and accept their places within a system that includes others, writers construct and instruct readers embracing the social self to understand community as a system to which a clear strategy of response can be and must be devised. Turner's call for self-education emphasizes individual work even as it situates African Americans within the dual systems of an African American community and a broader context of the reconstructing country.

Shirley Wilson Logan's research on nineteenth-century African American rhetorical education illustrates how self-improvement texts became sites to engage in such individualized, social work. Within the diaries of the four prominent women and one male writer that she had researched, Logan found that the writers seemed to embrace qualities of resistance, self-denial, and control when they began to study such textbooks as Northrop, Gay, and Penn's book *The College of Life or Practical Self-Education: A Manual of Self-Improvement for the Colored Race*.[13] She notes that the popular conduct books that transmitted discourses on success, conduct, and self-help during the nineteenth century often "sought to regulate the behavior of women"—a characteristic that cannot be understated here—and included tips on etiquette. Frequently, manuals targeting African American audiences were compiled by Black authors or by Black authors collaborating with white authors, and those early books were focused on the project of "Negro improvement," a project readily accepted by African Americans who were focused on the work of "recovering" from the "devastating" impact and wounds of slavery.[14] The emphasis was not on reworking a broken system because reconstruction carried along with it the hope of a positive future. Instead, the focus was on getting individuals to "change themselves" into the types of men and women that would be acceptable members of white society.[15] Inventing oneself at this moment, then, meant developing behaviors that might enable one to become conversant with the dominating class.

Although the process Vanzant outlines in *Interiors* for readers to begin their journey towards wellness reflects many of these values, it also emphasizes the importance of consciousness-raising endorsed in twentieth-century nationalist and feminist movements as steps towards reinvention. Black women have to carve out time and space for self-exploration to begin the healing process because their power source is inside of them. "We must teach ourselves the things we need to know that we have never been taught, and we need to remember those things we have forgotten," she explains.[16] Moreover, she implores, "We need to redefine and describe our experiences, practices, and beliefs in the context of the experiences and traditions of our ancestors . . ." and "expand our traditional African concepts, ideologies, and understandings to make them conductive to the constructs and realities of our modern-day psyches."[17] This focus on cultural wisdom is one of the appeals of the American self-help genre. For readers seeking instruction on self-improvement, these books give them access to knowledgeable experts who can guide their pursuits.[18] For writers, the genre provides a space to offer analysis, interpretation, and cultural critique and calls for readers to "reinstate certain traditions and beliefs that have been unwisely abandoned or neglected."[19] While there is an element of consumerism, most readers become what Dolby calls "life-learners." Once they have completed one reeducation project, they keep undertaking new processes of reinvention. Learning never stops.

Perpetual learning seems to be the intent of Vanzant's healing process because the Afrocentric educational base she wants readers to tap into is rooted in ongoing resistance. By the end of the late nineteenth century, Anna Julia Cooper and W.E.B. Du Bois had begun to draw attention to the numerous Eurocentric ideologies that had taught Blacks to devalue themselves, and they both called for the incorporation of race or African customs into educational practices.[20] The assumption was that the reeducation exposed individuals to African traditions and epistemologies that would foster self- and community actualization. Afrocentric philosophies and organized educational programs such as Molefi Asante's *Afrocentricity* are extensions of this effort because they foster the type of shift in self, consciousness, and worldview necessary to challenge domination. As an extension of the forms of cultural nationalism to emerge from the Black Aesthetic and Black Pride movements, Molefi Kete Asante's theory of Afrocentricity posits that situating the perspective of the African person as a frame of reference to view phenomena and events is central to the production of knowledge and construction of self.[21] To facilitate such revisioning or shifts in perspective, Asante advocates a reeducation process for the politically and economically marginalized that draws upon an alternative canon of thinkers including Cheikh Anta Diop, Chancellor Williams, John Henrik Clarke, Martin Bernal and others emphasizing self-esteem and self-actualization as correctives to educational violence. Although Vanzant does not directly cite these figures in her early books, she positions her wellness attempts near these earlier discourses by suggesting that tapping into an Afrocentric consciousness is an appropriate way to begin a process for healing.

Vanzant also benefits from the gendered dynamics of African American self-help reading audiences. According to Michael Rowland, the majority of this audience is comprised of college-educated women whose access to advanced formal literacy instruction has allowed them to benefit from greater social and political autonomy than had African Americans of earlier periods. Some of these women turn to these texts for specific instruction on how to overcome specific traumas and forms of physical or emotional abuse. More of the members of this group consider themselves "oppressed" by European/white perspective[s] and . . . have come to believe . . . "the stereotypes that have been projected onto them."[22] Self-help books are resources for conventional and cultural wisdom for women who want to release themselves of internalized stereotypes, but are "too identified with [them] to be able to break out of them on their own." Revision could be a process of seeing oneself anew.

Fighting Words: A Crisis of Misinformation

Two different survival strategies ideas dominated conversations about the state of Black America at the start of Vanzant's writing career. On one end, there were the attitudes expressed by figures such as Jesse Jackson. Against the backdrop of a popular anti-apartheid effort, escalating Black-on-Black violence and unemployment, and a crack cocaine epidemic that media seemed to see only in Black communities, Jackson invoked the importance of finding "common ground," and during his 1988 Democratic National Convention appearance, he translated these social issues into a call for the country to "go forward" and "keep hope alive."[23] On the other end was a set of leaders, intellectuals, and music artists who saw these issues as signs that African Americans should return to other ways of knowing as corrective measures. In response to several murders at rap concerts, Boogie Down Productions' "Stop the Violence Movement" released the 1989 classic, "Self-Destruction." A collaboration featuring popular hip-hop artists of the time, the song saturated radio airwaves and afternoon video shows with socially conscious messages about the importance of understanding the enemy and staying awake to systemic attacks on African Americans.[24] With its focus on identifying threats to the nation or body of African Americans, the song was one of many among conscious rap artists such as Public Enemy and X Clan in the late eighties and nineties. With repurposed themes of responsibility and the individual's obligation to turn his or her attention inward to inspire revolution and survival, the crisis-driven nationalist rhetoric of this moment seemed to stand in contrast to the integrationist appeals Jackson had called on Americans to adopt as a strategy for survival.

Shahrazad Ali's controversial 1989 book *The Blackman's Guide to Understanding the Blackwoman* was also published at this time. The follow-up to the 1985 book *How Not to Eat Pork, or Life Without the Pig* and the predecessor to *Are You Still a Slave?*, published in 1994, *The Blackman's Guide* was an intervention. In it, she attempts to redress what she saw as the central problem facing Black men and, thereby, the Black nation, during the late eighties: the unruly, unconditioned, and disrespectful Black woman. As she explains in her chapter on communication, longstanding oppression had caused Black women to forget the "law of nature"—a law which posits the Black man atop the social hierarchy and the Black woman beneath—in their efforts to vocally assert themselves and their independence.[25] Like a widespread amnesia passed down through generations, Black women's insistence on being assertive and pursuing their own autonomy had created what Ali saw as a pervasive emotional condition that was destroying the family and "deterior[ating] the nation" by making women illegible to the Black man.[26] With the goal of enlightening men and creating a "revolution" of positive change in heterosexual Black relationships, Ali lists the factors that have caused Black women to fall and offers a set of corrective measures Black men can use to restore women to their rightful places. Among the "facts" and measures she points out are:

- [The Black woman's] brain is smaller than the Black man's, so while she is acclaimed for her scholastic achievement, her thought processes do not compare to the conscious Black man's.
- [The Black woman] will use her sexuality to snare a Black man and will misrepresent the intensity of her sexual desire to get his attention. She lays sexual traps for him and behaves blatantly like a trollop when she is alone with a Black man she is trying to lure.
- Although traditionally a fine dresser, the Black woman is subject to keeping a nasty house. She will spend long grueling hours at her hairdresser and not be willing to spend thirty minutes a day cleaning her living quarters. There may be roaches, rats, and bed vermin.

- If [The Black woman] ignores the authority and superiority of the Black man, there is a penalty. When she crosses this line and becomes viciously insulting, it is time for the Black man to soundly slap her in the mouth.[27]

Even with its animalistic imagery, damaging stereotypes, unqualified categorization of Black women into upper-, middle-, and low-class groups, and endorsement of physical violence, Ali's book still earned impressive sales numbers. To some, *The Blackman's Guide to Understanding the Blackwoman* was a viable step towards resolving Black America's crisis.

Unsurprisingly, the responses were vehement. As Ali made the daytime talk-show rounds on Donahue, Geraldo, and Sally Jesse Raphael, fights ensued. Indignant Black women got into verbal sparring matches with handfuls of Black men who felt like Ali was down for them. The battles were revealing. During the exchanges, deep disagreements over issues of male power, feminism, interracial marriage, and reverse racism came to the surface. In newspapers such as the *Seattle Times,* journalists published stories, weeding through the claims of support, outrage, and suspicion over capitalistic motives Ali's book was inspiring among readers.[28] Academics weighed in too. In 1992, Haki Madhubuti assembled the anthology *Confusion by Any Other Name: Essays Exploring the Negative Impact of the Blackman's Guide to the Black Woman,* a text speculating that Ali's book offers a "needed response, or reaction, to what some consider to be the 'negative images' of Black men in Black women's literature."[29] Regardless the level of anger or disdain audience members expressed, Ali remained resolute. She was doing the work to resolve a crisis.

With her September 1990 *Essence* essay "Fighting Words: *The Blackman's Guide to Understanding the Blackwoman,*" Vanzant joined these conversations. In it, she concedes that there is a crisis among African Americans but argues that *The Blackman's Guide* mistakenly places the blame on Black women. Ali's book contained pathologizing "antiAfrican" and "anticultural" claims that made no sense.[30] Claiming that Black women were damaged because of oppression while arguing they should be held accountable for the "manifestations of the damage" was problematic to Vanzant; and arguing that "one person (the man) has the divine right to control or rule another (the woman)" was illogical.[31] Because of this confusion, Vanzant considers Ali's book the source of a new crisis of misinformation and implores *Essence* readers to recognize this issue and work to resolve it. "The challenge we face as we work toward our healing is to consider all the factors that have driven us apart, recognizing both the positive and negative" she writes. Establishing common meeting ground was the work they would have to undertake. "For the advancement of the whole, we must move from the strongest base of commonality—the culture and tradition of our ancestors," Vanzant writes.[32]

"Fighting Words" is an important moment within the launch of Vanzant's wellness campaign because of her use of explication and reframing as strategies for establishing a mandate for reeducation. As mentioned in chapter 1, African American women essay writers have historically used the genre for the rhetorical purposes of exposure. The goal has been to reveal adverse situations and social discontinuities that require the reader's participation in making sense of these situations and movement towards change. Vanzant follows this tradition in "Fighting Words." After telling readers that *The Blackman's Guide* is a "classic example of the confusion we suffer and injury we inflict when we turn on ourselves," Vanzant points out the consequences of Ali's argument, stating, "To ask a Black woman to surrender control of her destiny to the Black man, who is equally oppressed and damaged, is to ask her to self-destruct."[33] While such terms as "deadly injuries" function as terministic screens that produce urgency, her organizational strategy of citing the exigency before the implication implicitly establishes a link between threats to the Black community and Black women that casts Ali's book as the actual problem and exposes the sexist discourses within it. In doing so, Vanzant makes her purpose for writing clear: Black women have to be aware of the misinformed ideologies within Ali's book and they must learn how to actively resist their effects.[34]

On the pages of *Essence*, "Fighting Words" is an attempt at intervention that sidesteps many of the persuasive burdens Black women writers have had to contend with to be published in major outlets. Historically, whenever they have attempted to join in, reframe, or undercut disparaging conversation in mainstream literary or publishing venues, they are often perceived as "going against the grain" of public opinion or, as Royster explains, being too dissident.[35] With their sense of authority in question, the burden is to be inventive enough to redirect the gaze of a suspicious or indifferent audience and to be authoritative enough to set the terms of what is possible and sensible within a communicative moment. Vanzant's language choices reflect her ingenuity in using disidentification as a technique. By using terms such terms as "self-destruct" and "damaged" to describe "the" women Ali describes, Vanzant constructs a binary between the women who embrace Ali's book and her *Essence* readers, premised on the likelihood that they would disidentify with the book's claims. Further, in using terms such as "anticultural," and "anti-African," Vanzant expresses her mutual indignation and constructs an ethos implying that her guidance and teaching are viable ways to move forward with the African principles she sees necessary for healing.[36] Her call for a culturally centered approach to healing becomes a solution to the problem of Ali's book. Being well can involve social work.

Miseducation as a Call for Healing

Medical professionals and therapists widely agree that healing is a long game. It does not occur in discreet acts. The task for the healer aspiring to guide someone through this process via writing is similar to the task Royster indicates Black women have ordinarily faced when attempting to address audiences from a position of authority: how to create the "situated" ethos or sustaining reputation that enables them to guide readers through the identifiable situations that their remedies or strategies resolve.[37] This task-based approach gives us a lens for understanding one of the qualities of Vanzant's approach to rhetorical healing because it shows how she successfully manages to merge and satisfy those audiences apt to respond to the project of social repair with those that respond to the other concerns of her work—in one curriculum. Although Ali's book was a hypervisible impetus for Vanzant to join and shape public conversations about wellness, the pressing crisis that compelled Vanzant more involved the plight of the abused Black women she had encountered as an attorney in the Philadelphia Defender's Office. After walking away from an abusive marriage and putting herself through college and law school while raising her children, Vanzant began to embrace the Yoruban religion and recreate what she calls the "canvas" of her own life in *Interiors*. The insights she gained and positive changes she experienced in this process inspired her to develop teaching materials and activities for battered women. Alongside the still-popular *Acts of Faith: Meditations for People of Color* that she published in 1993, Vanzant drew much of the curriculum she offers women readers in her early books from this moment.

Vanzant's early writings for Black women address two seemingly divergent groups. In "Fighting Words," she appeals to the "social" self of civic-minded women who feel compelled to work at resolving community crises. With her focus on giving battered women resources, she also appeals to the demographic of self-help readers Dolby describes as the "wounded" self.[38] Victims, in some respects, these readers are in need of repair. Writers who address members of this reader construct often encourage them to analyze the effects of culture, psyche, and personal history on their psychological state. To her credit, Vanzant merges both groups with the lack-liquidated strategy Dolby traces through self-help literature. Most of these works are "written with the aim of enlightening readers about some of the negative effects of our culture and suggesting new attitudes and practices that might lead them to more satisfying and effective lives."[39] The initial rhetorical strategy these writers adopt is to foster a state of injustice among readers by suggesting that the reader's lack of success in relationships or other pursuits is because something is wrong with the culture that guides them or the information they have and use within the world. By creating a sense of injustice, the writer not only appeals to the reader's sense of entitlement to a productive life, but also establishes a scenario where his or her prescribed strategies appear as suitable solutions for resolving these injustices. Although readers are encouraged to critique the elements in their life that lead to their "culture of lack," the empowered or healed individuals ultimately learn to see their transformation as a personal and collective victory. Achieving wellness is supposed to be a triumph over the structures that disempower and keep them from carrying out their intended roles within their communities.

The personal injustice Vanzant wants her readers to consider a mandate for healing in her early works is the systemic miseducation about their spiritual power that they may have experienced. In *Tapping the Power Within,* she offers readers a step-by-step course in how to not only recognize the spirit Black women have within them, but to also tap into it as a form of latent power. Her study of African epistemologies and religions is evident as Vanzant argues that living a life of spiritual power, or spirituality, is the form of self-empowerment and healing Black women need if they are to recognize and live their life's purpose. With this insight, readers can survive and overcome the difficult and hurtful experiences that have kept them from achieving the purpose of their lives. Self-knowledge and self-confidence are the base requirements because only when readers' thoughts lead them to perform "actions which serve others as well as make [themselves] feel good" can they encounter the form of spirituality Vanzant promotes.[40] Reading *Tapping the Power Within* is just the first step in this "journey toward peace, success and freedom."[41]

From the book's outset, politicizing the personal seems to be the strategy for making healing relevant to Black women. In the introduction, the African model of spirituality Vanzant promotes is placed in contrast to Eurocentric models that situate the individual at the bottom of a "divine" hierarchy. Yoruban spirituality is upheld as a belief system that imbues individuals with guidance through life and an inner sense of divinity. Skeptical readers are advised to take heart if the idea of an untapped source of divinity within them is difficult to embrace because such a shift, a reorientation of sorts, in African Americans that have been "oppressed, disenfranchised, miseducated, culturally and spiritually raped" would be difficult to understand.[42] The violent language here inscribes the book with a jeremiadic sense of purpose by inviting readers to go back and revisit a form of spirituality they did not initially receive. As David Howard-Pitney explains, the fundamental premise of the African American jeremiad is that Blacks, like the biblical Israelites, are a "chosen people" and thereby entitled to a better quality of life. Rhetorics of indignation, jeremiads have been particularly potent appeals for justice because they foreground African Americans' humanity and link justice for them to progress for the whole.

The term "miseducation" invoked in the book's introduction also has a particular sociopolitical history among African Americans. Most widely credited to Carter G. Woodson's *The Mis-Education of the Negro*, where the educator calls for a culturally centered education strategy that builds upon students' strengths, cultivates their "latent" powers, and trains them in the skills that will render them invaluable assets to society, the term is a multi-functioning rhetorical commonplace.[43] As a metaphor, it symbolizes a systematic process wherein African Americans have been conditioned into accepting second- or third-class citizenship through the education they have received and, at worst, perpetuating these systems. In recent years, songwriters have invoked the concept as an extended metaphor to call for and describe a process of unlearning. Arguably, "The Miseducation of Lauryn Hill" demonstrates this process. On the 1999 Grammy-Award-winning album, Hill reflects on learning to distinguish between negative forms of conditioning and resolving to act in her own state of autonomy. The final track, which happens to bear the same name as the album, ends beautifully as Hill sings about deciding that she will write her own future and destiny. Since this is the last song on the album, listeners are apt to believe that Hill's reeducation process is complete.[44] Though Hill uses the concept to focus on individual action, her ethos as a young Black woman searching for insight on family, relationships, and career makes the statement an implied social critique. At the macroscopic level, miseducation draws attention to institutional structures and agents who influence how people understand themselves as actors within the world. On a microscopic level, it allows the writer to define forms of agency for resisting and overcoming miseducation.

Within the didactic genre of the self-help book, the language choices in this introduction amplify the culture of lack among Black women that this commonplace invokes. As terms such as "disenfranchised" suggest broad-scale attacks on Black communities, the phrase "culturally raped" adds a violent gendering to the idea of oppression. The sting of this term suggests that *Tapping the Power Within* responds to previous efforts to analyze hegemonic cultures. Consider Abbey Lincoln's 1966 essay "To Whom Will She Cry Rape" that was republished in Toni Cade Bambara's *The Black Woman: An Anthology*. The Black woman Lincoln describes is a victim of miseducation occurring within and beyond her home communities because

> her head is more regularly beaten than any other woman's, and by her own man; she's the scapegoat for Mr. Charlie; she is forced to stark realism and chided if caught dreaming; her aspirations for her and hers are, for sanity's sake, stunted; her physical image has been criminally maligned, assaulted, and negated; she's the first to be called ugly and never yet beautiful, and as a consequence is forced to see her man (an exact copy of her, emotionally and physically), brainwashed and wallowing in self-loathing, pick for his own the physical antithesis of her (the white woman and incubator of his heretofore arch enemy the white man). Then, to add guilt to insult and injury, she (the Black woman) stands accused as the emasculator of the only thing she has ever cared for, her Black man. She is the scapegoat for what white American has made of the "Negro personality."[45]

Lincoln's rhetoric contains both the frustration of the feminist movement of the mid-sixties and seventies and the indignation of the Black Power movement. Within the context of these nuanced discussions about sources of Black women's pain, the crisis of miseducation invoked at the beginning of *Tapping the Power Within* is cast as a threat to one's quality of life. Miseducation is a systemic issue that breeds the misinformation Ali's book spreads.

Of course, we cannot assume that Vanzant foresaw the relationship between these two concepts when publishing her first book but, as a moment within her overall campaign, the ways she navigates these two concepts underscores how Black women cultivate audiences through ethos. In bringing to light the lack, or issues that cause miseducation, and offering a curriculum in *Tapping the Power Within*, Vanzant moves from the position of responding to crisis, to acting in her authority to teach individuals how to overcome the crisis. Equipped with her own personal testimonies about the value of spiritual vision, she becomes an argument for her own product. From this position, the culture of lack she illustrates allows her to shift readers' attention from the potential of miseducation to their need to be reeducated, and this move enables her to merge her two groups of primary readers into one audience. "Social" working readers, or those who consider themselves part of a collective group that must undergo the necessary training to prepare for and resist such oppression, and "wounded" readers, or those who must recover and redress the trauma of such issues, are constructed as one group of miseducated women. In her teacherly ethos, Vanzant's call for readers to embark on a course of spiritual reeducation, is personal and poetic: "Like cotton, which grows in an ugly thorny pad and is transformed into beautiful color garments, you can transform your experiences into beautiful lessons. How? By changing the way you think about them."[46] The call to undertake a process of healing through revision becomes the viable way to liquidate the lack that social issues cause within Black communities and to resolve the individual and community issues that stem from the abuse of Black women.

The numerous tasks Vanzant had to undertake within this stage of the rhetorical-healing process point to the kinds of challenges Black women rhetors face in taking the authority to publicly assert themselves and their agendas. Even though Vanzant's audiences were primarily women, making a compelling enough argument for healing required her to engage in rhetorical acts of explication and redefinition, create contexts of lack, and reinvent her ethos at each stage in the development of her wellness campaign. To her credit, the arguments she makes invoke the semblance of Black women's resistance traditions and reflect how these themes and topics appear within contemporary Black women's writing and rhetorical practices. In this way, the early portion of her campaign shows a continuation of the Black feminist project of centralizing Black women's needs in relation to the well-being of their broader communities.

Despite Vanzant's agility in making an argument for her curriculum, the cautionary signs foreshadowing the critiques Five East would issue about her methods on *Fix My Life* are evident from the beginning of her campaign as well. The forward to *Tapping the Power Within* also reveals origins of one of the persistent consequences of her efforts to link spiritual vision and urgency: the over-amplification of Black women's agency. In what appears to be an appeal to self-resilience and fortitude, the discussion of historical oppression, disenfranchisement, and miseducation precedes the observation that "African Americans have relinquished their spiritual power to those who appeared to be more powerful than themselves."[47] Because the underlying warrant in this framing of miseducation is that it can lend itself to self-pity and apathy, the motive behind the theme's use in this passage seems to be an effort to appeal to readers' sense of individual agency and autonomy. Unlike jeremiads where the idea is that some widespread injustice has robbed a group of its chosen potential, the term "relinquished" adds an additional layer to the expectations of personal responsibility and consciousness to which this type of nationalist rhetoric appeals. Implicit here is a suggestion that Black women have been deceived into willingly allowing themselves to be oppressed and culturally disenfranchised and the brief-but-subtle insinuation that if they had been more perceptive of the schemes and structures designed to thwart their spiritual power, they would not have willingly allowed themselves to be miseducated, or abused. Blame is an undercurrent.

This misuse produces one of the problematic consequences in this stage of healing: a reinforcement of destructive and sexist mythologies about how Black women have hurt the progress of society. Patricia Hill Collins illuminates the process and evidence of this trend through her analysis of images of poor Black women in *Fighting Words: Black Women and the Quest for Social Justice*. As she explains, the media's circulation of the images of the "welfare queen" and the "bad Black mother" constructs Black women in ways that rob them of individual autonomy and overemphasize their impact on society at large. Cast under the light of their economic condition or social status as poor or single mothers, some Black women lose their individuality and visibility even as they are made to be hypervisible symbols of Black women as a collective. Because these women are largely working class and poor members of what Collins calls an "intensely-raced group," the forms of domestic violence, family strife, and personal adversities that are already exacerbated because of their race and economic positions take on greater visibility. When these adversities are "reinterpreted through an ideological apparatus that initially blames these women for their own poverty and for that of African-Americans as a class . . . Black women's poverty becomes . . . identified with and blamed for the deterioration of the American public sphere."[48] In a negative way, the Black woman's struggle within these social systems is constructed as a preventable virus that infects the African American community at large.

Since Vanzant claims that America's wellness depends on Black women's healing, the consequence of these efforts to promote individual accountability is an argument that not only invokes blame but possibly foregrounds shame. By enhancing a need for reeducation with the suggestion that readers should be intellectually vigilant within a culture of lack transfers responsibility back to women for the social conditions and forms of oppression they encounter. For survivors of abuse, this could be an offensive message because even as it acknowledges violence against women, it also foregrounds a notion of a social responsibility that suggests the woman who is smarter, more perceptive, or more spiritually strong could have avoided it. As I discuss later in this chapter, this trend resurfaces in Vanzant's campaign when she begins to undertake healing work on television. Blame, in this instance, becomes a conversation-shifting social rhetoric. When it saturates public discourses and policies on domestic violence, rape, marriage failure, or other issues that impact Black women specifically, it invites discussions of the kinds of self-regulating and group responsibility women must exercise. These messages about accountability run counter to the generative forms of feminist rage against misogyny and violence that June Jordan gave voice to in "Poem about My Rights" where she says: "I am not wrong. Wrong is not my name / My name is my own my own my own / and I can't tell you who the hell set things up like this / but I can tell you that from now on my resistance / my simple and daily and nightly self-determination / may very well cost you your life."[49] Consequently, blame discourses can promote social forms of shame and distortion that, among Black women, have fostered what Melissa Harris-Perry describes in *Sister Citizen: Shame, Stereotypes, and Black Women in America* as a "crooked room" where they have had to learn how to stand up straight. At a minimum, overcoming shame is a process that requires understanding social conditions.[50]

With the personal narratives Vanzant includes in *Interiors* to show her process and the rousing call for Black women's healing as a catalyst for American wellness, readers are apt to assume that she understands the internal consequences of shame. What she considers as the beginning of her healing was her realization that she, herself, was "the wall" to be torn down because she had become emotionally separated from her spiritual center. "I had many lessons to learn," she writes. "I had to become reacquainted with the part of myself that held the secrets I needed to flourish in life."[51] The first-person narratives throughout *Interiors* add dimension to Vanzant's ethos as a healer. Her focus on the actions she took to embark on the healing process and the realizations she makes throughout her text send the message that part of the healing process means being critical *only* of oneself. In the chapter "An Exhibit of Peace," she traces her "flawed" sense of self-concept back to her mother's death and the lingering resentment she harbored as a result. Feeling abandoned by the death and the subsequent forms of abuse she experienced from relatives and other adults, Vanzant allowed herself to give voice to the depths of her anger at her mother for staying in an unhealthy marriage and leaving her to be raised by her grandmother. "One day, I got so mad at my mother that I taped her picture to my bathroom mirror and cursed her out, but good. I called her every name in the book. I told her what I really felt about what she had done. About her dying and leaving me, and about what had happened to me as a result."[52]

Vanzant's grief and disappointment over the parental care and protection she did not receive are understandable responses; her vulnerability is a result of her sense of abandonment. What complicates the first-person narrative technique of *Interiors* is a focus on acceleration that also becomes a problem within the television stage of her healing campaign. Because of the capacity of death and other forms of trauma to stunt an individual's emotional growth and well-being, the choice to emphasize self-action as a means for attaining peace comes quite quickly in the narrative. Vanzant writes that after "a moment of contemplation and soul searching," she realized that forgiving her parents and accepting that they did the best they could was the only way for her soul to arrive at a place of peace. "If I wanted to survive, I had to let go of any negativity I felt about my parents," she concludes.[53]

I do not contest the relationship between survival and forgiveness that Vanzant makes here. Given the appearance of this argument in conjunction with the other socially conscious and nationalistic discourses Vanzant relies on to cast miseducation as a crisis and Black women's wellness as a national matter, this argument is too inwardly directed. Even if a woman is miseducated, emotionally abused, traumatized, or hurt by another individual, the suggestion is that critiquing individuals or systems that lead to such abuse is ultimately a futile response. When coupled with Vanzant's claims about the cultural resources her readers have at their disposal to aid them in the healing process, the message appears to be that Black women have few reasons to blame anyone. Vanzant's return to the link between Black women's healing and America's at the end of *Interiors* is an example of the ideology this take on agency upholds. In order for healing to occur, "we have to stop kicking and complaining about our wounds while relinquishing responsibility for our own healing to others."[54]

At this point within Vanzant's process of rhetorical healing, the ideas of vision as a spiritual and social resource and the cultural critiques of the activists her discussion of miseducation seems to invoke are reversed. Given her savvy in exercising these practices to discredit Ali's book and to link miseducation with injustice, it is ironic that her concept of healing does not foreground the critical acts of vision she had practiced to make reeducation persuasive for her audiences—acts that have been central to the Black women's intellectual tradition she seems to appropriate.

Revision: A Curriculum for Healing

Throughout her first three books, Vanzant argues that the pathway to redressing miseducation requires Black women to shift their outlook and change their vocabulary. Revision is an essential process to healing because Black women's bodies are tools and instruments of interpretation that shape their sense of self-understanding and social engagement. If Black women don't learn to see themselves and their circumstances differently, they may lose the most "sacred" parts of themselves.[55] Correspondingly, self-reclamation and preservation are discursive endeavors for Vanzant. "We must use different language and terms to describe and define ourselves and communicate with each other," she explains. "We do not want to continue to use the language and terms that have been used for centuries to dismiss and denigrate our culture and our very beings."[56] In other words, Black women cannot apply the same wounding words to each other if they are to become well.

As my discussion of Black women writers' perspectives on pain and wellness in chapter 1 indicates, these arguments are not necessarily new. What distinguishes Vanzant's approach, however, is the series of practices she models and teaches as means for attaining wellness through spirituality and the arguments she makes to instruct her presumably miseducated readers on why it is important to "do the work." Depending on the book, the name of the practices change; however, in general, five courses emerge, forming what I see as a three-sequence healing curriculum. They are: rereading the past through self-examination (i.e., detachment) and interpretation (i.e., discernment); revising one's concept of self through alteration (i.e., enlightenment) and articulation (i.e., integration); and finally, resuming one's intended life purpose or future through evolution (i.e., action) (see figure 3.1). Following these steps should imbue readers with the spirituality to proceed through life "making better choices and wiser decisions."[57]

Rereading the Past through Self-Examination and Interpretation

The initial exercises in Vanzant's books function as a preliminary course in self-examination intended to redirect women's energies inward for the purpose of deep introspection. In *Tapping the Power Within*, Vanzant models an activity called "Looking in the Mirror of the Self" in the chapter of the same name, relaying the story of how a girlfriend's betrayal taught her about the relationship between self-examination and self-acceptance to demonstrate the importance of finding areas in need of repair.[58] The betrayal taught her that African American women frequently "spend most of [their] time trying to fix what [they] see," because they don't realize "that what [they] are seeing is actually a reflection of who [they] are." To encourages readers to engage in self-examination, Vanzant finishes the chapter with the assurance that by learning to distinguish "who *they* are from whom they have been told or taught to be," readers can become more adept at tapping into their latent spiritual power as the resource for moving towards self-acceptance and higher self-esteem.[59]

In what appears to be a second stage—that of interpretation—Vanzant models how expressive and reflective journal writing can be used to make sense of past or present issues and apply spiritual principles to decipher the roots of trauma, crisis, or miseducation as reinforcement and application of the deciphering activities of the first course. After a discussion of the low self-esteem she felt as a darker-skinned young Black girl, she shares in *Interiors* how journal writing helped her reach a crucial epiphany about the source of her fractured romantic relationships: her unacknowledged resentment toward her father because of his failure to

Iyanla Vanzant counsels Evelyn Lozada on the OWN series *Iyanla: Fix My Life*, in 2012. Fair use.

protect her from the uncle who had raped her as a child. Her anger internalized, she finally determined that many of her fractured relationships with men were the result of her deep distrust of men, yet need for their acceptance. That revelation caused her to realize that African American women have been conditioned to believe that they are "separated from God" and god-like qualities. "We think there is something we must be or do to attain god-like qualities. In order to find out what those qualities are, we are taught that we must behave a certain way."[60] Encouraging readers to tap into their spiritual power and the legacy of Black women who were able to "make it against all odds," Vanzant emphasizes that the value of this practice is that it allows readers to reinforce their own agency, to, in essence, "create the energy" of their environments.

These initial courses suggest an attempt to instruct miseducated women by reinforcing and cultivating forms of vision and voice. For example, in her choice to make self-examination a primary course towards healing, Vanzant's curriculum seems to foreground the same reprioritization of self-concern that Toni Cade Bambara called for in *The Black Woman* when she said, "Revolution begins with the self, in the self."[61] By demonstrating the insights she gained through journaling, Vanzant argues that writing is essential to healing because it enables the writer to "find the realities, as well as inconsistencies." Her argument also seems to echo broad claims about the therapeutic aspects of literacy. According to James Pennebaker, writing releases inhibition because "talking or writing about the facts of incident . . . allows people not only to confront the trauma but to make sense of it."[62] The process of composing is thought to decrease internal turmoil because it requires a writer to structure and organize a potentially traumatic experience into a narrative. Beth Daniell corroborates these claims in her literacy study on Al-Anon members. According to one of the study participants, the process of narrating and organizing events helped her gain a measure of control during her recovery process. "I had to let go of it being perfect," the participant explained of her past expectations, "and then it became perfect."[63] The state of satisfaction the participant reached about her composed narrative mirrors her sense of self-contentment. Writing was a potential way to reach peace.

What undercuts some of the revolutionary potential in the two early stages of this curriculum is Vanzant's failure to acknowledge the intersectionality of oppression that Black women must first identify and then work through in order to reach liberation. These shortcomings work to narrow forms of critical vision. Bambara's contention about revolution is premised on her identification of the "lies" and "poison" that "assault the ego" and "threaten the heart," as well as her insistence that such contaminants are eventually confronted and purged.[64] In fairness, Vanzant's discussion of the impact that colorism had on her self-esteem as a young Black woman shows a measure of this type of race-and-gender consciousness. Yet, her systemic analysis stops there. She does not apply, or encourage readers to apply, the same level of analysis to interrogating the "lies" and "poison" within the culture of violence that makes young Black women frequent targets of sexual assault. Instead, she supports her claim about the value of self-examination with the claim that since women cannot change others or control others, they should focus on themselves.

Whether this lack of acknowledgement was a missed opportunity, an intentional decision, or a reflection of the pessimism that happens when individuals feel that they cannot change systemic issues and give up searching for a deeper understanding of them is unclear. The absence, however, of this acknowledgement within her early books is a shortcoming that functions to homogenize the argument Vanzant makes about the value of literacy to African American women. As Elaine Richardson explains, the literacies African American females have developed in a world where they are made aware—earlier than other groups—of their construction as racially and sexually marked objects, have included ways of seeing, being, and knowing that enable them to decipher disparaging public transcripts and compose more empowering ones to "advance or protect the self."[65] With a lack of outward focus or acknowledgement of the disparaging public discourses and transcripts, one consequence of the process of rereading the past that emerges in Vanzant's first stage is that it foregrounds a politic of isolation that implies to Black women that the state of social wellness they may seek requires their intensive private work. This conceptualization of healing narrows the angles of vision and oppositional worldview Black feminists have encouraged women to cultivate.

Public shaming can also be a consequence of this phase in Vanzant's healing curriculum. During a November 2013 episode of *Fix My Life*, entitled "Fix My Dysfunctional Sisterhood," Vanzant showed how decontextualized processes of self-examination and flawed notions of agency could inflict verbal wounding among Black women. The show focused on the strained relationship between two middle-aged sisters, Barbara and her younger sister Geneva, who are at odds because Geneva ended up having two children by Barbara's boyfriend after moving in with her older sister at the age of seventeen. The pain between the two is palpable, and Vanzant spends much of the early segments of the episode getting the two to verbalize the source of their hurts. In what has become a ritual on *Fix My Life* where Vanzant encourages guests to "call a thing a thing," or use actualizing language as they reread their pasts and engage in self-examination, the host chided Geneva into calling herself a "hoe." Geneva explained that she felt unduly forced into a sexual relationship with her sister's boyfriend, coerced into remaining silent when the boyfriend gave her money, and betrayed that Barbara did not believe her when she confessed that she had slept with the boyfriend. Despite these clear conditions, Vanzant's use of the practice of "calling a thing a thing" as a pedagogical strategy of supposed truth telling and accountability makes revision a form of slut shaming. In this moment, the host seems to ignore the factors that made Geneva vulnerable in exchange for amplifying the monetary exchange by stating repeatedly, "So you were hoeing?"[66] Nearly all of the blame is redirected back at Geneva.

Revising One's Concept of Self through Alteration and Articulation

What we should understand as a third course in alteration involves Vanzant teaching readers to re-create and reinforce their energy and environment as steps towards healing. For Vanzant, internal forms of disease and discontent often stem from the toxin of unforgiveness. As she explains in *Tapping the Power Within*, unforgiveness is an "investment in hate, not healing" that creates a state of mind and being that blinds one to the possibilities of the present or future by keeping the hurts of the past in the forefront of one's consciousness.[67] To move past this, she teaches readers to follow a seven-day "Forgiveness Diet" that involves responding each morning to such writing prompts as "I (your name) forgive (a person you blame) totally and unconditionally" as a means for learning how to release internal bitterness and hurt. The night version of this exercise focuses on personal forgiveness. Readers are taught to follow such prompts as "I (your name) forgive myself totally and unconditionally" to develop a practice for removing pain and negativity from their own consciousness.[68]

Vanzant's fourth course in what I call articulation contains instructions on how readers can exercise these forms of spiritual and discursive power within their lives. A two-part process involving prayer and affirmation, shifting language becomes the means by which readers can further change their reality, because, according to Vanzant, negative speech produces negative outcomes. Language is a resource that enables an individual to articulate his or her faith for Vanzant; thus, an affirmation's language has to avoid negative connotations and focus more on positive outcomes. Vanzant provides these examples of how affirmation works:

Example:	"I do not want to be sick."
Effective Affirmation:	"I am whole and healthy."
Example:	"I do not want to be alone."
Effective Affirmation:	"I am one with all life."
Example:	"I am not fearful."
Effective Affirmation:	"I am facing my challenges with courage and faith."[69]

To Vanzant, the benefit of this course is that "when we believe what we say and focus our mind on it, it will become truth. It may not be reality, but it will be our truth."[70] Ironically, this practice holds a different value for men. As she explains in *Up From Here: Reclaiming the Male Spirit*, affirmations enable them to "rewrite the programs that were given to [them] through pain and fear."[71]

Micki McGee and bell hooks both stress the rhetorical benefits of the recursiveness and affirmation that Vanzant's curriculum emphasizes.

According to McGee, repetitive writing exercises are thought to help readers tap into the belief system necessary to "anchor" the "truths" they must rely on to read and make sense of their worlds.[72] For Vanzant's primary reading audience, grounding "self-affirmation" is a step towards empowerment because, as bell hooks explains, too many women see harsh critique as character strengthening. Ideally, the self-affirmation exercises enable Black women to "silence the negative voice within" and model to "observers of [their] social reality that [they] deserve, care, respect, and ongoing affirmation" by talking the talk of care.[73] To Vanzant's credit, this course seems to function like the forms of self-communication Shirley Wilson Logan discovered among nineteenth-century diarists who, in order to prepare for greater citizenship roles, engaged in forms of "self-deliberation" by serving as their own audiences and arguing for a particular understanding of their experiences as they would with others.[74] In this way, this course indicates the role of literacy within models of self-education aimed at action.

The extent to which that action becomes sociopolitical action remains questionable given what I see as Vanzant's apparent failure to require intertextuality in her curriculum. What hooks considers as the tendency of self-help books to suggest that women "[can] change everything in [their] lives by sheer acts of personal will" appears in the emphasis Vanzant places on forgiveness without examination or confrontation.[75] To reinforce her claim about the value of forgiveness as a freeing endeavor, Vanzant argues that "racism and sexism in and of themselves are not what limit Black women in America," but rather it is their "perception of them." Readers, then, must understand that "their political realities . . . are not nearly as powerful as [their] fear of them, belie[f] in them, and reliance on their operation as an excuse to operate within the status quo." While this argument is an effort to appeal to her readers' sense of resiliency and personal agency, the rhetorical consequence is a homogenization of the specific external oppressions that can influence Black women's lives. Although some women may find the process restorative, the pedagogy of meritocracy that emerges when readers are taught to see their wellness as the sole result of intense self-scrutiny is dangerous. Since hooks argues that "talking back to elite discourses" is a sign of critical consciousness and Collins claims that oppositional knowledge is only oppositional when it is put into relation to other forms of knowledge, this portion of Vanzant's revisionary curriculum promotes a politic of silence that can ensure the political does not become personal in this vision of healing.[76]

Resuming One's Intended Life Path through Action or Evolution

The process for healing culminates in the action or evolution course where Vanzant teaches readers to adopt and perform behaviors she considers indicative of wellness. What she describes as a state of making better and wiser decisions in *The Value in the Valley* is termed as a "Spiritual Code of Conduct" in *Tapping the Power Within*. Living by this code requires readers to accept their "oneness with the Creator" as the source of their power. Through this relationship—the ultimate relationship—readers can follow the following principles of the code of conduct to engage in a more productive and happy life: unconditional love, truth, willingness, righteousness, responsibility, discipline, humility, compassion, perseverance, patience, speaking with a conscious tongue, selflessness, and tithing. By undertaking these actions, women can reconceptualize their pasts, revise their sense of self, and reimagine their sense of the future.

Given Black women's historically complex and often subordinated roles in the traditional Black church—one I discuss at length in the next chapter—and within other social institutions, the ways that conceptions of "selflessness" uphold these institutions through Black women's financial, emotional, and physical labor cannot be overlooked. Moreover, since Vanzant's emphasis on "speaking with a conscious tongue" as a way of enacting one's self-evolution is ultimately audience driven, her codes of conduct suggest a set of criteria for the outward demonstrations of wellness women are to perform as a sign of their healing and participation within their community. Within this context, the historically subversive practice of relanguaging that Gilyard describes takes on the opposite function, promoting what can become a form of self-censure that keeps women more conscious of their surroundings and the recourse of their words and behaviors. Although revision is the healing practice Vanzant teaches women to undergo, her curriculum does little to advance a form of revolution and does more to leave women simply recomposed.

Assessment

Vanzant's approach to healing does offer us some insights into contemporary Black women's intellectual practices. At times, she assumes the role of a critical teacher who speaks out against instances of misinformation and teaches women some processes for doing so. Her approach to healing also seems to make reeducation a bridge between the writer's sociopolitical action and the types of literacy-retraining that individuals may need to resist personal attacks and to ideally engage in intervention-type activities themselves. Since "literacy is the ground upon which rhetorical education develops," as Shirley Wilson Logan explains, the books and projects Vanzant has chosen as sites for her work are advantageous.[77] Vanzant's process of rhetorical healing shows us how these efforts can contain elements of a tradition of Black women's intellectualism where women can move from testifying about overcoming struggles, to theorizing the source of those struggles, to, ultimately, teaching others how to overcome their struggles. This aspect of Vanzant's work is one of the reasons why her arguments remain as popular and necessary as they are today.

Still, as Audre Lorde's message on empowerment in "The Transformation of Silence into Language and Action" reminds us, a curriculum that promotes strategies of submissiveness and self-censure does too little to aid in Black women's wellness because, in the face of intersecting oppressions, "your silence will not protect you."[78] Vanzant's wellness campaign is a conundrum. It is propelled by a rhetoric of revision that foregrounds arguments about literacy and strategic rereading, yet also contains reframing performances that stop short of meeting their liberatory potential. Her notion of revision promotes a politic of isolation, meritocracy, and blindness while instantiating Black women into the role of perpetual students who must be reeducated, revised, and recomposed to navigate a world they are taught to think they cannot actually change. Since these efforts to reeducate are imbedded within a self-help genre that seems to make the homogenization of the intersections of race and gender easy and amplified weekly through series such as *Fix My Life*, the consequences of Vanzant's message about "doing the work" cannot be overlooked, particularly as OWN featured a special episode of *Fix My Life* entitled "Healing in Ferguson" after the summer 2014 murder of Michael Brown. Revision, in this instance, functions like a campaign slogan that privileges community belonging and recovery even as it obscures internalized gender oppression and promotes narrow forms of critical vision.

CHAPTER 4

Come Ye Disconsolate
The Rhetoric of Transformation in T.D. Jakes's Women's Ministry

> Come Ye Disconsolate, where'er ye languish,
> Come to the mercy seat, fervently kneel.
> Here bring your wounded hearts, here tell your anguish;
> Earth has no sorrow that heav'n cannot heal.
> —Traditional Christian Hymn

Claps echo. A woman shouts, "Halleluiah!" An organist plays a somber chord in the background. "I believe that God can make me whole," a voice says. "I believe He can deliver me. I believe He can set me free." The voice increases in momentum. "I believe he can fix me. Even me. Even me. Even me. In spite of everything I've done, even me."

A glance around the room reveals the occasion; it is a revival service and there appears to be at least a thousand people in attendance. A preacher paces across the pulpit, imploring the weary and broken to make their way to the altar. "Come down out of that balcony!" His voice booms. Scores of women and a sprinkling of men rush forward.

A Black woman in her twenties rushes past the ushers into the double doors leading into the sanctuary. Her white dress is modest. Her nerves are visible. Her pause before beginning down the aisle suggests that she is uncomfortable. Church is not her home.

"You need this Word. You need a good anointed church like this where you can get the Word of God and be set free, and be healed," the preacher states. "Healed. Healed. Healed of your issues and your angers and your dilemmas. Healed. Healed. Healed. Healed. Healed."

Tearfully, the woman makes her way down the aisle. The preacher chants, "I want to be loosed. I want to be free. I want to get over it." He begins to sing, "There's room at the cross." The choir follows his lead.

"Somebody's mama is coming to the Lord!" the preacher announces. "Somebody's little girl is coming to the Lord!"

The woman walks to the altar. She stands for a moment before pulling out a tattered trash bag. Inside there is an old, white garment. She kisses it before bending down to place it on the altar.

Something catches her eye. Confusion overtakes her. She slowly stands.

"There's room at the cross," the preacher sings. "There's room at the cross, for you."

Engulfed in rage, the woman at the altar screams before firing three shots. The screen goes Black.[2]

* * * * *

The invitation is an appeal to embrace a denomination or to join a congregation that tends to come at the end of an evangelical Christian service. In the 2004 film *Woman Thou Art Loosed*, the scenes described above are a symbolic invitation that appears at the beginning. Moviegoers familiar with T.D. Jakes, the Dallas mega-church minister, may have recognized the gesture immediately. The first few minutes of the film contain the same messages about restoration and forgiveness, preaching cadences, and images of crowds rushing to the altar that are characteristic of Jakes's appearances on the *Trinity Broadcast Network* and his popular *Manpower* and *Megafest* conventions. What probably seems less familiar to viewers is Kimberly Elise's jarring portrayal of Michelle, the teary young woman who fires at the altar and kills her mother's longtime, alcoholic boyfriend, Reggie, who, as viewers learn throughout the film, had raped her when she was a child (see figure 4.1). Despite the contrast, the movie garnered praise by mainstream news outlets such as the *Los Angeles Times*. In dramatizing the message within the lyrics of the hymn "Come Ye Disconsolate," Jakes had successfully managed to bring elements of the Black church to the big screen. *Woman Thou Art Loosed* was a feat that helped solidify a market for church-sponsored films, opening the door for companies such as Sherwood Pictures to release *Facing the Giants, Fireproof,* and *Courageous* and have profitable box-office returns.[3]

At the time of its release, Jakes's 2004 film was the latest entry in a ministry franchise based on the Sunday-school curriculum the preacher developed for female members of his West Virginia congregation struggling in the aftermath of abuse or divorce. Included in the franchise was the self-published 1993 book *Woman, Thou Art Loosed!: Healing the Wounds of the Past,* an instructional workbook, a customized bible for

Kimberly Elise portrays Michelle, the battered protagonist who retaliates against her abuser in the 2004 Magnolia Pictures film *Woman Thou Art Loosed*. Fair use.

women, musical CDs, massive conventions, several reprints of the 1993 book, a gospel stage play co-written and directed by a then-unknown Tyler Perry, a novel, and, some years later, the 2012 sequel *Woman Thou Art Loosed: On the 7th Day*. The 2004 drama was a sharp departure from the 1993 book. The plot focuses on a young woman's efforts to rebuild her life after a childhood rape propels her into prostitution, drug use, sexual violence, and a stint in prison. The film's R rating prompted some Christian journalists to question the minister's shift in tone, and he responded. In a 2004 interview with *Christianity Today*, Jakes explained that the church needed a reality check if it was to fulfill its function as a hospital for the broken because continuing to promote the message that "praying the sinner's prayer" would sustain individuals who had undergone trauma was not a sufficient strategy. "When we perpetuate that myth, people who are in crisis are more worried about their reputation in the church and less secure in their opportunity to be healed," he explained. "In this case, instead of an outsider blowing the whistle on the church, it's the church blowing the whistle."[4] Ideally, books and films were a way to take the message of healing to an increasingly despondent and wounded world.

San Francisco Weekly film critic Julie Lyons lauds Jakes for another form of whistle-blowing. In her 2004 review, Lyons argued that the film was an intervention into the larger issue of sexism within the Black church. Citing his choice to address the needs of Black Christian women and to give female preachers such as Juanita Bynum their start, Lyons argued that Jakes was proclaiming spiritual liberation to women who had endured generations of "dogging and degrading" within a church tradition that had, to borrow Richardson's term, desired their tithes and talents but devalued them by subjugating them to a male clergy that had "free reign to operate under a different set of moral rules."[5] His messages were refreshing to the female fans who have helped sustain his career by purchasing his books. Within the market for self-empowerment literature that Vanzant joined in the early nineties, Jakes's books were a departure from community-based gospels that either ignored the realities of Black women, or exploited them for the purposes of admonishment and teaching. "I think that's why it's resounding today," said the bishop's wife Serita Jakes in a 2011 interview about the continued popularity of his *Woman Thou Art Loosed* convention. In her estimation, Jakes's messages "struck a chord in the hearts of women" and let them know they could find liberation. "It doesn't matter where you came from. It matters that you heard HIM and he identified who you are, who he intended you to be—and he beckoned you out of it."[6] The "He" is implied.

Beckoning is an outcome of the rhetoric of transformation in *Woman, Thou Art Loosed!: Healing the Wounds of the Past* and *Daddy Loves His Girls* that links these two important distinctions for Jakes. Despite wide-scale agreement on the social and political influence of the traditional Black church, there has been a much broader crisis of purpose to occur than the one to which Jakes alluded when defending his first film throughout the last twenty-five years. In his provocatively titled 2010 essay, "The Black Church Is Dead," religion scholar Eddie Glaude attributes this crisis to an abandoning of the historical social-justice mission that made the church a place of refuge and voice of the disenfranchised, and he cites the prevalence of contemporary African American ministers preaching prosperity gospels as evidence of this shift.[7] While Glaude considers this death an opportunity to reimagine the church's function, Jakes is one of a number of Black ministers including Creflo Dollar, Noel Jones, and Eddie Long who boast congregations in the thousands despite criticisms of their perceived focus on prosperity. Among this group, Jakes has remained the most visible and influential due in part to his ability to expand the message of forgiveness and transformation. Even though Black women have had a tenuous history within the church, Jakes has been able to develop a multi-genre ministry that draws from some of the most sustaining aspects of the church's social role to develop a wellness campaign where invitations are institutional interventions.

Reading Transformation: Preaching as Action

In *T.D. Jakes: America's New Preacher*, Shayne Lee argues that the much of the minister's success is the result of his innovation within an increasingly postmodern religious climate. As individuals have attained greater career access and social mobility, their spiritual needs and tastes have shifted; and ministers have had to appease populations with diverse psychosocial needs, cultural customs, and preferences.[8] Lee believes that Jakes's endorsement of such "American" ideas as self-reinvention and his choice to use postmodern features such as email to disseminate his message have enabled the minister to "saturate" a religious marketplace with an "incessant" stream of images and products. These images and products incorporate mixed codes from contemporary secular culture that coalesce to offer Christian consumers a form of therapeutic religion. The result, according to Lee, is that Jakes has become a visible figure within a broader paradigm shift of "religious realignment"—one where mainline churches that hold fast to denominational traditions experience decline while innovative, independent churches experience phenomenal growth.[9] Although I question Lee's use of the term "postmodern," I still find the concept of realignment useful considering the tasks figures such as Jakes face when attempting to balance their male privilege and institutional authority while redressing crises in their communities through instruction.

Throughout this chapter, I draw upon scholarship in womanist and liberation theology, dramatism, literacy studies, and rhetorical perspectives on preaching to contextualize Jakes's ministry within histories of the traditional Black church, identify his strategies in constructing an audience, and interrogate the implications of his modes of instruction for healing. First, I provide an overview of the Black church's history as a community institution and the social location many women occupy in Black churches. Second, I provide a discussion of Black women's experiences as what Jacqueline Grant describes as "the backbones of the church." Third, I examine the persuasive strategies Jakes adopts in the 1993 version of *Woman, Thou Art Loosed* to identify with his readers and call them to the work of healing within scholarship on Black preaching, womanist theology, and self-help culture. Afterwards, I interrogate the process of affirmation Jakes enacts in *Daddy Loves His Girls* as a distinct factor within his approach to healing to determine the gender politics in his construction of female readers. Finally, I draw upon Katie Cannon's womanist hermeneutic for preaching to examine the process for recovery he offers as a healing curriculum, replete with instructions on ways they can renew their minds, revise their behaviors, and restore their relationships. Katie Cannon's womanist hermeneutic centralizes the standpoint and experiences of Black women in its analysis of forms of power, and it excavates the ways in which patriarchal forms of power and disparaging constructions of womanhood operate within sacred discourses. As I show, Jakes's early books contain a potent rhetoric of healing that constructs and beckons infirmed and "disconsolate" women back to the church for transformation in order to transmit the inspirational messages within his Sunday-school curriculum into written texts broader audiences can access. In doing so, his process for rhetorical healing also inscribes a confining discourse of realignment that aims to keep women in line and ensure churches remain relevant.

Individuals and the Nation: The Influence of the African American Church

Several years before Eddie Glaude published his provocative article, Martha Simmons was one of the earliest journalists to categorize pivotal shifts within the Black Christian church throughout the last thirty years. With information drawn from a survey of ministers, laypersons, scholars, and preachers, her 2007 article "Trends in the African American Church" cites the growing numbers of mega churches, the increase in national retreats and conventions, and the rise in publications by preachers and ministers as a few of the major trends within the church. Number thirteen on the list of trends is one of the most contentious: the shift from "Christocentric" preaching to "me-centric" preaching. Most visible in sermons that focus on individuals getting their breakthroughs, entering their seasons, and walking into their destinies, me-centric preaching departs from social-justice focused messages that call for holy living and from the community-driven sermons, which have historically characterized the messages within the Black church.[10] In her article, Simmons does not draw a connection between the proliferation of these sermon topics and the broader focus on rugged American individualism that the self-help scholars I cite in previous chapters have pointed out. Similar to

Jakes's earlier reference about whistle-blowing and Glaude's essay, Simmons's critique is intended to be self-reflexive. With so many people facing hurts and seeking direction, Black preachers who continue to present a "we are all filthy rags" gospel lose their social relevance because "they have stepped out of touch with those who sincerely need words of healing and self-esteem enhancement."[11] The Black church's survival would depend on its responsibility and ability to address the social as well as the individual concerns of African Americans.

The concern for institutional survival is a departure from the focus on the church as a form of a community that has historically characterized the institution. Since the post-enslavement era when African Americans began to formalize the invisible, hush harbor-type meetings they had developed to engage in a religious practices away from the surveillance of their masters, the Black church has been a complex organism. As a site of literacy development, the church was a transgressive space where African Americans refashioned the scripture messages of servitude and submissiveness that their former masters had preached into messages of liberation and acceptance. Moreover, these "hidden" religious meetings were also means for African Americans to transfuse the projected Christianity of their masters with the spiritual expressions brought with them from Africa and transmit ways of knowing and subversion necessary to survive or escape transgression.[12] Beyond fostering a sense of community literacy, the church has also focused explicitly on community identity. Richard Allen's famous break from the white Methodist church in Philadelphia in 1816 is one of the more well-known histories within discussions of the Black church's development, but it is a regional narrative of displacement. For many African Americans, particularly those coming out of slavery in the South, building a church was the primary project on a list of structures and institutions they sought to create that would enable them to start creating their own social worlds. Through collaborating on which customs would define a space of worship, the task of creating the Black church became what Evelyn Brooks Higginbotham describes as a "domain for the expression, celebration, and pursuit of a Black collective will and identity."[13] In this manner, the African American church has always functioned as a counterpublic space, replete with the forms of shared knowledge, cultural views, collective aims, and the distinctive rhetorical practices that have come to characterize what scholars such as E. Lincoln Frazier call the "nation within a nation."[14]

The notion of a "nation within a nation" suggests uniformity, but there are numerous areas within the church community where different interpretations of thought and practice reside. In her discussion of the church as a community that influences how African Americans interpret texts and employ their literacies in *A Community Text Arises: A Literate Text and an African American Literacy Tradition,* Beverly Moss includes Lincoln and Mamiya's list of the pairs or poles, which operate as the major organizational frames within the church. Moss argues that it is the dialectical tension between how individual churches negotiate and enact where they reside within each set of poles that best characterizes the African American church community. Common characteristics and practices do exist; however the "dynamic rather than static nature" that these tensions reflect illustrate the ways that the church community tries to shift with the times.[15] The six poles she cites include: an orientation towards priestly or prophetic functions, an other-worldly versus this-worldly perspective, universalism and particularism, communalism and privatistic concerns, charismatic versus bureaucratic organizational structures, and resistance versus accommodationist philosophies.

Although each pole influences the context of Jakes's work, the communal and privatistic poles and other-worldly-versus-this-worldly perspective enables us to see how Jakes's decision to address the perceived needs of women in crisis through writing and publishing inspirational and instructional texts fits within the broader spectrum of the Black church and church community. According to Moss's description, "communal" orientations refer to the long-standing assumption that the Black church should be involved in every aspect of its members' lives. From political, to economic, to educational and social aspects, the Black church is supposed to have a form of influence. On the other hand, the privatistic pole represents the end of a spectrum where the church has withdrawn from the concerns of the larger community in order to focus solely on addressing the religious needs of the members.[16] Collectively, these orientations are shaped by an other-world perspective that emphasizes a concern with only heaven and eternal life or a this-worldly perspective that describes a church with an involvement in the "here and now" affairs of the world.[17]

Considering how Jakes's choice to address such private issues as substance abuse, rape, and depression reflects where he positions his ministry within the communalistic and privatistic orientations and the other-worldly-versus-this-worldly perspective on faith, his concern about the image of the church becomes relevant again.[18] If, as he asserts, "people who [are] in crisis [are] more worried about their reputation in the church and less secure in their opportunity to be healed," then the innovative intervention he seems to make by writing and publishing books for women must be understood alongside his concerns about the church's reputation.[19] In situating the needs of Black women, Jakes appeared to model the worldly shift that seemed to inspire Simmons to claim that ministers who rail against me-centric preaching are out of touch.

Jakes is not alone in making the shift to address the needs of women a major focus of his ministry. With her famous "No More Sheets" sermon, Juanita Bynum became one of the most prominent African American female preachers during the late nineties to gain widespread popularity for addressing women's emotional baggage. Her preaching style relied on frank forms of logic, personal testimony, and such dramatic illustrations as wrapping herself in a bed sheet to show the type of emotional binds single women place themselves in by seeking out male companionship through sexual relationships, with the hope of marriage, rather than waiting on a notion of divine timing.[20] Bynam's preaching during this moment in her career was as compelling as that of Jakes, and, to her credit, she did attain moderate success with her book *No More Sheets: The Truth About Sex* and her musical CDs and videos. Yet, even though Bynum had the benefit of an actual testimony she could draw upon when addressing the thousands of African American women who would attend her speaking engagements around the country, she did not have the same institutional authority and ethos as did Jakes. Despite what appeared to be her best efforts to franchise that message, she could not acquire the same mainstream status with her call for healing as sexual purity as Jakes did.

One of the most potent claims among feminist and womanist scholars is that church leaders, and church communities by default, have ignored, overshadowed, or caused the oppression of certain individuals and marginalized groups. Given the seemingly holistic emphasis in Jakes's ministry, carrying out his ministerial duties would require him to "deal with the problems and realities confronting . . . [all] people as they cope with the demands and stresses of daily living."[22] As such, addressing private and seemingly personal topics as the impact of child abuse on women, divorce, sexual abuse, and incest was the natural progression of a ministry mandate. Assuming Jakes's books, conventions, films, and recordings are a mass production of his sermons and teachings on healing, then other trends such as the rise of national revivals and the increase in publishing that Simmons cites suggest that one of the causes for the current trends in the Black church is the emphasis on dealing with "the nation's" problems.

"Backbones" and the Background: Women in the African American Church

The "nation within a nation" phrase is useful in conceptualizing the church's role within African American communities. Where Black women are concerned, the idea that they are the "backbone of the church" is the necessary frame for understanding their work and experiences within this institution. Comprising more than two-thirds of contemporary Black church populations, women have a long history of service to the church, frequently performing such essential tasks as serving on auxiliary boards and music ministries or supplying the financial funding through paying tithes to ensure the church's daily operation. These works have helped sustain the private arm of the church; Black women were equally active in performing the types of public good works that have helped make the traditional church the most influential site of racial self-help.[23] Through helping to establish schools, orphanages, and community centers, spreading messages of discontent at racial and gender discrimination, or contesting lynching and other forms of terrorism or disenfranchisement, Black clubwomen assumed teaching and evangelist roles that enabled them to transgress racial and gender boundaries on behalf of the church. The clubwomen's outreach and activism efforts did promote the politics of respectability that I described briefly earlier and Evelyn Higginbotham discusses at length in *Righteous Discontent: The Women's Movement in the Black Baptist Church, 1880-1920*, but their contributions sustained the institution. During the racial struggles of the clubwomen's time, the spiritual gospels they preached and the sociopolitical messages they helped spread with their teaching and writing propelled the Black church's contributions to post-reconstruction era efforts. Through a combination of private and public works, Black clubwomen exemplified the motto of "lifting as they climb[ed]," by helping the church extend its mission within and beyond African American communities.[24]

As a term, the word "backbone" bears additional significance. In her frequently cited essay, "Black Women and the Church," Jacqueline Grant suggests that the real significance of that phrase is in the word "back" which indicates where most women and their issues often reside within the church: in the background.[25] Grant's move to shift our attention from the backbone metaphor to the background indicator reflects feminist and womanist scholars' critiques of the tradition of patriarchy that has shaped the evolution of Black churches. For example, even though some Black women were active in religious meetings during slavery and frequently served in leadership capacities, male church leaders began to restrict their participation after emancipation. In *The Gendered Pulpit: Preaching in American Protestant Spaces,* rhetorician Roxanne Mountford explains that some Black male church leaders attempted to model their newly constructed families and religions after patriarchal antebellum white families once slavery was over, adopting equally narrow gender politics that regulated women's activity and blocked their leadership.[26] Although Mountford notes that Freedmen's Bureau agents reported that Black women "vigorously" resisted these efforts, this example speaks to church leaders' efforts to align themselves with presumed models of respectability at the expense of Black women members.

Early Black church leaders pursued goals of respectability through inter-related textual practices. Many of the male leaders of the religious denominations Blacks formed after slavery explicitly restricted women from ordination at their inception. The founders of these denominations reasoned that the Apostle Paul's scripture in 1 Corinthians 14:34 which reads, "Let your women keep silent in the churches: for it is not permitted unto them to speak," meant that God had not intended for women to preach or speak from the pulpit.[27] Ironically, many male leaders arguing for abolition renounced literal interpretations of the Apostle Paul's scripture that "slaves must obey their masters" to advance the cause for racial equality, a practice womanist theologians point to as evidence of the hypocritical forms of patriarchy circulating within early Black churches. The attempts of the itinerant preacher Jarena Lee to be ordained by the African Methodist Episcopal (AME) Church is an example of how some Black ministers' interpretation of scripture worked to restrict women's participation. Lee's 1836 biography reveals how in 1811 she approached Richard Allen, the well-known leader of the AME church, to obtain the right to preach and was told that their "discipline knew nothing at all about it—that it *did not call for women preachers.*"[28] Allen finally acknowledged Lee's call to preach, but only after a visiting preacher began to stumble through his sermon, and she stepped in and completed it.[29] Thank goodness for Lee's independent rhetorical education. Still, this incident is illuminating. By relying on literal interpretations of such biblical passages, some Black male church leaders used the same interpretive practices to make scripture a hegemonic discourse that white slave masters had used. In this instance though, Black male leaders were using these readings to monopolize leadership and relegate women to the pews or "backbone" of the church through an institutionally sanctioned textual politic that promoted Black women's silence.[30]

To be sure, there were many Black Christian women who actively rejected these textual politics and conditions. In response to the attempts to constrain their participation within formal ministries or block it altogether, some women channeled their energies into creating separate denominations such as the Church of God in Christ (COGIC) and the National Baptist Convention. Others chose to use these injustices as inspiration. In *The Black Megachurch: Theology, Gender, and the Politics of Public Engagement,* Tamelyn Tucker-Worgs cites nineteenth-century orator and abolitionist Maria W. Stewart's 1833 "Farewell Address to Her Friends in Boston" lecture as an example of this practice.[31] To make space for Black women to participate in abolitionist efforts, Stewart reasons,

> What if I am a woman; is not the God of ancient times the God of modern days? Did he not raise up Deborah to be a mother and a judge in Israel? And Mary Magdalene first declare the resurrection of Christ from the dead? . . . St. Paul declared that it was a shame for a woman to speak in public, yet our great High Priest and Advocate did not condemn the woman for a more notorious offense than this; neither will he condemn this worthless worm. . . . Did St. Paul but know of our wrongs and deprivations, I presume he would make no objection to our pleading in public for our rights.[32]

Tucker-Worgs acknowledges the Black women's intellectual tradition Stewart helped launch with this move to seize the authority to participate publicly within racial uplift and justice endeavors. Given the mixed audience she addressed with her appeal and the subsequent backlash, these efforts constitute what I see as a *within and beyond* set of practices that have marked Black women's engagement with this institution. When faced with hegemonic discourses, patriarchal policies, or wounding traumas, many Black women have not decided to leave the church en masse. Instead, they have resisted by creating new spaces within the existing structure that transformed the conditions where they worship or by going beyond the walls of the church and critiquing it publicly. This legacy helps us understand how Black women who might fall into the "wounded self" and "social self" audience constructs Sandra Dolby identifies among self-help readers might turn to Jakes's books. They have invested in rebuilding where they are with the hope of moving beyond their current dilemma.

The history of male preachers who have regulated women's issues outside the realm of concern or have exploited them for other purposes is an equally problematic textual practice that has shaped Black women's experiences in the church. As James Cone notes in his discussion of Black Liberation Theology, there is a contradiction in liberatory efforts that overlook issues of sexism, be they secular or spiritual. Like most other churches, the traditional Black church is male dominated but this dominance exacerbates the adverse forms of treatment some Black women receive because Black male leaders lack criteria for liberation that accounts for more than one form of oppression. "It is truly amazing that many Black ministers, young and old can hear the message of liberation in the gospel when related to racism but remain deaf to a similar message in the context of sexism," he notes.[33] Cone suggests that Black male leaders often do not have models for uplift and freedom that are rooted in biblical scripture and current enough for the present struggles of oppressed people.

One cause for the lack of clear liberation criteria is the textual trend of placing men at the normative center in traditional Black preaching. As Katie Cannon observes, by placing the concerns and perspectives of men at the normative center of their biblical preaching and teaching, many Black ministers have relied on and advanced disparaging characterizations of Black women to illustrate the world of sin that man must navigate in order to reach heaven.[34] The prevalence of such terms as "sin-bringing Eve," "henpecking Jezebel," "whoring Gomer," "prostituting Mary Magdalene," and "conspiring Sapphira" within Black preaching creates a "frame of sexist-racist social contradictions housed in sacred rhetoric that gives women a zero-image of ourselves."[35] Not unlike the disparaging, controlling images of Black womanhood discussed in the previous chapter, these tropes become more potent and destructive to Black women's self-esteem when they circulate within preaching because they are, supposedly, excavated from the minister's reading and interpretation of the sacred text. For example, the "Sapphire" and "Black welfare mother" are images that have informed the secular discourses that public policy makers have considered when passing laws that police Black women's bodies and their access to social services, while the image of "conspiring Sapphira" and "prostituting Mary Magdalene" has informed how some Christians perceive women's participation in the narrative of humankind's fall from grace within preaching traditions.

In both spheres, these tropes become intertwined within misogynistic textual practices that promote the belief that Black women can be held to blame for problems facing the collective body and the specific conditions that wound them.

It is worth noting that many Black women employ critical literacies when deciphering these messages. As a context, though, these conditions make it imperative to place Jakes's books within this facet of the church's history. The seemingly holistic emphasis of Jakes's ministry suggests that his work to advance a healing ministry to Black women takes up the goals of Black women's survival and wholeness, which womanist theology foregrounds. As I show in the following two sections, Jakes's early efforts to address personal and church-wide crises through a discourse on healing suggest that his *Woman, Thou Art Loosed* books and *Daddy Loves His Girls,* are extensions of the church's efforts making a positive impact on the secular world. However, because Jakes relies on problematic constructions of Black womanhood, the rhetoric of transformation he employs to move Black women towards healing also carries forth some of the more problematic issues within the Black church.

Failure: A Crisis of Missed Opportunity

By the time the fifth edition of *Woman, Thou Art Loosed!: Healing the Wounds of the Past* was released in 2005, Jakes had franchised his message on the power of faith and scriptural teaching to deliver and heal women from their infirmities by diversifying the genre and making bolder promises about the incentives of healing. In the description of the 2005 version, readers are invited to let their hearts be warmed as the "oil of T.D. Jakes's teaching" flows through their minds and spirits. The book is described as a balm that not only soothes the traumas and disappointments that single parents, battered wives, abused girls, and insecure women might face but also offers a "deep cleansing" for those hardened areas of women's hearts. As a resource for fighting the "infections" women experience in life, "*Woman, Thou Art Loosed!* will break the bands off the neck of every woman who dares to read it!."[36]

Against the backdrop of the questions about the church's social relevance, the situation that Jakes cites as the impulse for writing *Woman, Thou Art Loosed!* was the prevalence of sexual abuse victims in his West Virginia congregation. Compelled to intervene, Jakes developed a popular Sunday-school curriculum for female members. By helping adult survivors of abuse see God's transformative power of the scripture and God's mercy, Jakes's book aims to teach victims how to overwrite the discourses of shame, guilt, and condemnation that prevent them from living the lives of purpose that God intends for them. It is ministry on the mass scale.

The goal of helping individuals overcome trauma and rewrite their future, per se, is the explicit impetus of his book. However, since Jakes also argues that it is because the church has failed to recognize that the adult problems it fights to correct "are often rooted in the ashes of childhood experiences" that many adults are unable to recover from, his rhetoric of healing seems equally influenced by a crisis of missed opportunity.[37] Calling for the church to "share God-given biblical answers to troubling questions" as it deals with the long-standing effects of childhood sexual abuse, Jakes admonishes church leaders to have more faith *in faith,* writing "ours is not a medicine that can be mixed by a pharmacist. Our patients' wounds are in the heart. We don't need medicine; we need miracles."[38] Evidence of the this-worldly orientation of his ministry, Jakes's crisis-driven critique of the church reveals the implicit impetus behind his publication of *Woman, Thou Art Loosed!* Loosing, transforming, and healing victims of sexual-abuse are the miracles that help ensure women have what they need for survival. It is also the role the church must play to maintain its relevance as a source of inspiration and strength within the community.

The "cure for the crisis" Jakes offers readers in *Woman, Thou Art Loosed!* is a process of steps women can learn and follow to receive and maintain the spiritual deliverance necessary for transforming their lives. Jakes argues that issues such as depression, low self-esteem, and sexual promiscuity or *immorality* are actually spiritual ailments that result from traumatic events such as domestic abuse, child abuse, rape, sexual abuse, and/or divorce.[39] Because women are not likely to interpret their wounds as such, they are unaware of the power that God has to cure them, and so they misread their own self-worth. This illiteracy of sorts renders them unable to move forward with their lives in healthy, productive ways. By transforming how women see and understand themselves, their relationship with God, the power they possess as believers of God, Jakes offers a course of healing that enables women not only to get over the past, but to move forward into the healthy future, relationships, and identity that God intends for them.

Problems, Promises, and Prescriptions: Infirmity as a Call to Healing

Beverly Moss's discussion of the preferences African American churchgoers express about sermonic arrangement is essential to understanding the implications of how Jakes calls women to the work of healing. Most of the sermons within African American churches have multiple rhetorical and pragmatic aims, she explains. Some ministers follow a deductive organizational approach wherein they construct a thesis and break it down into points, explaining and illustrating the points and applying them to particular situations of the hearers. Conversely, there is also the inductive approach where the minister begins with a particular experience that is familiar to the audience and then moves to a general truth or conclusion. The inductive approach requires ministers to construct a shared, knowledge-making experience. Their task is to establish themselves as "part of the group while at the same time maintaining the proper distance from the congregation."[40] Black preachers must be skilled rhetors who know not only what to say, but how to say it in a way that establishes community ties with the audience as well as leaves individual space for innovation. At a minimum, ministers must bring a message or a form of scriptural insight, to audiences in what Moss describes as "a cup they can recognize" to earn their respect.[41]

Moss's observations also correspond to genre conventions in the self-help literature market Jakes joined when he published the 1993 version of *Woman, Thou Art Loosed!* As Sandra Dolby explains, written self-help genres require authors to address notably different expectations than oral folk-culture traditions that attempt to pass on the same insights or forms of wisdom. The appeal of such oral folk-culture genres as the story, parable, or fable is the flexibility they afford speakers who want to modify their texts. Depending on the audience's expectations or engagement, speakers can easily alter their cadence, visual cues, figurative language, length, or tone on a whim. Book writers are not so fortunate. Their challenge is to draw upon the assumptions or values they share with their readers because, regardless of editorial mediation or marketing, the reader determines whether or not to buy a book or implement its strategies.[42] For some authors, writing self-help books is performance in context.

The argument Jakes develops in *Woman, Thou Art Loosed!* shows his sophistication in addressing these performance-in-context mandates. In order to convert a sermon and Sunday-school curriculum into an accessible book for broader audiences, Jakes had to illustrate a crisis, establish what Royster calls a "mandate" that readers feel compelled to actively resolve, offer a solution, and make visible the implications of their inaction. Jakes devotes the first chapter of his 1993 inspirational book to these tasks, moving between the roles of illustrator, interpreter, messenger, and guide to argue that women must embrace the everyday utility of biblical scripture. In the section "Unprogramming Life's Poorly Programmed Events," he cites a biblical scripture admonishing readers not to conform to "the pattern of this world" but, instead, to be "transformed by the renewing" of [their] minds, to emphasize the shift in perception that must occur.[43] Relying on a comprehension-based argument, he explains that a person's experiences shape their perspective, and when those experiences are "distorted," an individual's understanding of "spiritual truths" suffers. Much like Vanzant who equates spirituality to vision, Jakes asks readers, "What do you do when you have been poorly programmed by life's events?" and then answers with an implied offer, "You reprogram your mind through the Word of God."[44] Reprogramming the mind through transformation and renewal is a learning cure that should equip a reader with access to spiritual truths and strategies for applying them to everyday situations.

To bring this message about transformation to his readers in a "cup they can recognize," Jakes opens the book by performing an exegesis of the scripture Luke 13:11–12. The scripture describes the infirm woman who suffered for eighteen years with a debilitating condition that kept her from lifting "herself" up or standing straight, before encountering Jesus who called out to her, "Woman, thou art loosed from thine infirmity." Framing it as the "testimony" of one of the patients of the "Divine Physician," Jakes suggests that even if the dilemma differs from his readers' experience, the infirm woman's "dilemma" offers a "point of relativity" for his readers or women they know. Offering his own interpretation, Jakes explains that the three components of this story are the person, the problem, and the prescription; therefore, "It's important to remember that for every person, there will be a problem," and "for every problem our God has a prescription!"[45] Although Jakes's analysis enables him to foster a sense of urgency for healing here, his presence and perspective remain implied. His explicit perspective does not emerge until he discusses how readers either overlook the command inherent in the statement "woman, thou art loosed!" or assume that simply discussing past trauma will lead to a sustained sense of healing. Analysis and application are key in Jakes's sense of healing because, after people understand the origins of their dilemma, it will still take "the authority of God's word" for them "to put the past under [their] feet!"[46] The appeal Jakes attempts in his introduction through this exegesis operates on three assumptions. The first is that the readers will identify with the infirm woman. The second is that the readers will have a problem. The third is that the readers will believe that they need to be able to put the word of God under their feet, or realize that they have not yet been able to do so. Assuming they do, the analysis Jakes offers in his introduction essentially places readers in a context of problems and promises where his offer to instruct women on how to use scripture to "put the past under your feet" becomes the prescription for transformation.

As a performance, Jakes's reading of the infirm woman's transition to wellness makes a convincing argument about why women must actively claim the forms of healing that are available through scriptural application. Unlike Vanzant, who could draw upon a shared sense of indignation at Ali's text and invoke her own personal testimonies, Jakes's participation in a church tradition that had, at times, ignored issues of trauma and abuse and used women as scapegoats in religious teachings was a constraint to the authority he might normally hold as a minister. His challenge was to make his ministerial qualifications clear to diverse audiences and to simultaneously establish distance between his ministry and claims of patriarchy and misogyny within the church. Making the "infirm woman" the primary point of identification for, presumably, female readers is a persuasive choice that defies the task of creating consubstantial space that rhetoricians would expect Jakes to undertake in this instance. Instead, Jakes's use of the "infirm woman" assumes readers will respond to her as a symbol, recognize her pain, and see in it their own reflections. By invoking her "testimony," he follows one of the strategies that Moss considers characteristic of African American preachers by establishing "distance" between himself and his readers, while also establishing the precedent for the "infirm woman's" transition to wellness and his call for healing as a resolution.

Distancing is a technique that takes on more resonance through the medicalized terminology Jakes employs to advance his argument about transformation. As Kenneth Burke's dramatistic theory on language use asserts, man*kind* is a symbol-using animal; therefore, his language choices should be read not only as modes of action, but also as indicators of the motive-driven nature of one's discourse.[47] In calling the "infirm woman" a "patient," Jakes establishes a terministic screen of sickness that enables him to select and direct his readers' attention from physical forms of pain to emotional issues they are to see as sources of personal crisis.[48] Naturally, most of the emotional issues fall into the category of trauma and involve such matters as childhood sexual abuse, rape, domestic violence and spousal abuse, grief, and divorce. Jakes defines these matters as "natural problems" that are "rooted in spiritual ailments."[49] It is unfortunate that at this point in his rhetorical healing process, Jakes misses the opportunity to acknowledge the troubled spirits that inflict these forms of pain on women or the cultures that objectify women and young girls. Such a dialogue could have been a step in the direction of helping women in trauma develop or activate their critical consciousness or making the church a more active vehicle within women's liberation efforts. The choice to use a discourse on infirmity as a call to healing makes sense though. Since the church is supposed to be a therapeutic place for individuals in crisis, a hospital even, infirmity is a discourse that makes the appeal of scriptural literacy more attractive.

The task of definition is the place where the consequences of the infirmity argument emerge. Infirmity is not solely physical ailments or adverse events in Jakes's healing effort. It is a social threat because, as he explains,

> many women also wrestle with infirmities in emotional traumas. These infirmities can be just as challenging as a physical affliction. An emotional handicap can create dependency on many levels. Relationships can become crutches. The infirm woman can place such weight on people that it strains a healthy relationship. And many times such emotional handicaps will spawn a series of unhealthy relationships.[50]

Jakes references no other tangible actors or individuals but the infirm woman here. In isolating her and obscuring discussion of external factors or conditions that shape women's lives, his claim that the emotional handicap that she carries places "weight" on people and relationships encourages women readers to identify within themselves similar personality traits or challenges and interpret them as burdens. The irony of this approach is that even though Jakes's book places women at the normative center, his choice to theorize sickness through a behavioral frame is no better. As Katie Cannon notes, traditional Black preaching has predominantly placed men at the normative center, while casting biblical women as the cause of humankind's sin-sickness. Jakes's attempts to place women at the center is equally problematic because, in using the "infirm woman" as the symbol with which readers identify, he implicitly constructs a context where female readers identify with sickness. When expanded through themes of burden and blame, the relationship Jakes encourages readers to develop with the "infirm woman" implies that women need not embrace transformation and healing for the salvation or rescue of their own sin-sick souls, but rather to protect their souls and the souls of their loved ones from the sin that their trauma-induced sicknesses and wounds cause. Though implicit, this appeal to Black women's presumed sense of self-lessness is dangerous because it reinscribes the "zero-image of ourselves" that Cannon claims some Black women learn through forms of preaching.

Jakes's definition of infirmity also makes interpersonal relationships an evaluative site where women are to determine whether they are infecting a union with their "issues." The problems in this causal logic appear throughout Jakes's discussion of how emotional illnesses spawn such "sin-sicknesses" as homosexuality, feminine-acting men, jealousy, overly critical parenting, and women distrusting men: issues that have all, at one point, been interpreted by conservative Black ministers as threats to the nuclear, heterosexual Black family.[51] Casting homosexuality in men and behaviors that fall outside of narrow, heteronormative conceptions of masculinity (ie., feminine-acting men) as emotional issues—for the sake of keeping illness a broad form of crisis—is an argument that promotes homophobia. With the move to pair the two with a behavior such as jealousy, this argument also creates a perpetuating logic. When readers embrace this logic and conflate identity categories such as sexuality with personality traits such as jealousy, the consequence of this rhetoric is that sickness, broadly defined, produces a perpetual source of issues that require healing. Infirmity becomes a replicating situation that allows Jakes to return to the notion of woman's wellness, publish multiple editions of this text in multiple formats, and appeal to diseased readers who would fall into the "wounded-self" category Dolby describes as well as women who are generally dissatisfied with the state of their lives.

Given critiques of the Black church for its failure to acknowledge women's issues and the pathologizing stance on homosexuality advanced by some of its most visible ministers, these initial efforts to establish a discourse about healing should direct us back to Katie Cannon's womanist hermeneutic which asks whose interests are served through this rhetoric. I do not doubt that Jakes created his initial *Woman, Thou Art Loosed* curriculum to accommodate the urgent questions and concerns of some of his female members or that his continued efforts to address these matters is part of the reason why he remains popular among Black women. When we consider the techniques he uses to establish a measure of distance between himself and his readers, as well as the way he defines sickness and moves the symbolic "infirm woman" through a context of problems and promises to offer his prescription, Lloyd Bitzer's famous explanation of the rhetorical situation becomes the answer to Cannon's question.[52] As Bitzer explains, the audience a rhetor chooses to direct his or her discourse to must consist "only of those persons who are capable of being influenced by discourse and of being mediators of change."[53] After complaints of women's neglect within the church and concerns about the institution's waning relevance, Jakes's efforts to make transformation seem urgent implies that Black women are the natural agents of such change because of their presumed self-lessness as mothers and backbones of the community. Transformation can be an institutionalizing discourse that, among other things, ensures that the church remains the site to take in women in crisis.

He Loves You Still: Intimacy, Kinship, and the Promise of Acceptance

As Black women have often defined pain on their own terms, it is not surprising that they have also sought to define the forms of compassion they should receive within healing efforts. Monya Aletha Stubbs does so in "Be Healed: A Black Woman's Sermon on Healing through Touch" by describing the extent to which infirmity can affect the self-esteem of young women. In the essay, she reflects on the physically and emotionally painful bout with impetigo she suffered as a teenager and her mother's choice to risk infection to provide her daughter with a "healing touch." When Stubbs asked her mother if she was worried that she herself would get sick, her mother told Stubbs that the shame she saw in her child's eyes as she went to school with her self-esteem shattered and soul troubled each day compelled her to act. "In order to heal you, I must touch you. I must feel you. I can't use gloves," said her mother.[54] Based on these acts of compassion, Stubbs developed a set of criteria for what ministry must accomplish for those with shattered self-esteem and confidence. A healing through touch or holistic ministry must reach individuals with damaged spirits and minds as well as side effects of physical illness, and it has to serve three functions: It has to meet people at the center of their affliction. It must reject "status quo sensitivity" or the inclination not to feel and empathize with the inward grief of others. Ultimately, it must empower those who feel shattered. The ministry that achieves these three goals, in Stubbs's estimation, embodies Christian principles of compassion and promotes whole and healthy recovery.

The shift from infirmity to intimacy Stubbs sets as criteria for holistic ministry also characterizes the shift in terrain that followed Jakes's release of *Woman, Thou Art Loosed!* Well before David Van Biema published his September 2001 *Time* magazine cover article coining Jakes the "next Billy Graham," the minister began to narrow in on the realm of women's relationships as a site requiring healing attention and began to gain a reputation as being the "Shepherd of the Shattered."[55] This gradual turn gains momentum with Jakes's 1996 book *Daddy Loves His Girls*. Marketed towards women with painful pasts and men who want the "courage to speak the healing power of love" to their daughters and the women in their lives, the book presents the premise that women who do not have healthy relationships with their earthly fathers cannot adequately understand the love that their heavenly father has for them.[56] This lack causes women to underestimate the extent of God's healing power and ability to resolve the "issues" they deal with in life. In chapters such as "Fatherless Girls, Fearful Women, and Faithfulness," and "Why Women War Against Each Other," Jakes draws upon his own experiences as a father and minister to explain how influential relationships are to a woman's well-being and to make the overarching call of his book: women need to develop and cultivate intimate relationships with their heavenly father if they are to be complete and whole. Ideally, cultivating these relationships enables women who have not experienced healthy relationships with their biological fathers to regain what they lost.[57] In addition to helping women deepen their sense of personal spiritual connection, Jakes attempts to demonstrate how men can express the power of healing to women in their lives.

The epistolary format of *Daddy Loves His Girls* aids in the shift to intimacy that characterizes this stage of Jakes's healing campaign. Composed primarily as a set of love letters, the book begins with Jakes affirming the uniqueness and beauty of his own two daughters and reminding them that they are "never ordinary" in his eyes.[58] He then transfers these messages of admiration to his readers, explaining that his message extends to all the "Father's daughters" and inviting readers to listen as "the Holy Spirit weaves a warming blanket under which all may snuggle and be blessed. This is a rare opportunity to examine the inner channels of the Father's heart."[59] In his use of such terms as "warming blanket" and such phrases as "all may snuggle and be blessed," Jakes incorporates written forms of the strategy of touch Lyndrey Niles considers essential to successful sermons. In "Rhetorical Characteristics of Traditional Black Preaching," Niles argues that a successful sermon hinges on the speaker's ability "to touch the deep emotions of the audience very early in the sermon."[60] Strategies of "touch" include providing a short statement of interest in presenting the text, telling a humorous story to relax themselves and the audience, providing informal, generalized comments, offering an invocation that opens the text, or inviting a soloist or choir to sing to begin the sermon. These gestures enable the speaker to establish a situation in which the feelings of the preacher and the people can be shared in an accepting climate of faith.[61] Touch and acceptance are crucial to the preacher's establishment of credibility and ethos before beginning the text. They ensure a measure of engagement necessary for ministry.

The forms of engagement Jakes attempts with these messages do enable him to model a way of helping women overwrite the discourses of shame and articulate the messages of acceptance that Stubbs considers essential to holistic ministry. Through his role as messenger, he assumes the authority to figuratively "speak life" into his female readers by reminding them that healing is a process that can cheat human understandings of time: "He has sent me to tell you—even after all that has happened to you and with you and in you—that He has not changed His mind. He loves you still!" Jakes explains.[62] The good news in this affirmation is appealing because healing through transformation carries a promise of acceptance and assurance: "I wonder how many women realize they have a Father who never sleeps nor slumbers. . . . He will spare no expense to insure that you are safe. He will not rest. He will arise with healing in His wings. . . . He doesn't leave. . . . What you must come to understand is that He cares so much for you," the minister writes.[63] The message is endearing, particularly among women who may feel the internal shame or have experienced the external condemnation, blame, and guilt that Stubbs describes. It is also strategic. By reminding readers of these promises, Jakes links acceptance to individual empowerment and expands his audience. Healing through transformation is a way to achieve the intended destiny Christian women should experience as daughters of God, and he is beckoning his readers to this.

Casting women as daughters in *Daddy Loves His Girls* is a decision that can be read as a patriarchal discourse strategy, and it does foreshadow the kinds of logic that inspire questions about whose interests are served by a ministry act. In this instance though, the move to assume the father-figure role should be understood as an effort to promote spiritual kinship. In this capacity, Jakes appears to reject the kinds of "status quo" sensitivity that might cause him to skip over the gesture of appealing to his female readers' self-esteem in favor of these performances of touch. What this decision suggests in terms of strategies writers use to address Black women in forms of pain or crisis is that re-establishing and performing kinship, compassion, or acceptance are pivotal steps within the healing process. The rhetorical move seems to have enabled Jakes to expand the territory of his wellness campaign. After publishing *Daddy Loves His Girls,* Jakes made relationship interventions a core facet of his writings for women with such books as his 1998 guide *The Lady, Her Lover, and Her Lord* where he adds heterosexual women's romantic partnerships to the domain of instruction and the 1999 musical project *Sacred Love Songs,* which offers a soundtrack to the most intimate of relationships in songs such as "Pillow Talk" and "He Teaches Me to Love." The audience of Black Christian women Jakes cultivates at this stage is saved and possibly sexy. Wellness can be a state of satisfaction.

Transformation: A Curriculum for Healing

The chapter "You Are Not the Same" in *Daddy Loves His Girls* contains the clearest indication of the worldview that informs Jakes instructional approach to healing. In it, he says,

> We are all students now in the school of life. Heaven is our only diploma. Any living person who isn't there hasn't graduated; they are still taking classes. You will learn from everyone. The discerning person learns wisdom from the idiot and folly from the intelligent. You must have the perception to look deeply into life and then apply what you see. You will see that every incident, every feeling, every fear is a class. Each one has its own curriculum. The ones who hurt you the worst teach you the best. Survival is taught in the wilderness. Loneliness is best taught in the crowd.[64]

According to Inger Askehave, the life-as-a-school-term Jakes uses is one of the more popular governing metaphors in self-help culture. As a pedagogical device, the figure of speech enables a writer to compare the familiar sphere of a school to less abstract entities of life such as people, goals, experiences, relationships, difficulties, feelings, states of mind, etc."[65] Although Jakes uses this metaphor, we can better understand the concept of discernment or wisdom, he advocates according to the Christian ideology that the world is a hostile temporal site filled with sin, toils, and snares that requires individuals to develop a sense of vision. Vision is a survival tool and skill as it enables individuals to navigate a world filled with sin, snares, and blocks to their heavenly reward. The prevalence of biblically inspired discourses promoting revelation and encouraging believers to seek Christ-like wisdom and understanding are a reflection of the influence that vision as a concept holds. As the incentive for believing and following God, vision is the blessing God grants to assist people in seeing the life course they must follow to mature and earn their eventual heavenly reward.

Throughout Jakes's ministry, passing through the school of this world with wisdom and vision is a process that requires women to undertake the critical pedagogy mandate inherent in scriptural charge to be "not conformed to this world," but to be "transformed" by the "renewing of their minds" and performing the "good, acceptable, and perfect, will of God."[66] The two-stage series of strategies Jakes teaches in his *Woman, Thou Art Loosed!* book and helps readers enact through his corresponding workbook pursue the idea of what is "good and acceptable" by bringing women into what Jakes considers as *realignment* with the goals God has for them. The first stage of renewing the mind involves what appear as courses in releasing the past and rejecting the enemy's plan. Revising behavior and restoring relationships are the processes for the second stage of resuming their destiny. Ideally, when women follow these processes they can remember scriptural messages of affirmation and acceptance, recall their responsibility to pursue the destiny that God intends for them, and respond to the charge to "be loosed."

Renewing the Mind by Releasing the Past and Rejecting the Enemy's Plan

The first stage in Jakes's curriculum teaches readers how to break the social and emotional stagnation of previous traumas in their lives by releasing the past. Somewhat expectedly, Jakes's work as Christian minister causes him to perceive issues such as divorce as life-altering events that not only shatter some women's self-esteem but can also alter children's understanding of the healthy life and relationships they are supposed to have. To help women break free from what he calls a "prison" of guilt and regret he assumes they are in when they "rage loudly about others" but "secretly blame themselves" for these events, he teaches readers a three-part strategy for getting perspective and placing distance between themselves and the past. The first step of exercising forgiveness, which he argues is "one of the greatest healing balms of the Holy Spirit," as a way of breaking links to the past, features corresponding workbook activities that combine scripture and short-answer questions about the external sources of pain, discord, or abuse. The assumption is that identifying these sources will enable women to recognize the roots of their traumas and place distance between themselves and the root even if they have committed inappropriate actions. This shift is essential to the second step in this process where readers use writing and prayer to confess their secrets and issues to God with the expectation that the past does not dictate the future for them because there is no "condemnation" or guilt for the Christian women. A culminating step in this process features women using writing to practice the relanguaging strategies necessary to continually reject the causal logic that people's troubled past is an indication of their future. These processes of release are pivotal to Jakes's conception of healing because "it is impossible to inhale new air until you exhale old." This step is prerequisite to receiving what "God has for you now."[67]

The second component in Jakes's process of transformation requires women to reject the enemy's plan. "Pain is not prejudiced" in Jakes's worldview, so the Christian woman should anticipate some adversity in her life. The challenge for her is to remain in line with the divine plan, which he describes through a discussion of gender construction. In the earlier versions of *Woman, Thou Art Loosed!*, he argues that men are constructed to be givers and women are to be the receivers both physically and emotionally. When a woman is emotionally or physically violated she becomes receptive to a flurry of other detrimental attitudes, perspectives, and potentially unhealthy relationships. The remnants of this violation produce behaviors and mentalities that work to thwart the "divine" plan for her life. Therefore, women must resist the enemy's plan to keep them from the transformation they need to embrace their destinies. The language domain is the first arena Jakes teaches women as a site for engaging in resistance. As he explains, Christians are often tripped up by the words they speak. "The enemy would love to destroy you with your own words. Satan wants to use *you* to fight against you. He will use your strength to fight against you. Many of you have beat yourself down with the power of your own words and have twisted your own back. . . . But now is the time is to reverse his plan."[68] By learning to identify and reject self-defeating attitudes, readers can make one of the first steps towards transformation because subtle statements such as "This is just the way I am," or "I am in a terrible mood today" reflect a person's acceptance of the state of failure and defeat characteristic of *this* world.[69]

The process for renewing the mind Jakes offers also suggests an attempt to cultivate among Black women forms of vision, therapeutic-writing processes, and strategic language practices. Unlike Vanzant who teaches women to use writing for self-reflection and examination, Jakes uses a curriculum that incorporates writing as a way to connect readers to a specific text and to foreground its "truths." According to Micki McGee, writing activities such as listing, sentence-completion exercises, inventories of skills or shortcomings, mission statements, "morning pages," deathbed reflections, fictional autobiographies, and fantasy ideal days, are the mainstays of self-improvement culture because they cement in readers a sense of direction and accountability. The self-knowledge these exercises promote can then be used to inform goal-setting and life-planning exercises.[70] In this way, the first step in this curriculum extends the process of creating the shared knowledge Moss considers essential to community building beyond the moment of the sermon and the walls of the church. The extracurriculum of healing Jakes offers within this stage is potentially subversive because it teaches women strategies to explore and engage with scriptural principles and acquire or cultivate oppositional knowledge to navigate *this* world within the truths of their faith.

Deep gender essentialism thwarts the radical potential in this stage of Jakes's curriculum. Christianity's appeal among many Black women resides in the fact that despite the "troubles of de world," as the familiar hymn attests, there is an intelligent design and a unique plan for each life. Although Jakes acknowledges this plan in "Broken Arrows," his attempt to emphasize the forms of compassion institutional leaders must extend to individuals recovering from forms of abuse is flawed by definition. "Perversion is the offspring of abuse," he writes in the chapter "Broken Arrows," and this abuse is made legible through a person's performance of gender. "Every time you see a bra-less woman in men's jeans, choosing to act like a man rather than sleep with one, and every time you see a handsome young man who could have been someone's father walking like someone's mother—you are looking child abuse in the face," Jakes writes.[71] It is interesting that Jakes abandons this pathologizing argument in the 2012 version of *Woman, Thou Art Loosed!*, which is simply entitled *Healing the Wounds of the Past*. In the newer version, he addresses men and women with his prescriptions for healing, offering fewer specific discussions of sexuality in exchange for broader discussions on how Satan is "attacking femininity" through a man-shortage.[72]

The arguments in the 2012 book are far less pointed but the results produce similar interpretations of gender. Jakes's choice to use these specific examples to signify and label abuse enables him to realign notions of gender essentialism with wellness as means of rejecting the enemy's plan. Although Black Christian women are apt to decipher the implications of this message, the consequence is that the renewing the mind involves learning how to conform to a standard, or script, of heteronormativity.

Restoration through Revising Behaviors and Restoring Relationships

The praxis portion of Jakes's curriculum begins with the third course on revising behaviors. Choice is paramount in the life of the Christian; therefore, to move upon God's vision, women must revise their behaviors accordingly. For Jakes, these behaviors include reading scriptures that affirm their faith and developing a more intimate prayer life. In addition to these more spiritual activities, women are instructed to pursue God's vision of transformation by conducting themselves with greater self-respect, resisting the urge to make excuses, abandoning overly critical attitudes, and actively appreciating themselves. Taken together, these practices are thought to transforms an individual internally and externally.

Subsequently, in the restoring-relationships stage, Jakes teaches single, married, and elderly women how to achieve the wholeness of life as a believer. In the chapters "Anoint me . . . I'm Single" and "A Table for Two," Jakes offers readers principles that they can use to ensure and restore positive relationships with others. Single women desiring to be married must take care of the Lord and learn how to savor the unmarried season of their life as an opportunity to cultivate a more devout form of spirituality. Jakes encourages women to restore their relationships with the Creator because, ideally, "single women ought to be the most consecrated women in the church."[73] Married women are to work on strengthening their marriages by (1) abandoning friendships that take more priority than their marriage; (2) honestly articulating their needs even at the sake of causing disagreement; (3) communicating in ways that produce action and emotion; and (4) improving the ministry of their marriage by being more compassionate to their husband's needs. In *Daddy Loves His Girls,* Jakes extends this discussion, advising readers to evaluate the motives that drive certain relationships and to examine how their own distorted senses of purpose could influence their parenting skills.

The arguments about survivorship and appropriateness used to justify this curriculum stage reveal the limitations of the life a "worldly" school woman must learn to navigate. Although Jakes explicitly condemns acts of rape, molestation, and sexual violation, he implicitly emphasizes women's responsibility to discern and avoid these traps in his discussion of the causes of these acts of sexual violence. Jakes's analysis of the biblical story of Tamar, King David's daughter, who was raped by her half brother Amnon, illustrates the vague interpretive strategies he promotes while warning women about Satan's plan to use men in evil ways.[74] As he explains, Amnon is emblematic of the ways Satan wants to violate Christian women; and he presents the plot the "enemy" uses to do so:

> He is planning and plotting your destruction. He has watched you with wanton eyes. . . . Satan lusts after God's children. He wants you. He craves you with an animalistic passion. He awaits an opportunity for attack. In addition, he loves to use people to fulfill the same kinds of lust upon one another. . . . Desire is a motivating force. It can make you do things you never thought yourself capable of doing. Lust can make a man break his commitment to himself.[75]

Sentimentality and pathos supersede the systemic in Jakes's tone, and his discourse reveals a worldview where women are inherently vulnerable and men are victims of Satan's attacks on humankind or mere receptacles of evil. Within a process of transformation though, this worldview enables him to suggest appropriate self-regulating behaviors women must adopt. As he explains in the section "Manipulating the Maternal," women need to be aware of how facets of their personality draw manipulative and abusive spirits to them because,

> one of the things that makes many women particularly vulnerable to different types of abuse and manipulation is their maternal instinct. Wicked men frequently capitalize on this tendency in order to have their way with women. . . . It seems that the more helpless a man acts, the more maternal women can become. Women instinctively are nurturers, reaching out to needy people in order to nurture love and provide inner strength. But all too often, these healthy desires are taken advantage of by those who would fulfill their own lusts. The gift of discernment must operate in your life. There are many wonderful men. But I must warn you about Amnon. He is out there, and he is dangerous.[76]

This worldview is problematic for several reasons. First, it suggests that men who victimize women are, in fact, victims of Satan's plot to violate humankind. This conspiracy argument reduces serious issues such as rape, sexual violence, and molestation into one-time, evil occurrences enacted by questionable men who allow themselves to be used by Satan. It also obscures the systemic structures of rape culture, misogyny, and other ills through the umbrella term of "evil," a term that is far too broad and general to represent how women come to be seen as sexual objects. In this instance, Jakes's sentimentalizing discourse causes him to miss an opportunity to teach women to connect biblical principles about evil to social theories through his curriculum. Jakes could have made healing a way to "set the captives free" and aid in their true liberation and recovery by teaching women how to connect the terminologies sociologists and others have cultivated to identify these structures with what biblical scripture calls the "principalities" of this world. Spiritual vision does not need to be so otherworldy that it is removed from the insights of social theory. Instead, Jakes's curriculum teaches women to prevent these acts and survive them, rather than to engage in dialogues about how rape cultures can subside or to theorize the structures that keep rape cultures alive.

When theorizing does happen in Jakes's curriculum, it takes on an antifeminist tone. In the section "Gender Oppression: Deeply Embedded, Seldom Defined" in *Daddy Loves His Girls,* Jakes argues that the solitary nature in which women are socialized causes them to eventually war with each other. "Isolation syndrome," as he calls it, manifests itself in three primary ways: the difficulty women have relating to other women; the tendency of women to treat their daughters more harshly than their sons or to choose to have children outside of marriage; and the sense of lowliness that women develop because of oppression. The majority of the chapter is devoted to the issue of how gender oppression distorts women's interactions with others as Jakes explains how people who have been oppressed have a tendency to operate like crabs in a barrel. They cannot accept another individual's success. To illustrate this point, Jakes shares the story of an encounter he had with a pioneering female journalist who came to his home to interview him and his wife. What started as a congenial interview turned uncomfortable when the journalist began to question the morality of Jakes's expansive wealth on the grounds that it is inappropriate for a minister to live in such affluence when church members live in states of poverty and need.[77]

As one of the earliest members of the elite group of Black megachurch ministers to amass tremendous amounts of financial wealth, Jakes may have been taken aback by the journalist's questions; but the way he deals with his sense of indignation in this book does unearth another gendered consequence of his approach to women's healing and wellness. Midway through his interview, Jakes determined that the "spirit of oppression was at work in the mentality" of the journalist. To him, the audacity of her interrogation and critique of his wealth were both signs of how oppression creates "disgruntled victims" who lash out to blame others. "In the same way, sexism has left even women who have been victims of it bickering among themselves. Satan's tactics are still the same: divide and conquer. He is after women in the same fashion," he reasons.[78] Responding to the journalist's critique with the reminder that "it was only a few years ago that the media . . . would say that you should be at home making biscuits," Jakes goes on to convince her of the ways that sexism had made her an aggressor.[79] He explains that they have both accomplished feats that have placed them in front of public scrutiny. Like her role, his role as a Black Christian minister had also placed him in the line of fire from individuals who thought he was unfit or undeserving of the responsibility of their new roles. To move forward from instances such as these, Jakes instructs the readers to "discuss and define oppression in all of its forms" and to be the bigger person in their interpersonal relationships.[80] "Make things right. Do not blame anyone," he advises. "Just allow the Holy Spirit to work. . . . God wants to heal your heart."[81]

Jakes's interpretation of the journalist's critique and interrogation of his wealth as indicators of her internalized oppression suggests what construction of womanhood his project of healing prescribes. By casting the journalist's questions as an extension of her own "isolation syndrome," he carries forth the theme that sickness or trauma dictates a person's behavior in detrimental ways. Due to the sickness that trauma caused the "infirm woman," she and women like her had to act to heal and transform themselves for the sake of their families and loved ones. Women like this journalist—who vocally interrogate what they perceive as power or potential manipulation—also need to be healed because of their threat to others. Made all the more potent by the move to cast himself as the victim, Jakes's call for women to heal themselves through transformation is an appeal to their sense of accountability: women owe it to God and their church to be in line with the expectations placed on them as women. The implied message of this passage is that transformed and realigned women avoid using their critical voice to launch "attacks" on others, because the instructional message for women is that regardless of how you have been hurt, traumatized, abused, or oppressed, your responsibility to others requires that you be the bigger person and rise above it.

When placed within the broader project of renewing the mind and revising behavior that Jakes teaches as steps to healing, this broad message enables Jakes to prescribe a number of "appropriate" womanly behaviors, not the least of which include the importance of avoiding retaliation and resisting the urge to vocally critique others in power. As a clear indicator of the world that his rhetoric envisions, Jakes's transformed woman is God-fearing, wisdom seeking, and empowered: she is healed of the urge to retaliate and is self-regulated by a sense of accountability to others.

Assessment

In the final scenes of *Woman Thou Art Loosed,* the film shows the main character Michelle sitting with Bishop Jakes in a jail cell. Some time has passed since she had shot Reggie. She is contemplative, playing with a house she built out of matchsticks, as the bishop looks down upon her. After some time, she says, "I didn't understand how God could forgive a man like that. I didn't understand why I should have forgiven him. Now I do understand. You can never really get even."

In a compassionate tone, the bishop responds, asking," Michelle, do you believe that what you did was the right thing to do?" Shaking her head she replies, "No, I don't, Bishop. What I did was wrong. No matter what he did, it was wrong. When you talk to God again, ask Him if He'll forgive me. . . . I know I can't bring a life back."[82]

After some final instructions to "stay free," the pastor walks out of the cell and the film ends.

Michelle's realization of the futility of killing her rapist certainly suggests how powerful the discourse on transformation can be. Like the "infirm woman," Michelle is a symbol of identification for viewers, and her jail-cell confession validates Jakes's message that healing means being the bigger person. Transformation replaces the desire for revenge with the responsibilities that come with healing and membership within a Christian community. Transformation can keep women from stepping out of line.

The process for rhetorical healing Jakes uses does show us how some contemporary Black ministers invent, translate, and define crises they might normally articulate through their sermons into books and how they construct community and shared knowledge in new settings. Because the church remains one of the most influential and educational institutions for Blacks, these realignment strategies enable us to better understand how Black ministers interpret the scriptural charge to "go ye therefore, and teach all the nations" the good news, the topics that inspire their efforts, and the tools some of them use.[83]

Yet, with Oprah Winfrey's choice to record *Lifecast* at Jakes's 2013 *Megafest* convention and the bishop's short-lived talk *Mind, Body & Soul* talk show, the implications of Jakes's message are still clear. The rhetoric of transformation Jakes deploys to construct audience and place his readers in a context of problems, promises, and prescriptions results in him conflating broader social issues and transcribing them into individual women's behavioral defects. Even if the intervention is timely, the opportunity for Jakes, as an agent of the institution of the Black church, to make a broader outreach statement is diminished when social issues such as rape and domestic violence that warrant public discussions become absorbed into less visible issues such as the low self-esteem some Black women develop. Instead, infirmity, as a means of identification, becomes a way for Jakes to secure church intake and expand its platform as Black women are encouraged to invest in acquiring scriptural literacy to navigate a world they are not encouraged to think they can change. Since the sermon, as Moss explains, is primarily instructional, this healing campaign teaches Black women that their transformation is the antidote to the sickness that has attacked nuclear heterosexual relationships and family structures within the black community. It is the prescription necessary for rewriting the church community's broader image.

CHAPTER 5

Take Your Place
The Rhetoric of Return in Tyler Perry's Films

Judith is a marriage counselor in her mid-twenties with grand dreams of launching her own counseling firm. Her childhood sweetheart-turned-husband Brice has a similar dream. One day he plans to run a neighborhood pharmacy. Their life together is modest, carrying over many of the Christian values Judith's devout mother instilled in them as children. Judith has a plain and conservative wardrobe. Brice still drives the faded pickup truck that brought them from their small Virginia hometown to their current life in Washington, D.C. They live in a humble apartment. On most accounts, the couple is on a path to gradually achieving their career and life aspirations. When Judith's boss asks her to assist the firm on a lucrative account for Harley, an Internet entrepreneur who makes his romantic interest in the marriage counselor known, impatience sets in and curiosity develops in her. Soon, Brice's pragmatic approach to career growth, romance, and even sex seems tired alongside Harley's wealth, hypermasculinity, and intense desire. Even the cautionary warnings and prayers of Judith's mother seem to lose their effect on the marriage counselor. Eventually, Judith gives into temptation and embarks on an intense and life-threatening extramarital affair, learning the hard way that the proverbial grass is not always greener on the other side when it comes to infidelity.

The premise that ambition and opportunity can be a lethal combination driving Tyler Perry's thirteenth film *Temptation: Confessions of a Marriage Counselor* is simple enough; but, for the purposes of this chapter, it is emblematic of the causal logics that can become encoded in representations of Black womanhood when African American writers adopt film as a means for rhetorical healing. Moral messages are a staple of the career Perry has created upon the success of such films as *Meet the Browns* and *I Can Do Bad All by Myself.* With his string of films, the gospel-playwright-turned-screenwriter and film-and-television producer has achieved two seemingly unrelated feats. First, he has made films and sitcoms catering to working- and middle-class Black Christian audiences into mainstream commodities. Second, he has given Black women unprecedented opportunities to have leading roles in his films. Both achievements are noteworthy given that the majority of Perry's box-office-topping films are adaptations of his gospel stage plays—works he wrote to share the insights about overcoming personal crises he discovered after watching an Oprah Winfrey show episode lauding the cathartic potential of self-writing. Perry adopted journaling to process the effects of his own abusive upbringing, eventually releasing his 1992 play *I Know I've Been Changed*, which focuses on adult survivors of abuse.[1] For Perry, the motive driving his release of over ten films in the last seven years is simple: "So many people are in need of healing" that he eventually developed "an unbelievable pull to have people see [his] movies and be healed."[2] According to one female fan, Perry's plays and films offer Black Christian women rare opportunities to see family and community-oriented narratives that remind them of "home."[3]

Despite these achievements, Perry continues to garner considerable criticism for his work.[4] According to Courtney Young, the consistent messages to "be strong, but not too strong," "let a man be a man," and that "true fulfillment is found in the role of wife and/or mother" embedded in his modern-day morality tales eschew a conservative gender politic that "reinforces rather than revolutionizes" representations of Black womanhood.[5] Kimberly Springer echoes this sentiment, noting that Perry's frequent choice to have his female protagonists return home enacts a retreatist narrative that makes the "postfeminist" argument that a woman's independence comes at a high cost.[6] Finally, in his examination of Madea, the hyperbolic southern grandmother Perry developed as an homage to his aunt and dressed in drag to portray, Timothy Lyle debunks any notion that Perry's choice to depict Black women dealing with such issues as domestic violence and molestation reveal a feminist politic in his work.[7] Because Madea reinforces transphobic and conservative gender ideologies all while acting as the guide for wayward female protagonists, Lyle asserts that the films fail to destabilize hegemonic ideas about gender construction or to capitalize upon the transformative potential of drag as a subversive practice.

Perry has never ceased to defend the images his films promote even in the wake of these criticisms. In a 2007 interview discussing his plays, he argued that "as long as people walk away from my shows feeling better . . . whichever way I lure them to hear that message, so be it."[8] During a 2012 *Fresh Air* interview with National Public Radio's Terry Gross, he repeated this sentiment when asked about the effects of his narrative choices and frequent use of the Madea character. "The audience loves it," he explained. "They get it. They know. They understand. They know me. I know them. And it works. And that's where I'm leaving it."[9] Perhaps Perry is right. Yet, given the tenuous relationship African Americans and Black women, in particular, have experienced with representations of their lives in film, we must question to what extent the hope for a therapeutic end justifies these narrative means.

When read as a form of rhetorical healing, the narratives of female empowerment in Perry's earliest films contain a complex discourse on return that reveal the implications of the filmmaker's legibility defense. Perhaps more than the other mediums that African American writers have gravitated to as sites for possible connection and intervention into Black women's lives, film remains a complex textual and discursive space. According to Henry Giroux, films transcend entertainment by offering up subject positions, mobilizing desire, influencing us subconsciously, and constructing a landscape of American culture. As they reflect and transmit forms of "material and symbolic relations of power," film produces and incorporates "ideologies that represent the outcome of struggles marked by the historical realities of power and the deep anxieties of the times."[10] In this way, films become vehicles for power by "connecting the production of pleasure and meaning to the mechanisms and practices of powerful teaching machines."[11] Put more simply, films are not just entertainment; they are persuasive forms of instruction.

Although films are potentially subversive media for challenging hegemonic discourses, they have been equally effective resources in the subjugation of Black women. As a form of public pedagogy, films have perpetuated such controlling images as the Jezebel, gold-digger, matriarch, and mammy that function to define Black womanhood within the social imaginary. When such images are transmitted through discourse, or replicated in film, these constructions of Black womanhood become tropes that uphold binary ways of seeing Black women, their families, and communities; and they justify exploitation, oppression, and domination. Perry's films aim to give readers an illustration of a transformative process where protagonists arrive at a place of healing and wellness, but he has yet to explicitly state that Black women's healing is the goal or motive of his work. As such, his choice to invoke discourses about Black women's roles within the home and his choice to use Madea and other characters as teachers of his curriculum make his films susceptible to perpetuating these controlling images.[12]

Reading Appropriation: Narrative as Action

The popularity of the Madea character prompted Perry in 2007 to publish *Don't Make A Black Woman Take Off Her Earrings: Madea's Uninhibited Commentaries on Love and Life*. An expansion of the character's opinionated bits of wisdom, the book opens with a forward from Perry where he reveals why Madea holds the central role that she does in his films. "Madea has an opportunity to say everything that I can't say because, number one, I'm a man, and a women get away with saying things a lot more than a man would," he explains. "In our society, women are given much more latitude than men to have emotions and to express them. And, number two, she has been around for a few more decades, so she can get away with stating some opinions I'd be afraid to say."[13] Perry's conscious choice to borrow the complex forms of privilege Madea has as a recognizable character among Black audiences enables him to carry out the tasks involved representing a pathway to healing through his films. Appropriation is both a narrative and rhetorical device.

In this chapter, I draw upon scholarship on African American counterpublics, film, rhetorical theory scholarship, and the critical insights of Black feminism and womanist theology I incorporate in earlier chapters to read through the forms of appropriation he has adopted to advance a discourse on healing. First, I consider the role of the Black Urban Theatre as a potentially counterhegemonic space to contextualize some of the tensions and criticisms that have followed him throughout his career. Next I juxtapose those representations with the market for female-centered narratives that emerged upon the end of the Black Women's Literary Renaissance. Third, I examine persuasive moves within Perry's films that indicate the concern for the home site that, as I mention in the introduction to this chapter, female fans have considered a draw of the playwright's work. Since Perry routinely recycles conflicts and characters in his films, I focus on *Diary of a Mad Black Woman* (2005) and *Madea's Family Reunion* (2006) throughout this chapter as they are his two earliest films and contain most of the messages and strategies for healing within his oeuvre.

Diary of a Mad Black Woman is the story of Helen McCarter's journey to healing after heartbreak. The Atlanta socialite's life changes when her husband of eighteen years, Charles, announces his intent to divorce on their anniversary night. With no alternative but to return home to her grandmother, Madea, Helen begins a circuitous journey through grief, anger, hope, and rage that is punctuated by her burgeoning romantic relationship with Orlando, the moving-truck driver she meets on her anniversary night, and a freak accident that leaves Charles in her medical care. In *Madea's Family Reunion,* the focus is on two protagonists: Vanessa, a single mother living with her grandmother, Madea, whose long-standing distrust of men is challenged when she meets Frankie, a local bus driver; and Lisa, Vanessa's younger, pampered sister, who is hiding her fiancé Carlos's physical and emotional abuse. Against the backdrop of an overdue family reunion and Lisa's wedding, both protagonists must learn how to remove negative people and elements from their lives and move on towards better relationships and forms of wellness.

The broader argument across Perry's films is that African Americans can resolve a myriad of personal crises by restoring the prominence of Christianity, family, and the home place in their lives; therefore, I end this chapter by critiquing what constitutes a narrative and visual curriculum for healing in these films. Through a rhetoric of return that situates traditional concepts of home and gender as ideal and persuades protagonists to revise their concept of self, faith, and the future, Perry's films teach viewers a gender politic that emphasizes the home place and family as the epitome of women's safety and actualization and narrows Black women's roles within these sites.

The Precarious Space of the Black Urban Theatre

Before concerns arose about the gender implications of Perry's films, questions began to surface about the racial implications of his gospel plays. In 2006, Larry Hamlin and other organizers of the 2007 National Black Theatre Festival denied Perry an invitation to their biannual event.

At the time, Perry's plays were bringing in unprecedented audiences and were financially lucrative in Black Urban Theatre markets across the country. Hamlin was resolute in his decision though and invoked a perspective on taste: "There are people who like *that*, and that's fine," he said. "But then there's other people who really just like *quality* theatre of excellence and that's what *we* offer."[14]

The distinction Hamlin makes here highlights some of the historical tensions about representations of race, social class, and taste circulating within the space of the Black Urban Theatre that Perry entered when he attempted to stage his first gospel plays. The roots of the contemporary Black Urban Theatre are steeped in the best and worst elements of African Americans' struggle to participate in mainstream American society. Originally, Black actors and audiences flocked to the increasingly popular vaudeville entertainment culture developing near the end of the twentieth century. Despite the effects of Jim Crow and the use of blackface, performers and patrons wanted to participate. Theatre owners met these efforts with calculated resistance. As Mel Watkins explains in *On the Real Side: Laughing, Lying and Signifying—the Underground Tradition of African-American Humor that Transformed American Culture, from Slavery to Richard Pryor*, the increase in Black entertainers and, correspondingly, Black audiences inspired mainstream theatre attendees to voice complaints about having to socialize with Blacks. Their complaints coupled with the clear profits of the Black audience inspired businessmen to organize a theatre circuit that "both showcased . . . performers and catered to the Black masses" that these performers could draw.[15]

Black theatre historians claim that these efforts to capitalize on white audiences' resistance to socializing with Blacks and Black audiences' desire to see stories reflecting their own lives led to the creation of the "chitlin circuit," or the network of small, local performance venues that hired Black actors and singers and offered shows catering to working-class Blacks. Considered the predecessor to the contemporary Black Urban Theatre, the "chitlin' circuit" first gained what some consider its reputation for being a haven for low-class and low-quality Black performances during the 1920s when it became the site for the development of a new type of stage show, the precursor to the gospel play. The shows mixed elements of Christian revivalism, Negro spirituals, and minstrel humor and drew huge crowds of working people during tours in the South. They also inspired criticisms from such Harlem Renaissance aesthetes as Alain Locke and Black journalists who questioned the representations these plays gave of African Americans by considering the perception white patrons would take away if they saw a "chitlin' circuit" show. "I shudder to think of the impression he must take back downtown with him," one journalist wrote. "When the comedy remains absolutely in the sewer and seldom ever rises to the level of the gutter. I wonder how many of what kind of people will be content to have it reflect their lives, thoughts, and actions to the outside world."[16] Hamlin's statement does not foreground the white gaze in the same way that this journalist's fear over misperception does, but the two statements illustrate a continuum. To this day, Black critics are often the most critical of the Black Urban Theatre and its productions.

Despite these contentions, the Black Urban Theatre remains attractive for audiences and actors because of the freedom it affords. Much like the Black church—which developed out of African Americans' resistance to exclusion and desire for a space to escape surveillance and engage in their own ways of worship, world making, and critical resistance—the Black Urban Theatre is a counterhegemonic space that has transmitted politics, visions, and themes of nation building typical in the Black public sphere.[17] The incentive for audiences—even those that Hamlin seems to dismiss—is that the theatre offers rare opportunities to gather together in "racially sequestered" space where they can see reflections of themselves and laugh "uninhibitedly" without worrying about what dominant groups may with think of them. In this way, the Black Urban Theatre is an institution that has played a role in distributing the messages and reflections of life that Perry's fans read as illustrations of home.

Perry acknowledged this appeal during an interview before the release of his 2004 play *Why Did I Get Married?* According to the playwright, African Americans have never had a venue where they could see or deal with life challenges, struggles, and problems; and Black theatre serves this demand. "Lots of Black audiences want to see real people coping with and overcoming real problems, so I talk about that. That's what my shows are about," he explains.[18] Understandably, Perry does not mention how the moralistic nature of the gospel play invites the messages of hope, uplift, and family survival that draw fans to his work. The form has certainly worked to his advantage in the market that Vanzant, Jakes, and others helped cultivate with their books. The Black Urban Theatre is precarious because even as it has originated out of exclusion and serves a necessary counterhegemonic role, it can also be a venue for an opportunistic writer. Dearth and demand can invite supply.

Characters in Someone Else's Story: Subjectivity and Black Women's Film

Although Perry's films have been credited with providing unprecedented opportunities for Black women actors in Hollywood and his female-centered films benefit from the audience created by a string of popular and commercially successful Black-female protagonist films of the eighties and nineties, the discourse on healing in Perry's films exists in an equally complicated context where Black women have had to fight to retain control of their images and narratives on the silver screen. Best characterized by the dichotomy between being invisible, and thereby subordinate, or hypervisible to the point of caricature, Black women's historically tenuous relationship with film and cinema is an extension of their efforts to become autonomous subjects within literature and social discourses. Hazel Carby's well-known discussion of the impact of race on the cult of true womanhood within antebellum literature in *Reconstructing Womanhood: The Emergence of the Afro-American Woman Novelist* offers one point of origin for this historical dichotomy. As she explains, the discourses aimed at preserving patriarchal family and economic structures relied on a system of behavioral organizations that domesticated white women by suggesting their social value was linked to motherhood and subordinated Black women by constructing them as property and sources of labor. While a white woman's behavior could be read as a sign of her internal character, a Black woman's behavior and physical appearance became signifiers of her internal character or lack thereof. Once again, these constructions of Black womanhood have preserved the tropes of the Black mammy, Jezebel, Sapphire, or welfare mother that have permeated the discourses within the social imaginary that I discuss in previous chapters. In this way film as a tool—and vehicle for an individual's perception and selection of reality—has often reified such historically disparaging tropes and representations of Black womanhood before mass audiences. Fortunately though, with the recent successes of Dee Rees's coming-of-age film about a young African American lesbian struggling to come out to her family, *Pariah;* and filmmaker Ava DuVernay's 2010 film *I Will Follow* about a woman grieving the loss of her aunt; and her 2012 film *Middle of Nowhere* about a woman reassessing her life after her husband is sent to prison, there is a growing body of Black female-written and female-centered narratives that challenge and revise these disparaging constructions of Black womanhood.

Perry's success predates Rees and DuVernay's success; therefore, it may be easy to overlook how influential the Black Women's Literary Renaissance was in fostering the market for films about Black women that he tapped into with the 2004 release of *Diary of a Mad Black Woman*. Galvanized by commercially lucrative adaptations of such novels as Terry McMillan's *Waiting to Exhale* and *How Stella Got Her Groove Back,* the market for films focusing on Black women as subjects—not objects—moving from states of disempowerment to empowerment, or navigating obstacles in their interpersonal relationships and careers, flourished during the mid-nineties. The mainstream release of films such as *Set It Off* (1996) and *Love and Basketball* (2000) furthered the development of this market. In these films, Black women appear as dynamic protagonists dealing with real-life dilemmas and exercising forms of agency forecasted in the literature of Black women writers decades earlier. Enhanced by the market for gendered approaches to self-help and the public debates over race and representation in Black Urban Cinema, films focusing on Black women gaining their voice, per se, or maintaining relationships as autonomous subjects, grew in popularity. With the support of faithful audiences of Black women who wanted to see positive representations of themselves and their communities, the success of these films was an early indication that Perry's narratives about Black women could appeal to a popular and powerful media demographic.

Despite the influence of Black women writers and, correspondingly, readers and film viewers, the market for narratives that appear to centralize them has also been subject to questions of authorship and commodification. For example, despite the critiques launched against Alice Walker that I discuss in chapter 1, the audience for narratives about Black women she tapped into with her portrayal of Celie was profitable enough that Warner Brothers decided to adapt it for film and allow Steven Spielberg, a white male director, to direct it. The differences between Walker's novel and Spielberg's film adaptation reflect the ease with which narratives about Black women coming to self-realization and agency can reinscribe notions of hegemony. In *The Color Purple* novel, Shug, the free-spirited singer that was Mister's mistress and Celie's lover, represents a form of Black womanhood that exercises sexual and social agency. Walker's choice to have Shug defy conventional norms of sexuality and womanhood enables the character to compliment Celie's eventual self-realization and evolution into a woman empowered to question existing definitions of faith and spirituality and normative romantic relationships.

Due to film executives' insistence that a storyline concerning Shug's fractured relationship with her father be inserted into the film, viewers never see Walker's version of Shug. Instead viewers see a female character obsessed with regaining her minister-father's affection; they see a woman who, by virtue of her "loose morals" and movie executives' efforts to implant a more "suitable" redemption narrative in the film, ultimately undermines the significance of Celie's struggle to value herself.[19] Assuming Walker's intention was for Shug to be a representation of assertive Black womanhood *and* one of the pivotal agents in Celie's journey towards self-actualization, the manipulation of Shug's image for film audiences not only shows how Black women have had to struggle to retain control of their own narratives, but also shows whose interests are served in these texts. Characters in someone else's story, the cinematic representations of Celie and Shug differ from Walker's vision in ways that render them as tools in an effort to capitalize on the scarcity of positive portrayals of Black womanhood and the potency of Black women's trauma and self-realization narratives. Given this context, the market for Black women's films that Perry tapped into and benefited from with his discourses on healing and restoration is as complicated as the Black Urban Theatre where his work originated.

The Regressing Family and Home Place: A Call to Healing

Unlike Jakes and Vanzant who make illustrating a culture of lack one of the first strategies in their healing campaigns, Perry does not offer a noticeable indication of the social concerns that inspire his films until the end of his second film, *Madea's Family Reunion*. Myrtle's speech reveals the broader crisis about Black families and homes that inspires his rhetoric of return. As older relatives get reacquainted at the reunion, younger relatives gamble and dance provocatively. The generational disconnect is so distressing to the ninety-six-year-old matriarch Aunt Ruby, that she calls the family together at their ancestors' slave cabin yards away to ask, "Is this what we paid for?" The question confuses the younger relatives, prompting Myrtle, Helen McCarter's mother from *Diary of a Mad Black Woman*, to deliver a speech about regression and family responsibility that ends with a call for the younger relatives to "take [their] place" in preserving the family's legacy. She begins by discussing the occasion, explaining that

> family reunions are about uniting the family. Bringing together the young and the old . . . and thanking God . . . for getting us over. . . . Do you see this shack? The men and woman who were born here gave birth to this generation. They were slaves. They worked this ground, but they bought it from the widow of the slave owner! The blood we have running through our veins. That's the stock we're made of! What happened to us? . . . Do you know who you are? What happened to the pride, and the dignity, and the love and respect we had for one another? Where'd it go? And how, how do we get it back?[20]

Myrtle's speech also employs elements of African American jeremiad appeals: namely, the citation of the group's promise and the criticism of their retrogression from it.[21] With her questions about her family's lost values, Myrtle's performance of this internally directed rhetoric of indignation creates a discursive space to call for younger relatives to take their place in preserving the traditions and legacy of the home and family institution.

Perry's choice to use Myrtle as the messenger and the ancestral home place as the site is particularly advantageous given how some Black women have been taught to conceptualize their roles as mothers within the home. According to hooks, one of the ways Black mothers have contributed to liberation efforts is by creating home places where African Americans learn how to resist dehumanization and "strive to be subjects, not objects."[22] In constructing safe spaces where Black people could "affirm one another" and, by so doing, "heal many of the wounds inflicted by racist domination," Black women's keeping of the home enables them to participate in liberation struggle. This work allows them to offer individuals the "opportunity to grow and develop, and nurture [their] spirits" away from contexts of white supremacy.[23] For hooks, watching her mother create a home place that fostered her sense of individual wholeness and her resolve to strive for the wholeness of her community modeled "degrees of critical consciousness" she used to navigate the outside world.[24] Perry's staging of Myrtle on the steps of their ancestor's home place and question about self-knowledge suggests his awareness of this tradition.

This discussion of home places and critical consciousness shows us a historical context for the crisis of poor parenting that appears to motivate Perry's work. As Perry explains in *Don't Make a Black Woman Take Off Her Earrings: Madea's Uninhibited Commentaries on Love and Life*, Madea—an abbreviation of the phrase "mother dear"—is a version of the rapidly vanishing southern Black matriarch of yesteryear. A fixture within Black neighborhoods, "she used to be everywhere," he explains, "but today she is missed. Back around the 1970s, the Madeas in our neighborhoods began to disappear and they have left an unmistakable void."[25] This void has created a decline in traditional family values because, in the past, "if somebody's child was doing something wrong, Madea got to them and straightened them out or she would go directly to the parents, and the parents straightened the kids out. . . . Because there are so few Madeas, children are pretty much raising themselves."[26] The suggestion is that children who are left to raise themselves not only miss the lessons on critical consciousness that help them navigate the world, but also fail to acquire the values that make them future contributors to their home places. When faced with crises in their relationships or other issues, these lost children can become the "mad," "bitter," "fragile," and "distrusting" female protagonists of Perry's films, women that figures such as Madea and Myrtle must help heal and take their places.

Given the impact of such historical documents as Senator Daniel Patrick Moynihan's 1965 report on the Negro family, which essentially blames Black mothers for the perceived dysfunctions of Black families, the reasoning Perry uses to validate Madea's value to African American communities and his films is problematic.[27] Citing the issue of children "raising themselves" as evidence of disintegrating Black families and proof of Madea's continued relevance—without acknowledging men's roles as husband, fathers, or parental figures—is a move that absolves men of their responsibilities in preservation of the Black family and places sole responsibility on women. Moreover, by situating the origins of the disintegrating Black family during the seventies when Black women first began to claim defined feminist identities en masse and assume roles as chief breadwinners in many households, Perry provides a veiled critique that chastises women who exchange their family obligations for career aspirations and other individual pursuits. The evidence of this critique appears in such Perry's films as *Daddy's Little Girls* (2007) and *The Family That Preys* (2008) in the form of the ambitious, upwardly mobile female who must be taken down a notch or taught to reprioritize her values. In consistently showing women returning home and revising their notions of "appropriate" relationships with their families, faith, and suitable partners, Perry's films teach viewers what amounts to a confining message: Black women may aspire to forms of success beyond the home, but they must honor and prioritize the needs of their families and communities.

"I Won't Tell Your Secrets": Appropriation and Black Women's Self-Writing

Helen McCarter is a wealthy Atlanta socialite. She shares an opulent mansion in an upscale neighborhood with her husband, Charles, a prominent attorney. The clothes she wears are of the highest quality. Her staff awaits her every beck and call. The car she drives is luxurious and European. To the casual observer, she is a vision of affluence and privilege. Her diary tells another story. As audiences watch her attending a prestigious banquet recognizing Charles's "Attorney of the Year" award on the eve of their anniversary, they hear in her daily diary entry the thoughts and voice of a woman in despair:

> I'm so proud of him. He's worked so hard. To look at us, you'd think we have it all together, but looks can be deceiving. Some days are good and I think he loves me. Then other days, I think he doesn't care. He is so into appearances. What looks one way on the outside, can be a totally different matter on the inside. I don't know the stranger I sit next to. All I know is with every dime with every case, he has changed.[28]

With an almost painfully fake smile, Helen displays happiness at the awards banquet despite her husband's evident disregard. The extent of Helen's emotional poverty is confirmed in the following day's diary entry. After waking to find that Charles had chosen to spend the entire night leading up to their anniversary somewhere else, she writes, "Tell me, why do I love that man so much? Maybe if I could stop thinking about how good things used to be, I could find the strength to leave."[29] By the end of the night, Helen would not only need to find strength but shelter too, as Charles rebuffs her attempts to celebrate, reveals his plan to end their marriage so he can live with his mistress and secret children, and throws her out of their house. As Helen cries and sobs on the steps of her mansion, beating on the door to be let in, she is a vision of emotional despair. She is lost and in crisis.

For Perry's primary audience of Black Christian theatre-goers, *Diary of a Mad Black Woman*'s concise yet dramatic portrayal of Charles's abrupt termination of their marriage is ample evidence of the individual crisis Helen undergoes; but the task of translating his overall message about the importance of forgiveness and restoration to mainstream audiences involved several constraints. At the time, there was little indication among Hollywood film executives that a film with such overt religious overtones and heavy moral messages would be marketable to mainstream audiences. Save for the adaptation of *Woman, Thou Art Loosed!*, the template had not yet been established for the kinds of images and messages that Perry would eventually bring to mainstream audiences. Moreover, despite his following with Black Christian audiences, there was still a resounding tentativeness among conservative African American leaders who were concerned with negative cinematic portrayals of their communities in the wake of films such as *Boyz n the Hood* and *Menace II Society*. Persuading audiences to receive and apply the model for healing displayed in Helen's journey to self-realization required Perry to build a relationship with his audiences that did not raise these concerns.

Whereas Vanzant and Jakes could rely on personal testimony, institutional authority, and analysis as meaning-making strategies to illuminate hermeneutical problems and create their ethos, Perry uses Helen's self-writing in her diary to illustrate the crises in his protagonist's life in depth. Through the diary, he complicates stereotypes about angry Black woman by giving audiences intimate access to the range of emotions Helen experiences during the six months following her ill-fated wedding anniversary. As audiences watch her struggle to rebuild her wounded self-esteem and regain her faith in relationships, they hear diary entries, such as the one from April 25th containing her varying stages of despair, suspicion, hope, joy, and anger: "Today was a bad day. I got up and came to church because I was so angry. When I think about all the blood, sweat, and tears, I put into my marriage, it makes me want to hate him."[30]

Slightly more acerbic yet still reminiscent of Celie's letters to God expressing the pain and isolation of her oppressive relationships in Alice Walker's *The Color Purple*, Helen's diaries act as a different form of character development and advancement. Through these forms of personal writing, Perry voices the depth of Helen's pain in her post-marital betrayal. In providing audiences—many of whom are Black women—with access to Helen's unheard voice, Perry's use of the diary appears to be an endeavor to move Helen from the state of being the object of Charles's betrayal to an empowered subject. This move from silence to speech is, according to hooks, "a gesture of defiance that heals, that makes new life and new growth possible."[31] Through attending to Helen's unspoken voice, Perry uses the diary in a gesture of sensitivity, concern, and demonstration of his intimate knowledge of the subjects of films—Black women in crisis. For his primary audience, the perspective Helen's diary offers about the painful and traumatic experiences some women encounter in relationships is a pivotal part of the ethos Perry constructs for his viewers. He appears to know the way Black women feel and their secrets.

Perry's use of the diary form to give voice and nuance to his representation of Helen's experience leads viewers to expect that journaling, self-rhetoric, and notions of reinvention might figure prominently in Helen's journey to healing and restoration. They do not. Instead, Perry uses Helen's diary to provide audiences with narration about key characters in his films. Through Helen's diary, characters learn that Charles was not always the "evil" and cruel man he appears to be at the beginning of the film. Her memories about how "good things used to be" makes Charles a more humanized villain. He is a symbol of the disregard for family and home that Perry's films attempt to redress, not a manifestation of the cruel, Black-brute stereotype that Black male critics have evoked in their critique of films such as *The Color Purple*. In contrast, the diary entries Helen writes when she begins to date Orlando work to cast him as the ideal mate. He is, as Helen's September 1st entry describes, "strong, beautiful, sensitive, and Christian," essentially everything that Charles, at this point of the film, is not. Although the diary is a tool of narration, Helen's entries become for audiences more persuasive evidence of the necessity of recognizing good opportunities and seizing them as a step in the healing and restoration process.

While Perry's use of Helen's diary to provide additional narration about Charles and Orlando redirects the agency she could be utilizing in self-writing and self-discovery into providing more information about male characters, it is the connection of the diary to forms of rhetorical containment that shows how Perry's attempts to demonstrate crisis work to objectify Helen. As shown in my previous discussion of the opening scenes of *Diary of a Mad Black Woman*, Perry uses forms of juxtaposition to illustrate Helen's emotional and marital state. By juxtaposing images that show her isolated in visible affluence and privilege with the images and sound of her diary entries, Perry amplifies for audiences the emotional impact of Charles's cheating and invokes the popular adage that warns of the dangers in gaining the world and losing one's soul.[32] The fact that this adage would be one of the preliminary impressions evoked by Helen's story reflects how juxtaposition, as a narrative device, can produce a sense of containment and, ultimately, culpability. As rhetoricians have explained, the arrangement of actors within a scene can produce the idea of synecdoche through containment. Based on the language, or image in Perry's case, a writer uses to arrange a scene, the principal actor within the scene will take on the essence, or nature, of the scene. In other words, as Kenneth Burke explains in his discussion of the pentad, "the contents of a divine container will synecdochically share in its divinity."[33]

Perry's choice to begin his film by juxtaposing images of the despair Helen experiences with images of affluence creates for audiences the initial impression that Helen's crisis is not just a result of her husband's infidelity, but is also one of containment. Because Helen sacrifices her sense of self to be with Charles—a figure who not only symbolizes the ills of *that* world but also persuades Helen to distance herself from her family—the diary becomes a visual symbol of how out of place she is initially when forced to move in with her grandmother Madea. Helen's speech, dress, and treatment of others, which are all remnants of the attitudes she adopted while married to Charles, are not only signs of how she's detached from her family community, but also indicators that Helen was in *that* world too long. In this respect, Helen's intimate compositions are not serving her interests. Instead, they are strategically placed bits of evidence of the broader crisis Perry's work attempts to address—able-bodied Black women who, by means of picking the wrong mate, are isolated from the Black family or disinterested in relationships with "good" Black men. That the private writings of Helen's diary would serve these uses and not directly contribute to the character's evolution and healing are reflections of the consequences that ensue when writers appropriate rhetorically rich tropes, messages, and practices to serve their own interests.

Bitter Black Women: An Impetus for Healing

Although less explicit than Vanzant's and Jakes's efforts, Perry's early films show efforts to portray Black women in ways that would invite readers to see healing as an action they need to take. In *Diary of a Mad*

Black Woman, Perry does this through his characterization of Helen. Promotional trailers for the film contain a montage of images illustrating Helen's opulent home, her husband Charles's adultery, her return to her grandmother's house, her descent into revenge, and the choice she must make between staying with her husband after he is paralyzed in a random act of violence or moving forward with Orlando, her new romantic interest. The pivot point is a shot where Helen throws a drink in Orlando's face and defiantly states, "I'm not bitter! I'm mad as hell!" Following scenes in the trailer show Helen beginning her rocky journey to emotional and spiritual wellness.

It is doubtful that Perry created the promotional materials for the film, but the emphasis on the shot where Helen asserts that she's "mad as hell" does suggest an attempt to invoke discourses regarding Black women's disappointment over the nature of their love lives. While numerous writers and recording artists have given voice to some of the dilemmas these women experience in their romantic pursuits, Black female-centered films of the nineties helped cement the "bitter" Black woman trope. Best exemplified in the shot of Bernadine setting her adulterous husband's possessions afire in the film adaptation of *Waiting to Exhale* (1995), the image of the mistreated woman who refuses to silence her resentment and acts out makes the bitter-Black-woman label time sensitive. Women are labeled "bitter" when they stay in the mode of critique, lament, or retaliation too long.

To his credit, Perry's use of Helen's diary entries complicates the stereotype of the bitter Black woman. However, his use of her bitterness and "misplaced" agency as catalysts for the family interventions show one of the hegemonic undertones in his representation of the crisis that should inspire his viewers to invest in healing. Through her diary entries, Helen shows viewers Charles's neglect, her own despair, the reasons why she stays, and her hopes to salvage their marriage. The effect is endearing but short-lived because of the interactions Perry stages between Helen and Orlando—the moving-truck driver Charles hires to escort Helen off their estate—to propel their romance. During their initial meeting, Helen lashes out at Orlando when he asks her for a destination, yelling, "All you men are just alike. You don't think about anybody else but yourself! Just stop the truck!" When she attempts to grab the steering wheel, Orlando finally relents, pulls the truck over, and departs the vehicle, saying, "Now I see why you're going through what you're going through!" The scene ends with Orlando watching her drive away and a following shot showing Helen arriving at Madea's house in the middle of the night.[34]

While Kimberly Springer asserts that Helen's retreat to Madea's house is a post-feminist "coming back to Blackness" argument about the "true" source of middle-class Black women's identities, this scene also shows how Perry's representation of healing casts women's acts of "misplaced" agency as threats to the innocent or the collective wellness of their families.[35] Helen's stereotyping of Orlando as being "just" like Charles is a feature that works to validate the stage of Perry's curriculum where protagonists learn to recognize good opportunities and seize them. The flaw in this technique is that it casts Helen as the aggressor and Orlando as the victim. Because Helen is too bitter to recognize Orlando's sympathy, her symbolic gesture of grabbing the steering wheel to reclaim a measure of control makes her a threat to others. She is lost, blind, and irrational. And Orlando, by proximity, becomes the undeserving target of her misdirected rage. Helen's act of agency is misplaced.

Karla Holloway's discussion of the unrecognized effects of the hegemonic gaze on Black women explains how these "misplaced" acts reflect expectations of Black women's appropriate behaviors. Constructions of ethnicity in literary, social, or cultural narratives have historically created and perpetuated the idea of "ethical" behaviors. As a result, "codes" such as "act your age, not your color" have become community-based epistemologies aimed at helping marginalized groups navigate the gaze of dominant groups. For Black women, the centrality of these themes in African American communities poses a dilemma where they must choose how to navigate encounters where their bodies, and therefore personhood, are read through disparaging notions of race and gender. In these situations, they must decide between inflicting damage upon themselves by ignoring stereotypes and behaving "as if race and sex are peripheral," or defying such codes of conduct and engaging in a practice Holloway defines as "turning it out."[36] When Black women decide to turn it out, they

> give up trying to respond to a situation as if both we and they (white people and/or men) are operating within the same codes of conduct. It can mean handing over to our adversary our version of the stereotype that motivates their disrespect to us—just to prove to them that they could no better handle the stereotype than they can determine and control our character.[37]

Holloway argues that "no one wins" in a situation where a Black woman resorts to turning it out; these acts of disruption are sometimes necessary for Black women challenging forms of objectification and control.[38]

Because Helen's second instance of "turning it out" at a family cookout is the impetus for the messages about restoration characters express through the remainder of the film, the suggestion is that her behavior, not necessarily her feelings, is a crisis that requires healing. The second meeting between Helen and Orlando carries over the tensions of the first. At a family cookout, Helen refuses to apologize for throwing Orlando out of the truck, and Orlando calls her "just another bitter Black woman" that makes every man she meets "pay for what he did." When she informs him that he doesn't know her and he responds by reminding her that he "watched a man drag [her] out of a house and treat [her] like dirt," she retaliates by throwing her drink at him and asserting that she's "not bitter," but "mad as hell."

Helen's choice to throw her drink in retaliation at being called a "bitter Black woman" could be read as an assertion of her agency against Orlando's taunt. Yet, Perry's decision to place their exchange within the scene of the family cookout, makes her choice to act out a signifier of how emotionally "lost" and disconnected she is from her family. While Orlando's antagonism is obscured, Helen's despair and irrationality is amplified against the backdrop of the cookout—a symbol some audiences may interpret as an indicator of the family's unity. Helen's retaliation becomes a willful breach of the proper code of decorum for family events and the indicator that the family needs to intervene. It is the confirmation women in the film and audience need to initiate and invest in the approach of family rehabilitation that Perry considers pivotal to healing.

What makes this attempt to identify with Black female viewers through the Helen character problematic is that it teaches viewers to see women's assertive behavior as a potential cause for intervention and to measure women's behaviors according to a code that privileges heterosexual, Christian men. For example, when Orlando tells Helen that he chose to reject the bitterness of his own heartbreak, his confession works to enforce the code that women must rise above mistreatment and get over it. Helen has no excuse to mistreat Orlando; thus, in her rejection of his marriage proposal in favor of honoring her commitment to Charles, viewers see the real threat to continuation of the Black family that Perry's rhetoric of healing resolves. When women such as Helen are unable to see, love, honor, or choose the good Christian men in front of them, families suffer and communities regress. This attempt to identify with Black women undercuts the positive potential of Perry's narrative for healing because Helen, at this stage, symbolizes the bitterness, blindness, and sense of loss Black women experience after traumatic relationship, and she signifies the attitudes and behaviors women must sacrifice so the nuclear Black Christian family can be preserved.

Practices, Processes, and Proofs: A Curriculum for Healing

Perry's use of film would lead us to think that his healing curriculum is less explicit than those that appear in written form. In reality, his films actually make more compelling arguments for the processes in his curriculum through his representation of women moving through the pain of heartbreak or trauma of abuse. By showing characters such as Helen, Lisa, and Vanessa undergoing the stages of restoration, resolution, and recognition—stages that define Perry's curriculum—his films teach viewers to see these behaviors as steps to healing that produce positive results. Coincidentally, the practices, processes, and proofs the protagonist's journey to wellness shows also teach viewers narrow ways to interpret women's behavior.

Restoring the Centrality of Faith

The first and most important action Perry's films show characters undertaking in their journeys to healing is to restore the centrality of faith in their lives. Through testimonies, sermons, and songs about the mercy, grace, and salvation, supporting characters encourage protagonists to make Christian faith their primary source of power and identity, or to restore the role of faith in their lives. And consistently, Perry's protagonists return to church, prayer, or a state of spiritual practice and later gain an improved sense of self-esteem and value. Because the protagonists eventually learns to forgive themselves of internal guilt or shame and move forward by forgiving those individuals that have abused or hurt them, the implied message is that restoring their faith and spirituality is the practice that enables them to take such pivotal steps towards healing and wellness.

The act of restoring the prominence of their faith is consistent within inspirational literature on healing, much of which suggests that cultivating a faith relationship affords an individual vision, wisdom, and discernment. What makes Perry's representation of this stage problematic is the values critique implicit in the scenarios and dialogues he stages to show women learning this portion of his curriculum. The nursing home scene in *Diary of a Mad Black Woman*, where Myrtle reminds her daughter Helen about the necessity of keeping God and faith first in her life, is one example of how sacred messages can be used to preserve the interests of groups in power and to reinforce worldviews. When Helen confesses how hurt she is by Charles's abrupt end to their marriage, saying, "I think I'm losing my mind, mama. He hurt me so bad. He was my everything," her mother responds with the statement, "God is your everything. Don't you know He is a jealous God? He don't want no man before him."[39]

Myrtle's response appears to be an act of sharing spiritual wisdom about the dangers of worshipping idols and conventional wisdom about the dangers of losing one's identity and sense of self in relationships. However, because viewers learn earlier in the film that Helen willingly allowed Charles to put Myrtle into a nursing home because Myrtle "didn't fit his model" of wealth and upward mobility, Myrtle's rhetorical question about God's jealousy not only implies Helen's complicity, but also critiques Helen's values. The suggestion is that if Helen's faith, self-image, and commitment to her extended family had been stronger, she would known that it was in her best interests to leave her fruitless marriage—symbolized by the lack of children—upon seeing Charles's shifting values and cold demeanor. By waiting for a divine change in a marriage that did not contribute to the preservation or extension of her family, Helen is shown in a situation where her faith pre-crisis is made to seem misplaced. Perry's message about the importance of women recognizing and preserving their own self-worth is valuable. His attempts to represent women revising their sense of self-efficacy in adverse situations lay the groundwork for one of the more troubling aspects of healing curricula—the idea that women must accept responsibility for the traumas they endure.

Restoring the Centrality of Family

Perry's films advance the idea that the Black family is as an institution within the broader Black community. Ideally, the family is supposed to be a refuge for individuals in crisis, a pillar of collective values, and a training site where individuals learn or relearn strategies and epistemologies to navigate hostile worlds. While the Black church has historically functioned as one of the civic arenas within African American communities, Perry's representation of the functional Black family casts it as a more private yet equally essential component; it is a site for the development of collective and individual skills for self-reliance.

While Perry's films do acknowledge how dysfunctional families can contribute to, or cause, women's crises, family gatherings and relationships are the commonplaces for the persuasive instruction women must undergo to arrive at healing. In these settings and scenarios, women are targeted with loving but didactic messages of wisdom that operate as forms of intervention aimed at redirecting or instructing the wayward protagonist. The lessons involve attitudes, behaviors, and practices the protagonist must adopt to overcome her crises. Delivered by such agents as the mother, sister, or grandmother, these messages remind the protagonist of her self-worth as an individual and purpose as a daughter, wife, and mother, while also explicitly or implicitly communicating to audiences that the woman needs the family to survive and the family needs the woman to survive. Within the scheme of the overall healing process, these moments work to shift the protagonist's focus away from her past trauma and present hurt to the future work she has to do as a functional member of the family and her community. This reprioritization is a crucial because it helps the protagonist forgive or resist individuals who abused her and move out of destructive relationships.

Madea's gritball lesson in *Madea's Family Reunion* is one example of the way Perry stages teaching moments to redirect women in crisis. In the scene, Madea shares important thoughts on selfhood and relationships, all while indirectly teaching her granddaughter Lisa, the sheltered and bourgeoisie princess trapped in an abusive relationship, how to fight back against her abusive fiancé, Carlos. The scene occurs in Madea's kitchen where Lisa confesses to her older sister Vanessa, the single mother of two, that Carlos is beating her. Although Vanessa immediately calls Madea into the kitchen to hear the news, she opts to keep her sister's secret after seeing Madea's initial look of skepticism. Instead, she tells Madea that a "friend" is in an abusive relationship. Seeing through the lie, Madea opts to play along and offers the following self-defense lesson about "gritball" instead of an admonishment:

> I'ma tell you this. Can't nobody help your friend until she wants to help herself. You can want all your life to help somebody but if they don't wanna get help, it ain't goin' happen. You listen to me, when you get tired of a man hitting on you, ain't nothin'

you can do but cook breakfast for him. . . . Bring him into the kitchen and get you a big ole' pot of hot grits, and when they start to boil like lava, after he done got good and comfortable, you say, "Good Morn'tink," throw it right on him.[40]

As reinforcement, Madea teaches them to hit their attackers with a frying pan. "I call it gritball," she says (see figure 5.1).

There is no direct endorsement about the centrality of family in this scene, but it does show some of the culturally situated literacy practices Perry appropriates to reinforce messages about the family as an institution. As Elaine Richardson explains, language and literacy practices such as storytelling that transmit the ways of knowing, reading, and responding to the world that Black women employ to "advance and protect themselves and their loved ones" are characteristically shaped by "a heightened consciousness" of the "rhetorical situation," or a sense of appropriate timing.[41] Because Madea is never directly told of her granddaughter's abuse, her ability to read the situation, respond with narrative instruction, and deliver the persuasive appeals about self-value Lisa eventually uses to get out of her relationship is supposed to symbolize a rhetorical intervention. Madea is intended to represent the many mothers who stay attuned to their loved ones and the challenges they face and are prepared to respond accordingly.

Perry's choice to have Madea deliver his message about women leaving violent situations and retaliating against their abusers contributes to the patriarchal logic his representation of healing advances. The parody of Black womanhood Perry (while in drag) enacts through Madea frequently involves aggressive and violent acts that work to reinforce his masculinity. Madea is far from respectable yet, ironically, her lessons to wayward women in crisis reinforce a gender politic that centralizes women's respectability. Madea's message that women must remember their self-worth and activate their agency against violence, for example, is valuable and necessary; but the suggestion that women wield a frying pan as an act of resistance does little to help characters such as Lisa, or viewers for that matter, understand how patriarchy works. Because the scene ends on a comedic note, Lisa does not come to understand how Carlos's male insecurity makes him possessive over her body and life. Instead, Perry's use of Madea as a tool to foster what hooks would call the "development" of Lisa's "self-will" instead of critical consciousness makes the victory Lisa achieves by fighting back a narrow one. As

Madea counsels her granddaughters in the sport of "gritball" in the 2006 film *Madea's Family Reunion*. Fair use.

viewers watch Lisa fight the inordinately villainous Carlos, this stage of healing is reduced to acts of retaliation rather than inquiry.

This facet of Perry's healing curriculum also reveals a troubling politic of proximity and critique of Black mothers. Lisa's estrangement from her family makes Madea's message about self-worth more poignant. As a strange text that must be brought home so Madea can read and teach her, Lisa is a character whose detachment implies that women are safer when they stay physically and ideologically closer to home *and* date family-approved partners. The politic of proximity embedded in Lisa's estrangement from the family and unrelated crisis of domestic violence works to reify the idea that the family is an institutional safe haven for women. Conversely, Perry's representation of Victoria, Lisa and Vanessa's mother, in opposition to Madea works to reinforce narrow conceptualizations of Black motherhood. Cast against Madea, who is made to seem like an appropriate, albeit nontraditional matriarch, Victoria, who inexplicably berates the older daughter and manipulates the younger into staying in an abusive relationship for the sake of marrying a richer man, is a villain. This binary upholds the forms of "Black mother worship" that occur when Black women's choice to be self-sacrificing is extolled and praised without complication.[42] Exaggerated, one-dimensional portrayals of characters such as Victoria work to reinforce the assumption that women who actively choose to be giving and self-sacrificing for the sake of their families are the "perfect embodiment of a woman's natural role."[43] Not only do these notions naturalize the idea that the "Black woman who works hard to be a responsible caretaker is only doing what she should be doing," but they also suggest that women such as Victoria pose threats to their families. As a result, Perry's use of Victoria as an antagonizing figure which Lisa and Vanessa must learn to reject or make peace with for the sake of healing makes his representation of Black motherhood, in this instance, a validation of the pathologizing rhetoric in documents such as the Moynihan report on the Negro family.

Resolving to Exercise Resilience

A praxis component of Perry's curriculum is the trend of characters resolving to exercise resilience. Motivated by the testimonies their relatives share and the skills they teach, Perry's protagonists press forward with their lives in the face of mistreatment and hurt. In *Diary of a Mad Black Woman*, Myrtle encourages her heartbroken daughter Helen to rely on divine assistance and courage to get a job and become economically self-sufficient after her divorce. When Helen explains how the pain of her broken marriage makes her feel too weak to carry on, Myrtle says,

> You've got the strength God gave us women to survive. You just ain't tapped into it yet. . . . Just let it go. There's nothing wrong with shedding a few tears. It cleanses the soul. You know, you need to stop thinking about what you think you lost and look forward to what there is to gain. It's a new life baby. It's right in front of you. All you got to do is reach out and grab it.[44]

When Helen asks how she is supposed to carry this out, her mother responds with the following charge: "By waking up every morning and thanking God, and then ask him to help you. Just ask the savior to help you."

Interestingly, the message of independence, survival, and faith Myrtle articulates to Helen in the film version of *Diary* is different from the play version. In that version of the text, Perry has Myrtle remind Helen of the legacy from which she came, saying,

> You come from a long legacy of Black Women who were raped, beaten, and separated from their families. But they sought strength in the Lord and they survived. You have to do the same. He will see you through this.[45]

Both versions show a concept of healing premised on individual action and the belief that one is divinely endowed with resources that enable one to survive difficult encounters. When viewers see protagonists such as Helen deciding to get their own jobs, returning to church regularly, or becoming financially self-sufficient, the argument is validated. As proof these processes work, Perry's films show protagonists enjoying their independence or talking about the difficult yet positive transformations they are undergoing, essentially rewriting their sense of purpose. Their progress, albeit not linear, reinforces the idea that exercising resiliency is a pivotal step within the journey to healing.

Consequently, the choices Perry makes to stage these teaching moments reveal how his concept of healing upholds forms of patriarchy through silence. Although it is understandable that a female-centered narrative focuses more on the dilemmas women face, in this instance, the form of domestic and emotional abuse Helen experiences is a two-person issue that requires a contextual view and analysis. Instead, Perry's film follows the trend that often occurs in self-help literature for Black women where writers accelerate the push to forgiveness. It is a way of helping readers in crisis reach the states of wellness through forgiveness and resume their roles as mothers, wives, or workers. As mentioned in previous chapters, the move is understandable as forgiveness may enable the reader to rid herself of anger and achieve the inner peace necessary for her survival; but too often the result is the failure to make a part of the curriculum the vocal interrogation or critique of systems of hegemony and oppression, which is a necessity for women's development of a critical consciousness. Myrtle's lament about "shielding" her daughter too much illustrates this oversight because in that scene, neither character acknowledges Charles's role. Instead, both women focus on their own complicity, with no attention to the complexities of race, class, and manhood that shaped the marriage or Charles's agency.

The focus in this scene reifies a problematic trend in rhetorical healing where women are taught to accept disproportionate levels of culpability for the traumas they or their loved ones encounter. In admonishing Helen to tap into the legacy of Black women who have survived trauma or abuse and critiquing herself, Myrtle perpetuates normalizing discourses about Black women's resiliency that, when misappropriated, exacerbate the silent and internal oppression that women in crisis or abused women sometimes endure. Songs, poems, emails, and other discourses lauding Black women's survival of attacks on their bodies, psyches, and families are commonplace; and these discourses often function as arguments that promote cultural pride and fortitude. Subsequently, these messages aimed at praising Black women for their strength preserve mythologies about Black women's immunity to pain. With her 2008 book *Black Pain: It Just Looks Like We're Not Hurting,* Terrie M. Williams relaunched an important discussion of the consequences of this cloak of strength by explaining how the signs of her depression went unspoken and misdiagnosed. Through her story and the testimonies of others, Williams verifies the link between these strength messages and Black women's internal oppression. Silenced by such familiar adages as "we don't air our dirty laundry" and her family's consistent messages about her success and Black women's strength, Williams spent several unfruitful years in therapy, unable to explain, communicate, or conceptualize the severity of her depression.[46] The normalization of Black women's resilience narratives and discourses contributed to a delay in Williams's healing. Thus, a consequence of Perry's appeal to resiliency is that his films perpetuate the myth that Black women are inherently capable of enduring and bouncing back from trauma or oppression, if they so choose.

Recognizing and Seizing Positive Opportunities

Enacting evolution is the last transformative step within the healing curricula African American writers have created to address and resolve individual crises. During this culminating stage, the healed individuals apply their new insights and perspectives to their relationships. The assumption is that healed individuals not only behave differently, but also make different decisions because they are better equipped with the resources or processes necessary to survive future crises. As proof, Perry's films show leading women taking actions and making decisions his audiences are primed to interpret as evidence of the protagonists' healing. Through appeals aimed at persuading them that they are not only entitled to a happy future but that they must actively decide to pursue it, protagonists such as Helen, Vanessa, and Lisa internalize messages of acceptance and praise that help them rewrite negative internal and external discourses that influence their self-perception post-crisis. These messages of acceptance and positive future opportunities are a critical element within rhetorics of healing because they foreground the importance of an individual recognizing good opportunities and seizing them.

The burgeoning romantic relationship is the most frequently used site where protagonists receive these messages of acceptance, and the character of the "good" Black Christian man is the most frequently used character to deliver these messages. Frankie, the bus driver, fulfills this role in *Madea's Family Reunion*. From the start of the film, he boldly expresses his interest in Vanessa, the single mother of two; however, she rebuffs his advances because of a deep-seated distrust of men, which viewers later learn is a result of her being raped as an adolescent by the husband of her mother. Compared to Carlos, the physically abusive man engaged to Vanessa's sister Lisa, Frankie is the model man. Patient and compassionate, Frankie takes time to formally court Vanessa and respond to her accusatory question of "What do you want? . . . All men come for something," with the answer that "some men come to restore."[47] In this capacity, Frankie is the strategically placed agent that enacts the crucial function of affirmation in the healing process. He delivers some of the messages the protagonist is supposed to use as a template of scripts to overwrite negative internal and external discourses, which influence her self-esteem or apathy, and shift her perception on relationships and her future.

In *Madea's Family Reunion*, Frankie's claim that "some" men can restore women to states of happiness reveals the narrow ways Perry's films teach viewers to conceptualize Black women's wellness. The irony in Perry's focus on Black women's healing is that protagonists are encouraged to expand their notion of desirable romantic partners to include "good," church-going, working-class men; but they are never encouraged to look beyond heterosexual relationships for sources of fulfillment, wholeness, or healing. More times than not, women do not relish in the fullness of their singlehood. They do not pursue advanced degrees, engage in body-affirming fitness projects, open new businesses, or take up activities that might offer them more balanced lives. Perry's films only teach viewers to see a woman's healing as the reward for choosing to take her place as a wife to the "good" Black Christian man. In *Diary of a Mad Black Woman*, Helen and Orlando's romantic relationship illustrates how the notion that healing is a result of proper decision-making creates a patriarchal system for evaluating women's behaviors. Despite his rocky start with Helen, Orlando, the moving-truck driver, is the strategically placed character who affirms her after her divorce. He does so on their first date by telling Helen that he sees her as a beautiful "woman that's been hurt," who has "taught herself to be tough."[48] The intent of this message is to restore Helen's desirability, and compliments are certainly welcome. In this instance, though, the focus on male affirmation and desire that makes the scene appealing later becomes a tool to measure Helen's progress towards emotional healing. When Helen learns that Charles, her soon-to-be ex, has been shot—as Orlando is proposing—and she opts to resume her wifely duties as Charles's caregiver, the suspended proposal and the sadistic forms of revenge she enacts on Charles become signifiers that Helen is not yet well or ready to move towards a positive future. In his impassioned plea for Helen to choose him and choose hope, Orlando reveals whose interests are actually served by the rhetorical healing Perry's films teach. He says,

> I . . . deserve to have good things and a good life and I deserve you. You're a good woman. You deserve me. The only reason you're going back . . . is because you're afraid. . . . I love you, but I need you to trust me. . . . I don't want just half of you.[49]

Since changes in perspective are an aim of rhetorical healing, the lesson about recognizing positive opportunities Orlando is supposed to deliver is actually a critique of Helen's values. When placed between an uncharacteristically one-dimensional male villain and, in contrast, a "good" Christian man such as Orlando, the protagonist's inability to choose the right option within this binary symbolizes her lack of progress towards healing and her threat to the good Black man and, thereby, the traditional nuclear family. All that is good seems to be represented in the positive life the affirming "good" man offers the wounded, yet recovering woman. A subversive motive to healing, Perry's prioritization of the "good" Christian man's happiness is most evident by the trend of women, like Helen, begging the good men to take them back—the good men they have "wounded" in their inability to recognize the man's love and acceptance. That the majority of his films end with a wedding is confirmation that healing is a restorative ritual that teaches women to take their places as whole, restored, and functional mates for Black Christian men.

Assessment

The second half of Myrtle's speech to her relatives in *Madea's Family Reunion* illustrates the culmination of Perry's message about restoring the place of faith, family, and home in an individual's life. After asking her family how to get back its commitment to each other, she turns to the men of her family and says: "Young Black men. Take your place. We need you. Your sons and daughters need you.... You were sold off and had no choice, but now it's time to stay. Take your place! Now. Starting now!" She continues, with a message for the women. "Young Black women. You are more than your thighs and your hips. You are beautiful. Strong. Powerful. I want more from you. Take your place." The scene ends with a shot of family members hugging. It is one of the most poignant parts of the film.

For the large body of contemporary African American Christians that are Perry's target demographic, the messages about family obligation and collective survival in his films are ones worth supporting. Much like the works of Vanzant and Jakes, his films have notions of resilience, an individual's entitlement to a happy future, forgiveness as a step towards wellness, and the importance of family, home, and faith. These are the strengths of his approach to healing. When read as an extension of a vernacular tradition devoted to the survival of African Americans, these themes, along with the messages of racial pride, perseverance, and unity in Perry's films show the positive and counterhegemonic elements of his work. Perry's movies make visible for broad audiences the ways of knowing and the reaffirming messages that have helped African Americans survive oppressive environments.

However, for the women who are cast as the students in his healing curricula, the binaries and narrow conceptions of gender roles his films advance are potentially dangerous. Two examples from Perry's recent films highlight the flaws with his rhetoric of return. In *The Family That Preys*, the final attack on Andrea is one of the most compelling scenes that shows the consequences when a woman does not take her place as a dutiful wife or mother. One of the film's storylines centers on the final road trip Charlotte Cartwright, a wealthy white businesswoman fighting off her son's attempts to take over the family company, takes with her best friend Alice Evans, a working-class Black diner owner struggling to keep peace in her family. The other plotline focuses on the exchange between the two matriarchs' families, particularly Andrea Evans's extramarital affair with her boss, William Cartwright, Charlotte's son. Throughout the film, Andrea embodies the negative stereotype of the blindly ambitious, gold-digging, emasculating woman who shows little respect for her "working-class" husband, Chris. When Andrea learns that Chris has withdrawn money from the private account William has established for her, Andrea verbally berates Chris with references to how he could never be "the" man William is and braggingly informs Chris that he is not the father of their child. Ordinarily, the rage Chris flies into when he slaps Andrea so forcefully that she flies over the diner counter would be identified as abusive; but the template for healing throughout Perry's films works to justify the act. Since Andrea is represented as the villain, her lack of marital loyalty and her disrespect for her husband make her a threat to Chris's wellness and happiness.

The consequences when Judith refuses to take her place as a dutiful wife are bleaker in *Temptation: Confessions of a Marriage Counselor*. Although Perry does suggest the extramarital affair she embarks upon with Harley is due, in part, to Brice's neglect and lack of attention, there are no grey areas when it comes to the penalty Judith has to pay for venturing outside of the tight radius of her life as a traditional, church-going, Christian woman. Despite the cautionary and didactic warnings and prayers of Judith's strategically placed minster-mother, Judith cannot hear or see how much she will lose by stepping outside of her marriage. When Judith finally does give into temptation, she steps all the way out of bounds by back talking her mother and emasculating her husband. Punishment comes quickly as Judith contracts the HIV virus, loses Brice, and, as the final scene of her limping down the street to church suggests, learns the hard way that the proverbial apple was not worth it. That one of the last scenes of *Temptation* shows Judith purchasing medicine to treat her HIV is the most stark indicator of the cause-and-effect logic and the punitive consequences that can occur when Black female characters are not ideologically or emotionally committed to their homes. In this instance, Perry's wellness campaign has evolved to the point where a woman's need for physical healing is the consequence of disobedience. It is a fear-based argument transmitted through an antifeminist pedagogy.

CHAPTER 6

With Vision and Voice
Black Women's Rhetorical Healing in Everyday Use

*E*ssence magazine drew little if any criticism the first time it opted to feature Steve Harvey on its cover in December 2009. As part of an issue promising an audience of presumably Black female readers tips from actual men on how to receive the love that was due to them, Harvey may have seemed like a logical choice. In January of that year, Harper Collins released the first book by the comedian-turned-actor-turned-radio-show-host. Titled *Act Like a Lady, Think Like a Man: What Men Really Think about Love, Relationships, Intimacy,* Harvey produced a "playbook" for women with out-of-date knowledge about the men in their lives. In the book's opening pages, Harvey explains that he drew inspiration for the project from the numerous female fans of his radio show who had sent messages to him seeking relationship advice.[1] The letters revealed to him just how many women were ignorant of the ways men process information about relationships and how many men, in turn, were able to manipulate and take advantage of women because women lack an understanding of how men think. In chapters such as "What Drives Men," "'We Need to Talk' and Other Words That Make Men Run for Cover," "Strong, Independent—and Lonely—Women," and "How to Get the Ring," Harvey attempts to "empower" women to assert control of their budding relationships through lessons such as the ninety-day celibacy rule. Ideally, the book provides women with the "wide-open look" at men's minds they will need to transform themselves into the type of catch men will see as a "keeper" rather than a mere "sport fish." By following the book's instructions, women should be able to "put into play [their] plans, [their] dreams, and [their] desires" and, more importantly, to "figure out if he's planning to be with you or just playing with you."[2]

Harvey's pathway to the cover of *Essence* was a quick one. By March 2009, he had made a second appearance on *The Oprah Winfrey Show*. This appearance was distinct because Winfrey gave Harvey the rare opportunity to address an audience of 300 female guests seeking follow-up advice from his book (see figure 6.1). By summer, the book was on the *New York Times* best-seller list. Months later, the popularity of *Act Like a Lady, Think Like a Man* inspired the producers of ABC's *Nightline* to feature Harvey as a guest-expert in an episode devoted to learning Black women's perspectives on a Yale University research survey documenting disparities in marriage rates of Black women compared with white women. Harvey reprised this role in April 2010 as the co-moderator of a *Nightline* "Face Off" episode on the "Black women's marital crisis," featuring comedian Sherri Shepherd; journalist Jacque Reid; Hill Harper, author of *Letters to a Young Sister: DeFINE Your Destiny*; and Jimi Izrael of National Public Radio.[3] The debate would later come to signify one of the more visible examples of the growing discourse of "crisis" concerning Black women's marriageability.[4]

Despite Harvey's successful year, the *Essence* editors selected a different approach in the December 2009 issue, opting to feature the comedian with his latest wife, Marjorie, on the cover. Mrs. Harvey is pictured on the cover leaning onto her husband's chest with a multi-carat diamond ring featured prominently on her hand. As she gazes into the camera, her smile and posture seem to embody the comfort of a woman confident in her husband's protection. Harvey smiles as well with shoulders taut from the tension of embracing his wife and positioning his chest so his wife may rest her head upon it. Glimmers of pride show in his eyes. It is clear that he relishes his role as man and caregiver. These themes reappear in "You're All I Need to Get By," the issue's feature article about the comedian's marriage and family. In it, the writer suggests the comedian's accomplishments of the past year were a result of his conscious choice to settle down in his third marriage and refocus his life on faith, family, and fidelity. "The thing I've learned in all of this is that you can make a lot of mistakes and you can mess up real bad and God can fix you up anyway," he confesses while describing how he originally met his wife decades before but had not learned yet how to treat her properly.[5] Peppered with images of the couple's blended family and Atlanta estate, the article and image effectively cast Harvey as a reformed and compassionate husband

Steve Harvey answers questions from an all-female audience on *The Oprah Winfrey Show*. Fair use.

and father. He is successful in life and love and, of obvious importance to the story's writer, he is authorized to guide women to successful relationships. By the time Harvey appeared by himself on the cover of the magazine's January 2012 issue to promote *Straight Talk, No Chaser: How to Find, Keep, and Understand a Man*, his second book teaching women how to "get the most out of their relationships," the career benefits of Harvey's personal penance were clear. As one of the few men to appear by himself on the magazine's cover, Harvey had become the most visible relationship consultant to Black women at that time.

By opening this conclusion with a discussion of Steve Harvey, my hope is not to suggest that *Essence* magazine is a bastion of cutting-edge or radical Black feminist politics or that the publication is immune to market trends. Rather, Harvey's appearances on the cover are an example of the work these wellness campaigns and learning cures require from those of us that understand the impact of language and language education on the quality of life that groups such as Black women strive to have. *Essence* is one of the public media venues like *The Oprah Winfrey Show* and *OWN* where scores of Black women turn for insight and instruction on matters of everyday living. Given the pedagogical and discursive function of these extracurricular forums and spaces, as Ann Ruggles Gere has called them, we have to question what it means that Harvey's redemption narrative about how learning to treat women better was the cure for his own love life and that the catalyst for his career ascent gets front billing.[6] Moreover, we must determine the consequences when a book promoting gender essentialism by telling women to "act like" ladies but "think like" men achieves best-seller status on a premise that seems to counteract the core tenet of Black feminist thought as a specialized oppositional knowledge. What are the implications when spaces such as *Essence,* which were once cradles for radical thought and platforms for burgeoning activists such as Audre Lorde and Bambara to communicate with Black women readers, lose some of their critical edge? What does the overall belief in a learning cure mean for the task of cultivating Black women's visions for equitable futures and their voices in bringing those futures to pass?

These questions mean that the next step in theorizing African American rhetorical traditions as a set of action-taking, knowledge-making, and community-sustaining resources is to figure out how we can put projects such as Black women's healing into everyday, critical use. In her short story, "Everyday Use," Alice Walker reminds readers that the remnants of a problematic tradition or practice do not necessarily need to be discarded. Instead, as African Americans have shown many times over, the undesirable and the complicated can be repurposed towards generative ends. Contemporary healing efforts require repurposing because of Black women's ongoing investment in wellness. As Jamilah King observes in the 2011 *Color Lines* article, "Three Feminists Talk About the Media's Obsession with Unwed Black Women," Black women are the group that have contributed the most in propelling Harvey to the status of "relationship" expert. "If Black women were not buying the Steve Harvey book," she reasoned. Furthermore, "if we weren't tuning into these specials . . . there would be no conversation."[7] King is right and, as my discussion of Winfrey's investment in these learning cures and role as literacy sponsor in the introduction suggests, these conversations are bound to continue. Even if Black women are enjoying overdue attention to matters threatening their wellness and are reading these texts discriminatingly, the costs for these types of life classes are just too high.

Consider, for example, how Harvey has been able to capitalize on Black women's investment in the promises of acquiring interpersonal literacies. In *Act Like a Lady, Think Like a Man* and his second book *Straight Talk, No Chaser: How to Find, Keep, and Understand a Man,* he makes no mention of healing as an impetus or goal for his writing and teaching. It is not necessary. By following the pattern of establishing a culture of lack and appealing to his readers' desire for happy futures, he has been able to seize the space to offer his product of information on how men think. Even as his books encourage readers to see themselves as ignorant about the ways of menfolk and to adopt forms of game play and deception, the form of wellness Harvey imagines for women could almost be confused with a feminist form of empowerment because it foregrounds the assumption that women deserve choices. When we consider this moment within the history of Black women's intellectualism, the contrast is stark. Sojourner Truth, one of the most effective rhetors of the nineteenth century, listed the educational credentials she had used to participate in civic affairs by boldly professing that she could read "men *and* nations." Now, over more than a century and a half later, one of the best-selling books among contemporary Black women offers to teach them only how to read men.

The depoliticization and the narrowing of these learning agendas mean that a critical turn must happen if we are to gain any everyday use out of these campaigns and projects. With the explicit emphasis the three primary writers in this study have placed on readers performing legible behaviors and communicative practices to signify their wellness, it is apparent that these campaigns are essentially rhetorical *reeducation* endeavors. When Black women writers of the seventies and eighties assumed the authority to define how to redress their pain and began to outline the types of literacies this work required by way of Black feminist thought, the result has been a resurgence in pedagogical projects that, as Jessica Enoch explains in her definition of rhetorical education, cultivates students' communal and civic identities and dictates the types of persuasive practices and bodily and social norms that prepare them to participate in various arenas of community life.[8] Moreover, through rhetorics of revision, transformation, and return, writers have been able create the discursive and hermeneutical space to teach women how to do so, essentially reconstituting the discursive borders of these communities and reinstating the importance of their institutions as Black women are retrained on how to be functional and, most importantly, working citizens. The irony, as this analysis has shown, is that while conversations about healing open up spaces for individuals to talk to Black women and define social problems, these rhetorics too frequently narrow perceptions about the spheres of Black women's participation, influence, and work. As Black women become increasingly visible and influential media consumers, discussions of pain and empowerment are becoming the type of commonplaces that can be easily coopted.

Addressing matters of pain can become a stepping-stone to all types of professional and commercial gain.

The possible coopting of these issues in the name of offering a learning product makes it urgent that we embrace the charge to cultivate the types of "critical thinking citizenship" that should emerge from our efforts to promote rhetorical education. In her 2010 Chair's Address, "It's Bigger than Comp/Rhet: Contested and Undisciplined," Gwendolyn Pough encourages us to make better use of the interdisciplinary insights that have already informed the fields of rhetoric and composition. She argues that even in our privileged positions within the academy, we can still foster change and interventions within larger society by expanding how "we think about teaching our students to be communicators: writers, speakers, listeners, but most of all thinkers."[9] The form of thinking Pough advocates involves using interdisciplinary frames to research and understand how groups use language and writing to take action and the specific knowledges and ways of knowing that have aided in survival. This thinking, this interrogative stance, also involves asking the difficult questions—talking back even—about what these practices mean and who benefits from them. "We have to teach them to think about what they hear," she argues. "To listen, really listen. If we do that, then we will really be helping to create a critical thinking citizenship."[10]

I cannot agree more. The campaigns I have analyzed in this book show us that we not only have to keep our eyes towards the reeducation efforts happening in plain sight, but that we also need to bring them into sharper focus by identifying similar types of efforts and establishing terminologies and concepts that aid individuals in navigating them. Striving for this shaper focus and clarity requires that we awaken students to adverse realities, to inconsistencies, to hard questions about privilege, and to moments of appropriation and misappropriation as well as just the possibilities of using rhetoric efficiently. It must begin with the understanding that teaching them how to be rhetorical critics has to incorporate the vernacular customs and traditions that may be trying to shape them, because a critical thinking citizenship must possess rhetorical awareness or, as I prefer to use the term, "discernment" about the discourses that seem most familiar, most affirming, and closest to them. This goal puts these messages into additional everyday use. With that in mind, I devote the final section of this conclusion to synthesizing some of the findings of this analysis, identifying avenues for future research, and charting some of the pedagogical objectives that should be on our agenda if we are to take up this work.

On Templates, Construction, and Tracking: Putting Campaigns to Use

Since approaches to healing are initially attempts at some kind of intervention, one of the primary ways to use these campaigns to enhance forms of critical thinking and discernment is to encourage students to identify the persuasive templates writers use to engage their readers. As the rhetorics of healing throughout the works of Vanzant, Jakes, and Perry show, there is a remarkable similarity in the initial steps writers take to construct a presumably instructive Black female audience for the purposes of intervention. Regardless of crisis, their own gender, and medium, the writers all followed a set of preliminary tasks that include illustrating a crisis by bringing a culture of lack to their readers' or viewers' attention, casting the culture of lack as a hermeneutical problem, performing or demonstrating an understanding of what we can understand as the Black women's rhetorical condition, and calling for action. The consistency of these steps and conventions suggests that African American writers find it imperative to address the personal needs of Black women as social members of their communities. Despite how individualized the appeal may seem or how personal a crisis may be, writers still read Black women in pain as members of families and broader units and workers within broader institutions.

Due to the consistency of these approaches, one area of research within African American vernacular culture should involve determining how writers within other campaigns construct audiences for the sake of group action. In the last two decades, for example, a number of prominent African American pastors and leaders have published books on how to manage finances and attain financial wellness. Given this market, determining the genre strategies these writers are using to promote their learning cures may help us identify both the important assumptions about social class, economic status, and material gain circulating within inspirational literature and the specific discourses these pastors use to address these individuals. Additionally, with recent shows such as TV One's *Save Our Sons* aiming to intervene into the lives of wayward Black males, analyzing the modes of discourse that African American charter-school principal and host Steve Perry used to address parents could also help us deepen our understanding of group action efforts in Black communities. Perry's show does not employ the same didactic approach found in the healing projects I've explored in this book, but the messages about salvation he and his guests invoke to rescue young men highlight cultural scripts about Black masculinity, endangerment, and group responsibility. In the wake of the Black Lives Matter movement and the conversations it continues to inspire in and beyond Black communities about African American humanity, these messages and styles are likely to reveal what we see as the threats to Black men's wellbeing and the types of affirmation and action thought to promote their survival.[11]

Making pedagogical use of these projects and approaches means that we must teach our students to develop a discriminating eye for detecting trends and movements as forms of social and pedagogical action. Even if instructors of writing, women and gender studies, or African American studies do not go so far as to read and teach specific genres such as Black women's self-help books or watch and interrogate gospel stage plays, teaching students to identify campaigns and track their function across multiple forms of media is a generative exercise in research, analysis, and criticism. At a minimum, these activities would push students to consider the implications of the rhetorical choices writers make and to think about the effect of mainstream visibility when a work originates from a specific urgency or in the interests of a specific group. The career progression of Vanzant is one of the clearest examples of why tracking the proliferation of a discourse such as healing should be on the research and pedagogical agenda for us. In the last few years, the self-help coach has released a series of twentieth-anniversary and reprinted versions of her early works. Books such as *Tapping the Power Within: A Guide to Black Women's Self-Empowerment* and *The Value in the Valley: A Guide to Black Women's Dilemmas* that were once directed to specifically Black female reading audiences are now released with no visible audience in mind even as they promote the same practices as pathways to healing. This trend may be a result of the publishers' influence but the decontextualization of these messages is another depoliticizing gesture that can be a site of inquiry for us.

Recently scholars such as Jonathan Alexander and Jacqueline Rhodes have challenged writing teachers to disrupt the need for "narrative coherence," or a tendency to privilege a universal human experience rather than exploring difference within multicultural classrooms, by showing how these appeals to collective comfort produce a form of "flattening" that erases the specificities of marginalized or under-studied populations.[12] This insight is not unlike Wanzo's concept of homogenization in that it also posits that conflation is a violent identity-stripping gesture.[13] Since cooptation has the potential to be violent as well, tracking the "crossover" of texts that once catered to Black women, for example, is the type of vernacular-based project that helps us understand what makes an audience a useful community at any given time and when those characteristics cease to have value to a writer or an agenda. Moreover, when we encourage students to identify instances where writers use homogenization, for instance, to achieve broader identification, we can help them understand forms of cultural production and knowledge making that have been packaged for mass consumption and equip them with gender-based lenses and terminologies to identify the consequences in instances where, for example, intersectionality is not at work.

On Ideologies, Vision, and Interrogation: Putting Pedagogies to Use

Rhetorical healing processes throughout these campaigns also reveal insights about which ways of knowing and being the writers see as important to the survival and maintenance of their institutions. As Jakes's analysis of scripture in *Woman, Thou Art Loosed* and Perry's choice to foreground the diary as a narrative device in *Diary of a Mad Black Woman* indicate, the images of the woman with some understanding of the value and application of the biblical scripture or with the resources to engage in personal journal writing is in and of itself a trope. This consistency may be because the three figures that I researched in this study all seem to be concerned with addressing Black women who are, apparently, Christian or adhere to a form of spirituality and are cognizant or concerned with the welfare of the Black family. Even so, it is necessary to determine if writers addressing different audiences or Black women of different spiritual backgrounds make the same assumptions about what behaviors their audiences will recognize as legitimate or authentic.

These campaigns point to several avenues for future research that can help extend the work scholars are currently doing to theorize relationships between African American literacies and rhetorical practice. For example, in the emphasis that Vanzant, Jakes, and Perry all place on their readers acquiring new ways to understand themselves or reread their past and reimagine their present circumstances, contemporary healing campaigns advance some of the ideologies of opportunity, progress, and emancipation among African Americans that Sonja Lanehart describes in her ethnography *Sista, Speak!: Black Women Kinfolk Talk about Language and Literacy*.[14] An immediate project would be to study the ways of reading Black women apply to these texts and to determine the insights women yield by completing the writing exercises commonly assigned in self-help and inspirational literature. Rhea Lathan's discussion of gospel literacies in *Freedom Writing: African American Civil Rights Literacy Activism, 1995–1967,* and Eric Darnell Pritchard's analysis of the literacy practices Black queer and LGBT communities use as forms of bibliotherapy and scriptural interpretation in his forthcoming ethnography are rich models for the work we're doing to expand our understandings of how sexuality, social movements, and spirituality influence African Americans' literacies. We can still ask more questions though. Is vision, for example, always a gendered resource? What are the circumstances that cause arguments about the incentive of literacy to shift?

Identifying these assumptions across different literacy campaigns can help students determine when a learning cure is essentially a form of deficit pedagogy. For instance, Harvey's initial angle of attracting readers in *Act Like a Lady* encodes an assumption of Black women's social illiteracy. With his depiction of men as "players" and "hunters" who are resistant to sharing their emotions or revealing their plans, he recirculates old notions that men are from Mars and women are from Venus, suggesting to women that some heterosexual men's masculinity is a culture of lack, with which they are simply ill-equipped to deal. Coupled with Harvey's argument that women must change in order to change men, the notion of deficit is compounded by his discussion of the mysterious "playbook" of man codes and other devices women must learn to decode if they hope to have a good relationship. The argument should be offensive to men as well as women but, more often than not, it isn't. Harvey buttresses his rhetoric of game play with arguments about the ease in which women can break these codes with his help. I observed in vivid color the consequence of the deficit argument one morning in 2014—ironically, it was Valentine's Day—while watching the *Steve Harvey Show*. During a segment on how to decode text messages featuring a panel of married and single women, Harvey translated the messages these women's husbands and significant others had sent them. He actually read to them.

Since women are the characters in these learning-cure dramatizations, our forms of rhetorical criticism and critical pedagogy have to interrogate images and assess the value of the knowledge they are supposed to receive in these representations. As the curricula I uncover in this study—and in Perry's films in particular—show, healing campaigns often contain narrow conceptualizations of womanhood, contradictory messages about Black women's agency and their propensity to survive trauma, and curricula that shift women's attention away from broader sociopolitical activity. Black women are indirectly taught to be more critical of themselves and other women than other groups are taught. When we encourage students to look at these types of texts, consider them as campaigns, and ask "whose interests are served?" by a particular representation of learning within these extracurricular spaces, we can cultivate the practice of asking the "hard questions," as Pough terms it, that are necessary to promote forms of critical media literacy through rhetorical criticism.

On Voice, Modulation, and Empathy: Putting Healing to Use

Asking "hard questions" of these projects cannot be the end goal if we are to get any everyday use out of Black women's healing discourses because rhetorics of healing and empowerment projects such as the ones in this study can still spark complicated forms of discomfort. I discovered this trend in the midst of a recent attempt to teach Elaine Richardson's memoir *PHD to Ph.D: How Education Saved My Life* in a 300-level cross-listed section of our Women Writers class I named "Learning from Life: Women Writing the Critical Memoir." In what I initially proposed as a hybrid memoir workshop where we would read books such as Audre Lorde's *Zami: A New Spelling of My Name,* Maxine Hong Kingston's *The Woman Warrior,* and Dorothy Allison's *Two or Three Things I Know for Sure,* I aimed to test my hypothesis that (a) women have written their way to forms of healing by theorizing the conditions that wound them, and (b) understanding the writing processes, narrative tasks, and argumentative choices within these memoirs can help students learn how to use life writing in a social way. In short, I wanted to see if my students and I could figure out how women had used the memoir to make theoretical arguments that could instruct other readers.

Based on what I knew of Richardson's then forthcoming memoir and the reading interests of the Black and Latina women who gravitate towards my courses, I decided it would have to be included. As mentioned in chapter 1, Richardson's book describes her childhood in Cleveland, the rape and subsequent abortion she had in her early teens, her descent into teenage prostitution and drug use, the years she spent performing sex work, her experience as a single mother, and the way she eventually earned three college degrees and became a tenured professor. The book is emotionally devastating at times. With vivid language and imagery,

Richardson juxtaposes the social messages she learned from peers and other sources with the forms of life wisdom her Jamaican mother had tried to instill in her. The lessons range from societal beauty preferences toward Black women, the importance of preserving one's self-esteem (beautifully rendered in her mother's saying "shame chree dead"), the street "literacies" necessary for survival, and, ultimately, the "game" one must know to advance through the academy without incurring damage to oneself.

The book's descriptions of sexual abuse and human trafficking prevent it from being a linear-progress narrative. To Richardson's credit, she exemplifies some of the best attributes of self-interrogation that Black women writers, Vanzant included, have advocated by taking wounding and trauma into the realm of possibility by naming the factors that contributed to some of her life circumstances. In one of the most poignant passages of the book, Richardson uses the term "soul sick" to describe the negative consequence that these physical and mental assaults had taken on her throughout much of her youth, writing,

> Ever since I was a little girl, bits of self-love had been creeping out of me daily. Mama and Daddy's big fight. Every time I got the message that "regla" Black girls weren't beautiful. Every time somebody looked at me like they wanted to fuck me. My first date/rape. Every trick I turned. Every betrayal of my loyalty. Every shot of dope. Every beat down. Every dollar I gave Mack or any man. No matter how "down" I was for him, he couldn't love me enough. And how could he? He was just as soul sick as I was. . . . Yes, my family loved me, yes my parents were hard working people, yes they took me to church and taught me right from wrong. But that was never enough . . . for me. Instead of believing who I was, I allowed myself to be defined by people, places and things.[15]

PHD to Ph.D is undoubtedly a memoir about healing because it showcases how a broad sense of self-learning and encouraging models of education can be one cure for overcoming low self-esteem, sexual and physical abuse, and cycles of perpetuating shame. While I did have some initial concerns about exposing students to the depictions of sexual violence within the book, I decided the yield was greater than the risk if I was responsible. It would be the final book of the class.

Despite the challenge of adapting what I envisioned as a twenty-person hybrid workshop course for the forty-person cross-listed, 300-level

Women Writers survey that I was assigned, and that, according to my department's curriculum, was supposed to give students an introduction to a literary tradition, I felt confident that my course plan would work. As I saw it, my pedagogical task was to guide students in establishing frames for understanding the craft of the memoir, identifying how these texts function as social arguments, and critiquing their effectiveness according to the experiences of a diverse group of women writers. After some deliberation between Sue Silverman's *Fearless Confessions: A Writer's Guide to Memoir* and Vivian Gornick's *The Situation and the Story: The Art of the Personal Narrative,* I chose Gornick's book as our primary craft text because it focuses on memoir reading as a step towards memoir writing. According to Gornick, memoirs reflect the writer's sense of obligation to excavate from the raw material of his or her life a narrative that will "shape experience, transform events," or "deliver wisdom" to readers.[16] The two-fold task of the memoirist is to address the question of "Who am I?" and discover "How did I become this way?" When done effectively, memoir writing becomes a way for a writer to achieve self-definition by moving away from what Gornick describes as the "murk of being told who you are by the accident of your circumstance," or your conditions I would contend, "toward the clarity that identifies accurately the impulses of the self."[17]

Gornick's conception of the memoir corroborated so much of the focus on "self-definition" I discovered while researching rhetorics of healing that I saw in her efforts to guide future memoir writers the basis of a heuristic we could use to identify the personal and political function of these texts. She suggests that readers must first imagine the narrator as an individual in movement and then consider the narrator as an "instrument of illumination" on a task of reflection and discovery. The writers' task, in this instance, is to rigorously "penetrate the familiar" details of their lives, identify their "situation," or their specific context and life circumstance, locate a form of "tension" or conflict by way of a specific moment or urgency, demonstrate "modulation" or emotional as well as chronological movement, and deliver the "story" or the emotional experience, wisdom, or insight the writers feel compelled to share.[18] From these conventions, I introduced a basic set of criteria for understanding these texts. It involved students looking for

1. The readers' sense of thoughtful introspection, or a purpose for revisiting one or more moments of "tension" within the "situation" of their lives.

2. A state of modulation, or a focus on internal movement, that shows the narrator working to clarify her perspective on the world and the way she understands her motives and behaviors. The narrator is learning at this point and moving towards what we in the class call an "aha!"
3. An identifiable "inner resolution" that suggests the readers have achieved some form of "self-knowledge" or "self-definition" that will better enable them to navigate and change their situation.

Since this was my first time teaching this course and I had no evidence that this framing approach would work, I stressed to my students that these conventions were one way to read memoirs and that they would offer us a common way to talk about them together.

The course progressed well. In the first unit on the craft of the memoir, we read Daniel Mendelsohn's brief history "But Enough About Me: What Does the Popularity of Memoirs Tell Us About Ourselves?", Barbara Christian's "The Race For Theory," and Gornick's book. During a substantially longer second unit, we situated memoirs within feminist literary-criticism history by reading Virginia Woolf's *A Room of One's Own*—a text I introduced as the first memoir to constitute feminist literary criticism—and then complicated Woolf's privilege and arguments by reading criticism by Fanny Fern, George Elliot, Joanna Russ, Adrienne Rich, and Alice Walker. By the time we got to the third unit on brief memoir excerpts, students seemed fairly adept at applying Gornick's conventions and concepts such as Rich's "revision." To prepare students for the fourth unit featuring Dorothy Allison's memoir, we reviewed concepts such as "social construction" and screened the majority of the *Showtime* adaptation of Allison's *Bastard Out of Carolina*.

Based on my class's reactions during the film, I held several discussions about perspectives on social class, whiteness, poverty according to geographic region, and sexuality—since more than half of the students were native New Yorkers or were from families of Latino/a and Caribbean descent who expressed a lack of familiarity with depictions of southern poverty. This contextualizing seemed to work as they began to acknowledge the adverse effects of poverty and the ways it made Allison's already humble beginnings worse. As we discussed *Two or Three Things I Know For Sure*, they expressed appreciation for Allison's use of the photograph as a way to engage in revision and "modulation" and found the statements she would make at the end of each section as evidence that she had experienced the all important "aha" about how life had shaped her and the work she could do to overcome these situations. By and large, they found the book an achievement.

Due to some of the content matter in *PHD to Ph.D*, I devoted the first part of the final unit to addressing context, conditions, and craft. We began by screening one of Richardson's YouTube videos describing her journey and discussed her professed motive of making sure her daughters and other women avoid the path she had taken. After having screened the documentary *The Souls of Black Girls* and having had what I thought was a frank and honest conversation about the destructive impact of colorism, I introduced Richardson's own concept of the "Black Rhetorical Condition." I used the concept in relation to the portrayal of Patsy in the then recently released *12 Years a Slave* to give them some additional grounding in the idea of being "desired and devalued" in relation to the control that Black women have had exerted over their bodies, and I raised issues of human trafficking. We ended the preliminary stages of the final unit with a discussion of bell hooks's essay "On Self-Recovery" in *Talking Back: Thinking Feminist, Thinking Black*. Not only does hooks make self-care a rhetorical act by explaining how language is a "place of struggle" and a means for Black women to "recover-ourselves—to rewrite, to reconcile, to renew," but she also acknowledges the need for women to be discerning in how they navigate the "voices that speak in and to us" if they are to reach a state of critical consciousness.[19] By all accounts, I thought I had set the stage for a discussion of Richardson's book as a critical memoir.

Given the lively discussion we had about the first three chapters, I assumed I had succeeded. My Caribbean and Latino/a students in particular expressed their familiarity with "Laney's" mother's sayings, relishing as they read aloud scenes featuring the narrator's mother in their versions of Jamaican patois. Many of my Black students compared the narrator's discussions of her childhood in Cleveland with their own experiences in Brooklyn, Queens, and other parts of New York City. As a whole, the class expressed what I interpreted as their understanding of assaults on her self-esteem that the narrator experienced through teasing and observations about her male peers' beauty preferences when it came to Black girls and women. During our discussion of Laney's first sexual assault and the obvious depression she experienced after aborting the pregnancy, they voiced what appeared to be respectful sympathy and some shared stories of young women they knew who had experienced similar encounters. Based on reflections such as the following one by

Denny, a Black transgender male, I assumed they understood the role of social conditioning in Richardson's book. As Denny writes,

> Both the rape and the abortion destroyed her already low self-esteem and placed her in a position where she would allow herself to be talked into anything if she felt someone was valuing her. Although she is trying to stay out of trouble, she is searching for her position and her worth in all the wrong places, and thus she is unable to. The only thing that really become[s] clear is the fact that while her environment had some folks that would try to keep her on the straight and narrow there were many more factors that would play in the hardships she would come to endure.

Melissa, a white female, also seemed to interpret a set of social and internal family conflicts that threatened the narrator's development of positive self-esteem. She, however, went on to consider the influence of environment and how it shaped the narrator's actions and choices, writing that

> the first tension I recognized was the description of the projects that she grew up in. She says, "No grass would grow there. Hardly anything or anyone could grow there without being torn down." Without saying much, Richardson reveals that her childhood was not a place of growth or sustainability. Her environment sets up a tension or a barrier for people, and herself, to succeed. The second tension is more of a personal conflict or identity crisis. One conflict in regards to her family occurs . . . when her parents fight. She writes, "that was the only fight they ever had, though it lasted all of our lives. And we just lived over it." This not only is a physical conflict but one that held its power in the family, so much so that it was never discussed and they all went about their lives.

Since the rest of the class made similar observations about this aspect of Richardson's childhood, I assumed that they were prepared for the rest of the journey she would take in the book.

What I did not anticipate was the lengths some of my female students of color would go to distance themselves from Laney and her story once the time came to discuss the middle portions of the text wherein Richardson describes her double life as high-school student and teenage prostitute. A mere forty-eight hours earlier, some of these young women had regaled the class with their observations about peer social and sexual pressure, Caribbean parenting, and negative beauty standards. Yet, when we got to a portion of *PHD to Ph.D.* where the narrator decides to go back to Andrew, the teenage pimp who had attacked her and launched her into prostitution, there was no discussion of memoir conventions, close reading, or even research documenting how frequently women who experience domestic violence go back to their lovers, adequate enough to cut through the air of respectability and dissemblance that swept through the room. In a huff, one Latina student exclaimed, "I'm tight! I can't with her" and descended into a discussion of parenting. Most of the male students and the white females in the class continued to talk, but the majority of the Black women fell into silence, offering little more than expressions of confusion and disappointment before they just stopped talking at all.

Although feminist rhetoricians such as Krista Ratcliffe have helped us refine the way we understand classroom resistance to uncomfortable discussions about race and gender with concepts such as rhetorical listening, different challenges may await those of us who aim to put vernacular projects or Black women's healing narratives and life writing to everyday pedagogical use.[20] As I drove home from class the evening after my talkative, young women of color students fell into nearly complete silence, I knew a different kind of crisis had emerged. I had not put my female students of color on the spot by asking them to respond to Richardson's book as though they were some type of cultural spokesperson speaking for all Black people or Black women. I had not told them that they had no grounds to critique or question Richardson's text, albeit I can confess that my investment in the work as one of the only full-length memoirs from a woman of color to end up on my syllabus was probably clear to them as well. My hope was that their questions would create opportunities for us to talk about the conditions that make life writing so vital for women who have experienced trauma, the craft of telling one's own story, and the possibilities of self-knowledge. I selfishly wanted them to continue engaging throughout Richardson's text and to stay in the journey with her, particularly since they had already demonstrated that they could use genre conventions and they found Allison's memoir completely legible, accessible, and worthy of their sympathy and understanding.

When I put to practice what Ratcliffe calls "listening pedagogically" or applying a kind of deep attention to and analysis of students' resistance and silence, I realized that their resistance was possibly a reflection of the same kinds of shame that Richardson overcomes in her book.[21] Based on their excitement during the first class discussion of the book, it is very plausible that my female students of color were deeply identifying with Richardson's book and using it as a way to bring their own experiences into the classroom in a way they assumed the entire class would welcome. They had certainly seemed to enjoy assuming the authoritative role during our early discussions. Listening to their silence when we got midway through Richardson's book taught me a profound lesson—even when teachers make space for such discussions as Black women's healing narratives in racially diverse classroom settings and instruct students on how to establish a critical reading lens that pay attention to context, craft, and the race, gender, and class conditions that impact writers, readers, and subjects of a text—that forms of discomfort and shame may still flare up that wound and impede how Black women and individuals in other historically marginalized communities see themselves as readers, critics, and citizens within these learning spaces. Sometimes, a performance of respectability is the result as students resort to drawing attention to how different they are from the events that they encounter in a text. On other occasions, it is an apathy that I imagine may come from seeing on the page the realities of people they may know or illustrations of events they may have experienced. In either case, the practice of distance is a result that requires us to reassess our approach to these kinds of painful and uncomfortable scenarios. If we, as teachers, let these types of silences fester under the assumption that we are avoiding triggers or keeping our students comfortable, we are complicit in keeping certain experiences, voices, and people out of our learning spaces even when we've made gestures to include this content on our syllabi.

A pedagogy that helps us to take advantage of rich but overlooked conversations such as Black women's healing and anticipates the kinds of discomfort these texts can produce must foster a language of critical empathy. The step towards empathy that is one of the best outcomes of rhetorical healing and other endeavors towards empowerment can come from adopting a writer's mindset. After scrambling to figure out how I could intervene in the remaining class discussions and reclaim the energy from the first session, I eventually resolved to introduce the concepts of the "voice of innocence" and the "voice of experience" that Sue Silverman describes as *Fearless Confessions*. Unlike Gornick, Silverman sees memoir writing as a way to interrogate motives, not just to understand *how* we become the way we are but to determine *why* we make the decisions we do. The "voice of innocence" is raw emotion.[22] It offers an unmediated account of an event and details without analysis or clarification. Conversely, the "voice of experience" offers insight and critique. It reveals the writer's maturity and the "progression" of his or her thoughts.[23] Silverman argues that when a writer fuses both voices well, a reader will "willingly follow" the writer through the "maze" of the text and, ultimately, gain insight into the "beautiful—if sometimes wrenching—pattern to it all."[24] Coupled with Gornick's framework, Silverman's concepts of voice offer a fresh way to look at a genre such as the memoir, which can sometimes be dismissed among more civically oriented composition teachers as expressivist writing, in critical as well as socially situated ways that recognize the rhetorical competence of a writer.

Naming patterns is one of the first steps towards this type of critical empathy. Teaching Silverman's concepts mid-unit helped steer my students away from silence because the act of listening for these two voices seemed to help close some of the space that the students who began to disengage had placed between themselves and Laney. By the end of the third class session devoted to discussion *PHD to Ph.D.*, they had started to identify the number of times the narrator said such phrases as "had I been in my right mind," "had I had the sense God gave me," and most explicitly, "this is insane." Though these seem like small gestures, I considered them a sign of progress because they indicated that students were moving from silent resignation to active attempts to identify with Richardson again through understanding her choices within context. In their final reflections, several of the students took the concept of "voice" as a way to think more about Richardson's technique as a strategy. Destiny, a Black female student, attempted to name and theorize the journey Richardson takes to wellness by coining the term "limbo." According to her definition, limbo is a state of suspension which

> happens in the everyday life. People battle with themselves (their current state and where they hope to see themselves). This struggle makes things more truthful and believable because essentially "nothing comes easy" and can be harder for people of color and women. "Limbo" provides veracity in the written memoir, not only for the reader but the writer as well. "Limbo" will also highlight the "aha" and show a direct connection between the "aha" and the modulation. With this technique in place, readers will interpret the text as something they can see themselves being a part of. The text becomes realistic to the reader just based on social beliefs of success and struggle.

Destiny's response does not contain the specific vocabulary writers such as Ntozake Shange developed decades earlier when she coined the term "metaphysical dilemma" to describe some Black women's plight. However, by analyzing Richardson's book as a rhetorical argument and naming the effects of her writing, Destiny moves in this critical direction. Her observation that adverse situations happen in "everyday life," for example, implies an awareness of systemic conditions; and her explanation that struggles are "harder for people of color and women" indicates an awareness of intersecting oppressions that influence the sometimes self-destructive choices people make that can impede their own wellness. Additionally, with her discussion of "veracity," Destiny acknowledges the kinds of hegemonic reading and listening practices that can make audiences less than sympathetic to the testimonies and personal narratives of historically disempowered groups. In this instance, Destiny gives her own name to the burden of the "writer's task" that Royster theorizes as constraint to Black women's rhetorical practice by describing the challenge of breaking the silence with ethos and authority.

Using genre criticism, one of the male students in the class gave an analysis of Richardson's book that also reflects an important move towards empathy. For Evan, Richardson's book illustrates a practice he calls "false clarification." As he explains,

> in *PHD to Ph.D.*, it was necessary for Richardson to include such events as her abortion to her encounters with pimps to her time in college as it all worked towards a final clarification. Yet, do not be fooled. In a memoir, modulation can suggest that clarification has already happened when it hasn't yet. For example, when Richardson had her abortion, it seemed as if she reached a place of self-knowledge that would make her focus only on school. This is not the case because she has encountered a false clarification. She has not arrived yet to a full understanding of how her social factors affected her.

To be fair, Evan does not acknowledge here how young Richardson was when the assault occurred. At the same time, his use of the term "false clarification" demonstrates a move towards critical engagement that we should strive to cultivate among our students. Building on the concept of modulation, he uses the term to place readers' expectation of tidy, linear, or respectable progress narratives into a more realistic context. He goes on to to explain that without modulation the reader would be unable to see the evolution of the author in the numerous events that led to the development of the self-definition of who the author is. But it is also necessary in the memoir because it helps the author see how they developed as a person. With modulation, a writer like Richardson can see that through the events they encountered, they developed to the person they are today and that allows them to be comfortable with who they are as well.

It may seem presumptuous for any undergraduate student to offer what amounts to an attempt at a diagnosis given the grave situations that are described in Richardson's book. Even so, Evan's explanation of "false clarification" is still important. As he explained during one of the early class conversations about *PHD to Ph.D.*, he was not a person of color and he had not grown up in circumstances similar to the majority of the students of color in the class; thus, it may have been easier for him to employ silence as a way to negotiate what Ratcliffe describes as a "speaking" or "writing block" that can happen when members of dominant groups lack the frameworks or lexicon to engage with matters of gender, race, class, and, in this instance, trauma.[25] His use of the word "comfort" here indicates a possible shift in his own investment. Although he begins the second portion of his response by discussing how writers should compose as a means of demonstrating their progress to the reader, he ends by stressing the importance in the writer's self-knowledge and ability to make peace with the decisions and struggles he or she has encountered. At its best, Evan's passage suggests his transition from the role of spectator and evaluative reader to empathetic and engaged listener because he wants to know and ensure that the writers know whether or not they are well. Ultimately, the passage suggests that we can centralize the experiences of Black women and other non-dominant groups and still teach members of dominant groups how to stay in the conversation when silence may seem easier and teach them how to engage these matters and narratives with sensitivity and respect.

A Final Assessment

We never fully regained the enthusiasm of the first class when we discussed Richardson's book, and I am not sure if end-of-the-semester fatigue or other factors were the cause. We also did not get to discuss whether the students saw in Richardson's embrace of education a form of healing in the same way that they were able to discern it in Allison's book—although the majority of the students agreed that choosing to invest in education had saved her life, leading me to think they may have come to this conclusion. I suspect that this lingering question is the point though. Black women have always been telling their stories and teaching themselves how to be well even when no one recognized this tradition and long before this tradition was coopted. The concepts of "limbo" and "false clarification" that Destiny and Evan developed show us that our work as scholars and teachers is to cultivate the vision to understand these stories and movements and to figure out how to listen, "really listen" as Pough states, to the voices within them even when they offer narratives we may not want to hear or see.

I am slow to call this healing work or to suggest that we do not have existing pedagogical models for bringing these kinds of commitments to our teaching. My aim in this book is not to provide definitive answers about the kinds of wellness strategies Black women need. Instead, my goal is to argue that we must pay attention to projects such as healing, empowerment, and wellness that show us the systematic ways African Americans go about solving social problems, and we need to generate critical models that recognize the agency of individuals who seek them out for themselves and may need them most. We need these practices of vision and voice if we, as scholars and teachers, consider positive social change a goal of our work because the concepts of allyship, assistance, and advocacy that we imagine as ideal outcomes of civic and rhetorical education are rooted in the relationships we have with each other, the compassion we show, and the ways we listen, identify, and empathize. Staying mindful of this goal keeps us sensitive to the power of discourse to construct subjectivity and to shape the way individuals understand the literacies and rhetorics they rely on in the practice of their everyday lives. Being well and promoting the wellness of others can begin with care.

Reverberations

Parallel to the commercialized attempts at healing I analyze in this book, Minnie Ransom's question and advice still reverberates in dialogues about contemporary Black women's wellness. *The Feminist Wire* is one of a number of periodicals that outline proactive and preventative steps women of color can take to remain well as they are socialized to place their familial duties, financial responsibilities, or personal relationships before themselves and their desires and they encounter various racialized micro-aggressions. In November 2012, the magazine featured a symposium addressing self-care measures for Black women, featuring essays such as Shanesha Brooks-Tatum's "Subversive Self-Care: Centering Black Women's Wellness" and Erica Lorraine Williams's "A Black Academic Woman's Self-Care Manifesto" where both writers consider myths of Black women's inordinate strength and reaffirm the inward turn.

Conferences have also become important formalized gathering spaces where Black women are proactively educating themselves about matters of sustainable living and growth. Founded by Lisa Peyton-Caire in 2008, Black Women's Wellness Day is a yearly health event and summit aimed at empowering women with the resources to live lives centered on their individual physical health and well-being.[1] Similarly, what began as a grassroots gathering of Black women interested in matters of wholeness in 2010 has evolved into the National Black Women's Life Balance and Wellness Conference. The yearly event draws hundreds of women to Atlanta to hear guest speakers and participate in workshops and breakout sessions on matters of holistic healing, writing as therapy, and fitness matters.

At the institutional level, Black women are also prioritizing matters of wellness and sustainability. In 2012, Dr. Beverly Tatum made the controversial decision to eliminate the athletics program at Spelman

College, the prestigious, historically Black women's institution in Atlanta. Citing the number of women suffering with diabetes, hypertension, obesity, and stress-related ailments as inspiration, Tatum decided to replace the small yet increasingly expensive athletics program with the Spelman wellness initiative. The campus-wide effort involved a renovation of the athletic facilities and a host of daily fitness classes designed to help the women of Spelman become "soldiers in the wellness revolution."[2]

Contemporary Black women singers are also addressing matters of wellness. On her sophomore album entitled *Recovery*, neo-soul artist Algebra Blessett takes listeners on a sonic journey to healing. In the song "Writer's Block," she describes how challenging the task of composing can be and the types of physical and emotional ailments that women develop when they invest in perfectionism or allow the expectations of others have power over them. Blessett does not include overt references to race or class, but her performance in the neo-soul aesthetic invokes the musical contributions of socially conscious women artists such as India Arie and Erykah Badu who explicitly endorse Black women's self-care. Ultimately, Blessett instructs her listeners that the only way to overcome their fear of rejection is to let go of their work and expose themselves to the world.[3] Vulnerability can be a source of strength.

Television screenwriters and producers are also exploring the range of issues and assumptions that can threaten Black women's sense of personal wellness. In comedies and dramas, screenwriters have challenged the dichotomies between the outward demeanors of strength many Black women are portrayed as having and their internal vulnerability. They have also shown the formal as well as unexpected ways Black women seek out solutions to personal crises and wounding. Under the direction of show creator Mara Brock Akil, writers for the BET Networks comedy *The Game* took a departure from its traditional ensemble focus format in August 2013 with an episode entitled "In Treatment." The episode focused solely on the out-of-character decision of leading female character, Tasha Mack, to visit a therapist in order to make sense of failed social and romantic relationships. The character eventually realizes the hardened demeanor she practices in her family and romantic relationships stems from the class-based shame and anger she harbors over being rejected as a teen-mother by her child's father. The subtle message within Mack's insistence on reaching this realization during a day-long session is that Black women cannot rush the process of healing or therapy.

The writing staff of Akil's breakout BET Networks series *Being Mary Jane* also characterize the show's protagonist in ways that push viewers to consider the types of masks Black women wear to conceal their disenchantment with their states of life and the ways they perform their social roles. Although the show's Atlanta-based news-anchor protagonist Mary Jane Paul is an image of upper-middle class sophistication and achievement, behind the mask and against the self-help affirmations and proverbs she writes on Post-it Notes and displays throughout her home, she still struggles to have healthy family, professional, and romantic relationships in ways that make her character flaws believable and sympathetic. As Mary Jane comes to terms with the inordinately high standards she places on her family, the show advances the message that wellness and happiness for Black women cannot be achieved through affair, career achievement, or Post-it Notes alone.

These discussions, and the dialogues they inspire, show us that the traditions of social, narrative, pedagogical, and independent wellness efforts that Black women have developed in pursuit of liberation are reverberating. Indeed, to channel the late Barbara Christian who cited Black women's use of "pithy language to unmask power relations" as evidence that they were always "a race for theory," these ongoing conversations and independent efforts suggest Black women are also a race for healing.[4] This race hasn't stopped and it cannot stop because if it does, Black women lose the right to define for themselves what wellness and healing can and should be.

I am in this race for healing because my goal as an educator and in all things is to get understanding. This search for understanding made me run to the altar of the Richmond Coliseum in April 1999. At that time, I was a first-generation college junior who went home once a month to play the piano for my church's youth choir but was still intensely private about the religious traditions I had grown up practicing. Somehow my college girlfriends managed to chip away at that reserve by that Friday night in April, and I agreed to go with them to hear T.D. Jakes preach to thousands in attendance about the importance of discovering the "destiny" of one's life. The message stirred me in a powerful way, and later that night, I read over the packet of literature he gave those of us who wanted to know more about how to set our lives on course. To this day, I can still hear his voice.

I was searching for understanding in my mid-twenties when I discovered that my same college girlfriends were turning to Vanzant's books. They were seeking some kind of understanding about how they should deal with their disappointments over the slow pace of their career growth and the then unnamed micro-aggressions they were encountering at work and in other social scenarios. I had a different crisis. I was dealing with the internal shame of being in a relationship everyone else assumed was good with a man everyone else assumed was right. It wasn't. That relationship was hurting me. Somehow though, the same books could address our dissimilar forms of hurt. For better or worse, we were all just trying to be the superwomen we had been led to think we were supposed to be.

I thought I had an understanding of the function of the vernacular and the power of representation on African Americans' lives until one afternoon back in 2006 when I walked into a Charlottesville, VA, *Target*. My mother had given me one assignment that day: pick up a copy of *Madea's Family Reunion,* which had been released on DVD that week. My task was nearly complete when I was stopped in my tracks at the cash register. The very nice white cashier began to gush about how much she loved Perry's films and, before I could chime in that I liked many of them too, she launched into a full-on imitation of Madea replete with her best attempt at the character's dialect. What I thought was a private or underground phenomena clearly was not.

I knew, though, that I had to get a deeper understanding of healing and some clarity about the assumptions embedded in the term and what it can involve one afternoon in 2013 after a phone conversation with my aunt. She was going through a painful divorce from her husband of more than twenty years, and she would call me periodically to talk. When she called that day, she began to tell me about the second job she had taken to cover the expenses she was now responsible for and the late hours she had to work. "Sometimes I get home after midnight and I have started to journal." She couldn't have known how cool I found that prospect. "Writing makes the pain go away," she said.

I know it's a start. That's why I will stay in this race.

Notes

Life Class: An Introduction

Epigraph: Eva Illouz, *Oprah Winfrey*, 24.

1. The phrase "better happier, bigger, richer" and "more fulfilling" appeared in promotional emails for the launch of *Lifeclass*. The phrase also appears on the OWN *Lifeclass* youtube site: <https://www.youtube.com/playlist?list=PLFAF0H GlvTj4gAh3WqikVaY1bPZOte6iU>

2. Kathryn Lofton, "Practicing Oprah," 603.

3. Here, I refer to Janice Peck's essay "The Secret of Her Success: Oprah Winfrey and the Seductions of Self-Transformation" and Kathryn Lofton's "Practicing Oprah," wherein both scholars situate the religious and self-help aspects of the talk show host's career in psychosocial histories.

4. I use the terms African American and Black interchangeably throughout this book. I do so in an effort to be in conversation with the authors who have written about people of African descent and to acknowledge my own alternating use of these terms

5. Lofton, "Practicing Oprah," 599.

6. I attribute the discussion of habitus, which Illouz relies on to interpret Winfrey's show, to Pierre Bourdieu's concept of habitus in *La Distinction: Critique Sociale du Jugement*. Bourdieu conceptualizes power as a cultural and symbolic creation that is reinstated and legitimized through a relationship between agency and structure. These processes produce a habitus, or worldview and set of intentions and rituals, that guide the way individuals feel and act.

7. Eva Illouz, *Oprah Winfrey and the Glamour of Misery*, 21.

8. Ibid., 149.

9. Thomas Miller, "Lest We Go the Way of the Classics," 18.

10. Ibid., 18.

11. Elaine Richardson, *African American Literacies*, 33.

12. See Logan's "Free Floating Literacy" chapter in *Liberating Language*.

13. Jacqueline Jones Royster, *Traces of a Stream*, 42.

14. Dana L. Cloud, *Control and Consolation in American Culture and Politics*, 15.

15. Illouz, *Oprah Winfrey*, 19.

16. See Nan Johnson's *Gender and Rhetorical Space in American Life: 1866–1910* and Shirley Wilson Logan's *Liberating Language: Sites of Rhetorical Education in Nineteenth-Century Black America* for more discussions of historical attitudes about the civic nature of reading.

17. Elaine Richardson and Ronald L. Jackson, *African American Rhetoric(s)*, x.

18. Malea Powell, "Down by the River," 58.

19. K.A. Ono and J.M. Sloop, "The Critique of Vernacular Discourse," 19.

Chapter 1: Are You Sure You Want to Be Well? Healing and the Situation of Black Women's Pain

Epigraph: Toni Cade Bambara, *The Salt Eaters*, 3–4.

1. Toni Cade Bambara, *The Black Woman: An Anthology*, 13.
2. Ibid., xi.
3. Ibid.
4. Kimberly Nichele Brown, *Writing the Revolutionary Black Diva*, 190.
5. bell hooks, *Sisters of the Yam*, 11.
6. Ibid., 11.
7. Patricia Hill Collins, *Black Feminist Thought*, 112.
8. Athena Vrettos, "Curative Domains," 458.
9. Ibid.
10. Zora Neale Hurston, *Mules and Men*, 195.
11. Ibid., 193.
12. Ibid., 195.
13. Ibid.
14. See Gay Wilentz's book *Healing Narratives: Women Writers Curing Cultural Dis-ease* for a more extensive discussion.
15. Vrettos, "Curative Domains," 455.
16. Ibid.
17. Ibid.
18. Keith Gilyard, "A Legacy of Healing," 99.
19. In this instance, I am referring to the section of Morrison's novel wherein Sethe is challenged to recall the last memories of her mother. When she does, Sethe remembers as a child seeing a woman lynched. In an effort to determine if the woman was in fact her mother, Sethe ran to the body in search of the identification symbol her mother had previously shown her before Nan, a fellow slave who also spoke her mother's African language, grabbed her. Undoubtedly, this instance is an example of traumatic memory loss, but I also see it as further evidence of how the brutality of slavery alienated African Americans from their traditional African languages.
20. Toni Morrison quoted in Gilyard, "A Legacy of Healing," 104.
21. Ibid., 99.
22. Ntozake Shange, *For Colored Girls*, 4.

NOTES TO CHAPTER 2

23. Jarrett, quoted in McDowell, *The Changing Same*, 120.
24. Ibid., 103.
25. Darryl Pinckney, "Black Victims, Black Villains," 81.
26. In *African Americans and the Culture of Pain*, Debra King references Elaine Scarry's work on trauma and the body as an example of how women compose trauma differently than men do. Scarry argues that "pain is the unsayable. It is that which cannot be spoken, although it can be signified through supplementation" in her book *The Body in Pain*, 20.
27. Debra King, *African Americans*, 16.
28. Ibid., 20.
29. Shange, *For Colored Girls*, 17–19.
30. Ibid., 19.
31. Ibid., 20.
32. Collins, *Black Feminist Thought*, 119.
33. Ibid., 299.
34. Alice Walker, *The Color Purple*, 283.
35. Duchess Harris, *Black Feminist Politics*, 64.
36. For a full definition of "womanish" that I draw upon here, see "womanish" in accordance with Walker's famous definition of "womanist" in her collection *In Search of Our Mother's Gardens: Womanist Essays and Prose*.
37. Kimberly Nichele Brown offers a more thorough discussion of the backlash against Alice Walker and other contemporaries in the prelude to her book *Writing the Black Revolutionary Diva: Women's Subjectivity and the Decolonizing Text*.
38. Clarke, "Lesbianism: An Act of Resistance," in *Words of Fire: An Anthology of African American Feminist Thought*, ed. Beverly Guy Sheftall, 242–51.
39. Royster, *Traces of a Stream*, 22.
40. Audre Lorde, *Sister Outsider: Essays and Speeches*, 145–75.
41. Lorde, "Eye to Eye: Black Women, Hatred, and Anger," in *Sister Outsider*, 155.
42. Ibid., 145.
43. Lorde, *Sister Outsider*, 150 and 147.
44. Elaine Richardson, *PHD to Ph.D.*, 2.
45. Lorde, "Eye to Eye," in *Sister Outsider*, 147.
46. Brown, *Writing the Black Revolutionary Diva*, 190.
47. Beth Daniell, *A Communion of Friendship*, 55.
48. Mark Hall, "The 'Oprahfication' of Literacy," 649.

Chapter 2: I Need You to Survive: Theorizing Rhetorical Healing

1. James Cone, *The Spirituals and the Blues*, 9.
2. Ibid., 5.
3. Anis Bawarshi, *Genre and the Invention of the Writer*, 30.
4. Ibid.
5. Carolyn Miller, "Genre as Social Action," 151.

6. Manning Marable and Leith Mullings, *Let Nobody Turn Us Around*, 6.
7. Geneva Smitherman, *Talkin and Testifyin*, 76.
8. Ibid., 73.
9. W.E.B. Du Bois, *The Souls of Black Folk*, 2.
10. Richardson, *African American Literacies*, 33.
11. Ibid., 35.
12. Marable and Mullings, *Let Nobody Turn Us Around*, 7.
13. See Hannah Arendt, *The Human Condition* (Chicago: University of Chicago Press, 1958) and Jürgen Habermas, *The Structural Transformation of the Public Sphere: An Inquiry into a Category of Bourgeois Society*, trans. Thomas Burger (Cambridge, MA: MIT Press, 1989) for extended discussions of the public sphere.
14. See Nancy Fraser's "Rethinking the Public Sphere: A Contribution to the Critique of Actually Existing Democracy," 56–80 for her take on this discussion.
15. Michael Warner, *Publics and Counterpublics*, 56.
16. Ibid, 56.
17. Vorris Nunley, *Keepin' It Hushed*, 283.
18. Ibid., 23.
19. Pough's definition of "wreck" as a practice of disruption that Black women use to break into public discussions emerges in relation to the concept of the Black public sphere that scholars such as Houston A. Baker, Elizabeth Alexander, and Michael C. Dawson defined and explored in *The Black Public Sphere: A Public Culture Book* (Chicago: University of Chicago Press, 1995) wherein the scholars rework the term to acknowledge a "critical social imaginary" that exists through the material spaces, texts, and specific discourse forms African Americans use to shape and reshape their lives.
20. Gwendolyn Pough, *Check It While I Wreck It*, 225.
21. Adam Banks, *Digital Griots*, 125.
22. Ibid.
23. Footage from this *Lifeclass* episode segment appears at http://www.oprah.com/oprahs-lifeclass/Lesson-8-When-You-Know-Better-Video.
24. See James Paul Gee's "The New Literacy Studies and the 'Social Turn,'" for a more extensive conversation of this scholarly term.
25. Royster, *Traces of a Stream*, 45.
26. Richardson, *African American Literacies*, 35.
27. Ibid.
28. Lindsey, quoted in Bambara, *The Black Woman*, 85.
29. Bambara, *The Black Woman*, xi.
30. Combahee River Collective, quoted in Hull, Bell-Scott, and Smith, *All the Women Are White*, 13.
31. Ibid., 14.
32. Collins, *Black Feminist Thought*, 9.
33. Ibid.
34. Joy James, *Shadowboxing*, 79.
35. Ibid., 92.

36. Ellen Cushman, *The Rhetorician as an Agent of Social Change*, 23.
37. Royster, *Traces of a Stream*, 26–31.

Chapter 3: I'll Teach You to See Again: The Rhetoric of Revision in Iyanla Vanzant's Self-Help Franchise

1. See Lee Hernandez, "Evelyn Lozada, 'Basketball Wives' Star, Writes a Letter to Her 7-Year-Old Self: 'I Will Try to Be Better,'" *Huffington Post*, June 5, 2012.
2. Iyanla Vanzant, *The Value in the Valley*, 73–75.
3. See Five East's open letter at http://fiveeast.tumblr.com/post/36029709439/open-letter-to-iyanla-vanzant.
4. Vanzant, *Interiors*, 405.
5. Anna Julia Cooper, *A Voice From the South*, 31.
6. Rebecca Wanzo, *The Suffering Will Not Be Televised*, 10.
7. Micki McGee, *Self-Help, Inc.*, 7.
8. James Anderson, *The Education of Blacks in the South, 1860–1935*, 17.
9. Heather Andrea Williams, *Self-Taught: African American Education in Slavery and Freedom*, 5.
10. Ibid., 75.
11. Ibid.
12. Sandra Dolby, *Self-Help Books: Why Do Americans Keep Reading Them*, 23.
13. Shirley Wilson Logan, *Liberating Language*, 54.
14. Ibid.
15. Ibid.
16. Vanzant, *Interiors*, 406.
17. Ibid.
18. Dolby, *Self-Help Books*, 8.
19. Ibid., 12.
20. See Cooper, *A Voice From the South* and Du Bois, *The Souls of Black Folks* for insight into these early manifestations of Afrocentric education.
21. Molefi Asante, *The Afrocentric Idea*, 1998.
22. Michael Rowland, "African Americans and Self-Help Education," 2.
23. Jesse Jackson, "Keep Hope Alive," 535–38.
24. Boogie Down Productions, "Self-Destruction."
25. Shahrazad Ali, *The Blackman's Guide*, 6.
26. Ibid., viii.
27. Ali, quoted in Vanzant's "Fighting Words," 55.
28. Yeye Olade, "Shahrazad Ali Points Finger at Black Women," *Seattle Times*, December 3, 1990.
29. Haki R. Madhubuti, ed., *Confusion by Any Other Name*, 15.
30. Vanzant, "Fighting Words," 55.
31. Ibid.
32. Ibid.

33. Ibid.

34. In his dissertation, "A Litany For Survival: Black Queer Literacies," Eric Darnell Pritchard expands on Royster's discussion of mandates explaining that Black women's literacy was always "mandated" to seek socio-political change for themselves and their communities. Mandates, in this instance, refer to these and other types of obligations that are "felt to be imposed on the learning, meaning, and uses of a person's 'literacy,' while still recognizing that mandates are interpreted and taken up through the will or agency of the individual" (5).

35. Royster, *Traces of a Stream*, 82.

36. As Kenneth Burke describes in his 1953 book, *A Rhetoric of Motives*, rhetorical identification occurs through the rhetor's creation of consubstantiality. He explains:

> In being identified with B, A is "substantially one" with a person other than himself. Yet at the same time he remains unique, an individual locus of motives. Thus he is both joined and separate, at once a distinct substance and consubstantial with another. . . . For substance, in the old philosophies, was an act; and a way of life is an *acting-together*; and in acting together, men have common sensations, concepts, images, ideas, attitudes that make them *consubstantial*. (21)

37. I use the term "situated ethos" to refer to what Sharon Crowley describes as the "existence of power relationships within the environmental context, which bolster a communicator's communicative ability, or . . . typically compromise it" (cited in Royster, 64). As Royster acknowledges, the greater the disparity between the "situated status of the writer and her audience, the greater the gap that must be traversed in order to communicate effectively and, given this model, to construct effectively consubstantial space for rhetorical engagement" (64).

38. Dolby, 22.

39. Ibid., 38.

40. Vanzant, *Tapping the Power Within*, 20.

41. Ibid., i.

42. Ibid., ii.

43. Carter Woodson, *The Mis-Education of the Negro*, 151.

44. Hill, "The Miseducation of Lauryn Hill."

45. Lincoln, quoted in Bambara, *The Black Woman*, 98.

46. Vanzant, *Tapping the Power Within*, iii–iv.

47. Ibid., v.

48. Collins, *Fighting Words*, 36–37.

49. The fuller segment of June Jordan's "Poem about My Rights": "*I am not wrong: Wrong is not my name /* My name is my own my own my own / and I can't tell you who the hell set things up like this / but I can tell you that from now on my resistance / my simple and daily and nightly self-determination / may very well cost you your life" (309).

NOTES TO CHAPTER 4

50. In *Sister Citizen: Shame, Stereotypes, and Black Women in America* (28), Melissa Harris-Perry uses the metaphor of the crooked room to signify an atmosphere of distorted stereotypes and policies that oppress women.

51. Vanzant, *Interiors,* 401.
52. Ibid., 401.
53. Ibid., 402–3.
54. Ibid., 406–8.
55. Ibid., xi.
56. Ibid., 406.
57. Vanzant, *The Value in the Valley,* 32.
58. Vanzant, *Tapping the Power Within,* 44.
59. Ibid., 64.
60. Vanzant, *Interiors,* 404.
61. Bambara, *The Black Woman,* 134.
62. James Pennebaker, *Opening Up: The Healing Power of Expressing Emotions,* 50.
63. Daniell, *A Communion of Friendship,* 45.
64. Bambara, *The Black Woman,* 134.
65. Richardson, *African American Literacies,* 75.
66. Video footage containing segments of this episode of *Fix My Life* is available through an internet search, but Akoto Ofori-Atta's November 2013 article for the online magazine *The Root,* entitled "That Time Iyanla Vanzant Accused a Rape Victim of 'Hoeing' and No One Cared," is a substantive summary of this incident.
67. Vanzant, *Tapping the Power Within,* 68.
68. Ibid., 71.
69. Ibid., 64–66.
70. Ibid., 64.
71. Vanzant, *Up From Here,* 19.
72. McGee, *Self-Help, Inc.,* 157.
73. hooks, *Sisters of the Yam,* 40.
74. Logan, *Liberating Language,* 34.
75. hooks, *Sisters of the Yam,* 4.
76. hooks, *Talking Back,* 38; and Collins, *Fighting Words,* 89.
77. Logan, *Liberating Language,* 4.
78. Lorde, *Sister Outsider,* 41.

Chapter 4: Come Ye Disconsolate: The Rhetoric of Transformation in T.D. Jakes's Women's Ministry

Epigraph: "Come Ye Disconsolate."

2. *Woman Thou Art Loosed,* directed by Michael Schultz. Dallas, TX: Magnolia Pictures, 2004.

3. *Fireproof, Facing the Giants,* and *Courageous* are the three latest releases from Sherwood Pictures, an independent film company that developed as an extension of the media ministry at Sherwood Baptist Church in Albany, Georgia.

4. Julie Lyons, "A bishop's book becomes a powerful movie about hypocrisy and salvation," 23.

5. Ibid.

6. "Thousands of Women Set to Gather," *Culvert Chronicles*, September 2011, 15.

7. Eddie Glaude, "The Black Church Is Dead," 8.

8. Shayne Lee, *T.D. Jakes,* 6.

9. Ibid.

10. Martha Simmons, "Trends in the African American Church," 13.

11. Ibid.

12. Nunley, "From the Harbor to Da Academic Hood," 223.

13. Evelyn Brooks Higginbotham, *Righteous Discontent,* 9.

14. Frazier, quoted in Higginbotham, 14.

15. Beverly J. Moss, *A Community Text Arises,* 22.

16. Ibid.

17. Ibid.

18. LaTonya Taylor, "Jakes on the Loose."

19. Lyons, "A bishop's book," 23.

20. Bynum, "No More Sheets." A version of sermon is available at https://www.youtube.com/watch?v=A4VpzfsEjN4.

21. Bynum, *No More Sheets: The Truth about Sex.*

22. Smitherman, *Talkin and Testifyin,* 87.

23. Higginbotham, *Righteous Discontent,* 1.

24. Here I am referencing Mary Church Terrell's often quoted statement, "Lifting as We Climb," which was the motto of the National Association of Colored Women. Paula Giddings discusses the formation of this organization in *When and Where I Enter: The Impact of Black Women on Race and Sex in America* (New York: Harper Collins, 1984), 94.

25. Grant, quoted in Hull, Bell-Scott, and Smith, *All the Women Are White,* 141.

26. Roxanne Mountford, *The Gendered Pulpit,* 98.

27. Tamelyn Tucker-Worgs, *The Black Megachurch,* 134.

28. Grant, quoted in Hull, Bell-Scott, and Smith, *All the Women Are White,* 142.

29. Mountford, 98.

30. As Audre Lorde explains in her oft-cited essay, "Age, Race, Class, and Sex: Women Redefining Difference," one of the misconceptions that hurt early women's liberation efforts was the tendency of white women to focus on their oppression as women and ignore differences of race, sexual preference, class, and age. Assuming there was a "pretense to a homogeneity of experience covered by

the word *sisterhood* that did not in fact exist," white women's subscription to the belief that there was a hierarchy of oppressions is one factor that contributed to the development of pluralized conceptions of feminism (114–23).

31. Tucker-Worgs, *The Black Megachurch*, 135.
32. Ibid., 135.
33. Cone, quoted in Grant, 145.
34. Katie Cannon, *Katie's Canon*, 114.
35. Ibid., 114.
36. A description of *Woman Thou Art Loosed!: Healing the Wounds of the Past* can be found here: https://books.google.com/ books/about/Woman_Thou_Art _Loosed.html?id= HcbJpK2FamcC.
37. Ibid., 33.
38. Ibid., 33.
39. Ibid., 17.
40. Moss, *A Community Text Arises*, 65.
41. Ibid.
42. Dolby, *Self-Help Books*, 13.
43. Romans 12:2 (King James Bible),
44. Jakes, *Woman Thou Art Loosed*, 30.
45. Ibid., 15.
46. Ibid.
47. In *Language as Symbolic Action*, Burke explains that any nomenclature necessarily directs the "attention into some channels rather than others" (45). In this capacity, terms reflect reality, however simultaneously select and deflect reality (45). Terministic screens direct our attention and thereby influence our understanding/perception of reality (45). They are inherently useful because "we can't say anything without the use of terms; whatever terms we use, they necessarily constitute a corresponding kind of screen; and any such screen necessarily directs the attention to one field rather than another (50).
48. Ibid., 45.
49. Jakes, *Woman, Thou Art Loosed!*, 18.
50. Ibid., 16.
51. In its emphasis on the importance of the nuclear, heterosexual family as a means of community survival, the Black church and its most conservative leaders have been criticized for perpetuating narrow, rigid, and exclusive views towards individual identity. Claims that the traditional Black church is homophobic remain the most frequent complaint. A number of academics such as Mark Anthony Neal in *New Black Man*, (2005) examine and critique the existence and practice of heterosexism and homophobia in the Black church; and fiction writers such as E. Lynn Harris in *I Say a Little Prayer* (2007) provide fictional accounts of bisexual members within the Black church.
52. Lloyd Bitzer, "The Rhetorical Situation," 8.
53. Ibid.

54. Monya Aletha Stubbs, "Be Healed," 306.
55. David Van Biema, "Spirit Raiser" *Time*, September 2001, 52.
56. See the description of *Daddy Loves His Girls* on Google Books: https://books.google.com/books?id=f5utAAAACAAJ&dq=editions:l912sPDm7OQC&hl=en&sa=X&ved=0ahUKEwjCvbSQ-tHLAhXEcz4KHVZNB4UQ6AEIKDAC.
57. Jakes, *Daddy Loves His Girls*, 6.
58. Ibid., 2
59. Ibid.
60. Lyndrey Niles, "Rhetorical Characteristics of Traditional Black Preaching," 47.
61. Ibid.
62. Jakes, *Daddy Loves His Girls*, 9.
63. Ibid., 27.
64. Ibid., 20.
65. Inger Askehave, If Language Is a Game, There Are Rules, 19.
66. Romans 12:2 (King James Bible).
67. Jakes, *Woman, Thou Art Loosed!*, 18.
68. Ibid., 139.
69. Ibid., 23–25.
70. McGee, *Self-Help*, 157.
71. Jakes, *Woman, Thou Art Loosed!*, 36.
72. Ibid., 81.
73. Ibid., 113.
74. The biblical story of Tamar and Amnon is often taught as an example of man's lust. Amnon, King David's son, was so enraptured by his half sister Tamar that he seduced and raped her. Later Absalom, Tamar's brother, enacted revenge on Amnon by killing him.
75. Jakes, *Woman, Thou Art Loosed*, 63–64.
76. Ibid., 64.
77. Jakes, *Daddy Loves His Girls*, 102.
78. Ibid., 105.
79. Ibid., 105.
80. Ibid., 105.
81. Ibid., 105.
82. *Woman Thou Art Loosed* film.
83. King James Bible, Matthew 28:19.

Chapter 5: Take Your Place: The Rhetoric of Return in Tyler Perry's Films

1. In a 2009 blog entry entitled "We're all PRECIOUS in His Sight," posted at http://www.tylerperry.com/messages/were-all-precious-his-sight/, Perry explained that the focus on forgiveness in his work is a result of his own abusive

upbringing. He urges his fans to try forgiveness, writing, "If you're having a hard time getting over something in your life, maybe you can try forgiveness too. It's not easy, but it does bring forth healing."

2. Rodney Thrash, "Playing to Their Crowd," 1.

3. Ibid.

4. For additional critical discussions of Perry's films see Benjamin Svetkey, Margeaux Watson, and Alynda Wheat's 2009 *Entertainment Weekly* essay, "'Madea': Bad for black America?: Tyler Perry: The Controversy Over His Hit Movies"; Robert Patterson's 2011 essay "Woman, Thou Art Bound: Critical Spectatorship, Black Masculine Gazes, and Gender Problems in Tyler Perry's Movies" in *Black Camera: An International Film Journal*; and LeRhonda S. Manigault-Bryant, Tamura A. Lomax, and Carol B. Duncan's recently released edited anthology *Womanist and Black Feminist Responses to Tyler Perry's Productions* (Palgrave MacMillan, 2014).

5. Courtney Young, "Tyler Perry's Gender Problem," 1.

6. Springer, "Divas, Evil Black Bitches, and Bitter Black Women," 249.

7. Timothy Lyle, "Check With Yo' Man First; Check With Yo' Man," 945.

8. Ruth La Ferla, "Sometimes Piety Isn't Squeaky Clean," 1.

9. See "Tyler Perry Transforms: From Madea to Family Man." *Fresh Air*, National Public Radio. October 2012, http://www.npr.org/2012/10/15/162936803/tyler-perry-transforms-from-madea-to-family-man.

10. Henry Giroux, "Breaking into Movies: Pedagogy and Politics of Film," 585.

11. Ibid.

12. Collins, *Black Feminist Thought*, 75.

13. Perry, *Don't Make Me Take Off My Earrings*, ix.

14. For more insight into the controversy of the 2007 National Black Theatre Festival, see "Black Theatre Festival Disses Tyler Perry, " 9 August 2006, www.youtube.com /watch?v=KIWM6XSn17Y.

15. Mel Watkins, *On the Real Side*, 365.

16. Ibid., 387.

17. Pough, *Check It While I Wreck It*, 16.

18. Thrash, "Playing to Their Crowd," 1.

19. Jacqueline Bobo, *Black Women as Cultural Readers*, 69–72.

20. Tyler Perry, *Madea's Family Reunion*.

21. David Howard-Pitney, *The African American Jeremiad*, 2005.

22. hooks, *Yearning*, 42.

23. Ibid., 44.

24. Ibid.

25. Perry, *Don't Make Me Take Off My Earrings*, vii.

26. Ibid., x.

27. Here I am referencing the Senator Daniel Patrick Moynihan's infamous report on the status of the Black family; it is a report that numerous feminist and

critical race scholars see as an indictment of Black women as the source of social problems within African American communities.

28. Perry, *Diary of a Mad Black Woman*.
29. Ibid.
30. Ibid.
31. hooks, *Talking Back,* 39.
32. I intentionally paraphrased the scripture Mark 8:36, which states, "What doth it profit a man to gain the world and lose his soul?" A similar sentiment is inherent in the idea that "money can't buy you love."
33. Kenneth Burke, *A Grammar of Motives,* 8.
34. Perry, *Diary of a Mad Black Woman*.
35. Springer, "Divas, Evil Black Bitches, and Bitter Black Women," 266.
36. Karla Holloway, *Codes of Conduct,* 31.
37. Ibid.
38. Ibid., 32.
39. Perry, *Diary of a Mad Black Woman*.
40. Perry, *Madea's Family Reunion*.
41. Richardson, "To Protect and Serve," 86.
42. hooks, *Yearning,* 45.
43. Ibid.
44. Perry, *Diary of a Mad Black Woman*.
45. Perry, *Diary of a Mad Black Woman: The Play*.
46. Williams, *Black Pain,* 117.
47. Perry, *Madea's Family Reunion*.
48. Perry, *Diary of a Mad Black Woman*.
49. Ibid.

Chapter 6: With Vision and Voice: Black Women's Rhetorical Healing in Everyday Use

1. Harvey, *Act Like a Lady,* 9.
2. Ibid., 1.
3. For footage and commentary from this debate, see "Video: ABC's Nightline Tackles Issue of Single Black Women," *Eurweb.com*, last modified April 22, 2010, http://www.eurweb.com/2010/04/video-abcs-nightline-tackles-issue-of-single-black-women/.
4. For a response about these concerns over marriageability, see Jamilah King and Noelle de la Paz's October 31, 2011 *Colorlines* appearance, "Three Feminists Talk About the Media's Obsession With Unwed Black Women," http://colorlines.com/articles /three-feminists-talk-about-medias-obsession-unwed-black-women.
5. Millner, "You're All I Need," 126.
6. I am invoking Ann Ruggles Gere's well-known term "extracurriculum" of composition here from her essay "Kitchen Tables and Rented Rooms: The

Extracurriculum of Composition," *College Composition and Communication* 45.1 (1994):75–92.

7. Jamilah King and Noelle de la Paz, "Three Feminists Talk about the Media's Obsession with Unwed Black Women."

8. A number of scholars have defined the term but I prefer Jessica Enoch's definition of rhetorical education in *Refiguring Rhetorical Education: Women Teaching African American, Native America, and Chicano/a Students, 1865–1911* (Carbondale, IL: Southern Illinois University Press, 2008), 172 because it accounts for the behavioral, communicative, and mental expectations that are encoded through the term "citizen."

9. Pough, "It's Bigger than Comp/Rhet: Contested and Undisciplined." *CCC* 63.2 (December 2011), 308.

10. Ibid., 309.

11. The Black Lives Matter movement is a multi-dimensional social and political effort to assert the humanity of African Americans in the wake of police violence. Birthed out of a social media hashtag that developed in response to the murder of Trayvon Martin in the summer of 2013, the movement has evolved from protests, awareness campaigns, social-media dialogues, marches, and scholarly efforts.

12. Jonathan Alexander and Jacqueline Rhodes, "Flattening Effects: Composition's Multicultural Imperative and the Problem of Narrative Coherence," *College Composition and Communication* 65.3 (February 2014): 441.

13. Wanzo, *The Suffering Will Not Be Televised*, 11.

14. In *Sista, Speak!: Black Women Kinfolk Talk about Language and Literacy* (Austin, TX: University of Texas Press, 2002), 3–5, Sonja Lanehart outlines three ideologies about literacy use among Black women in her family. The ideology of opportunity promotes the belief that literacy acquisition and "standard" English grants societal benefits. The ideology of progress asserts that those who are literate or those who speak "standard" English will (1) overcome the adversities and shortcomings of a deprived or deficient culture that does not use "standard" English or value literacy, and (2) develop greater cognitive and logical abilities that will facilitate abstract thought. Finally, the ideology of emancipation purports (1) autonomy, (2) empowerment due to the development of critical thinking, and (3) emancipation (real or symbolic) because of the control one will be able to achieve as a shareholder in what can constitute or lead to real power. In this view, literacy is empowering, transformative, emancipatory, and self-enlightening. It inspires confidence.

15. Elaine Richardson, *PHD To Ph.D.*, 163.

16. Vivian Gornick, *The Situation and the Story*, 91.

17. Ibid., 93.

18. Gornick does not attempt to delineate these terms in the way I did for the purposes of my undergraduate class, but the section of her book devoted exclusively to the memoir (86–165) outlines these concepts in greater detail.

19. hooks, *Talking Back*, 28, 30–32.
20. See Krista Ratcliffe's *Rhetorical Listening: Identification, Gender, Whiteness*.
21. In *Rhetorical Listening*, Ratcliffe defines "listening pedagogically" as a way of practicing what I see as deep sensitivity during classroom engagements to the various ways race, class, gender, and other identity categories impact everyday life. She writes, "Listening pedagogically targets classroom performances of students and teachers. By listening pedagogically, both students and teachers may become more open to hearing one another's metaphors (dead or otherwise) and, perhaps, more willing to celebrate the words of the stories that we all acquire during our lifetime" (134).
22. Sue Silverman, *Fearless Confessions*, 52.
23. Ibid., 53.
24. Ibid., 58.
25. Ratcliffe, *Rhetorical Listening*, 139.

Reverberations

1. More information about Black Women's Wellness Day and the origins of this yearly event can be found at http://www.blackwomenswellnessday.org/.
2. Richard Pérez-Peña, "Spelman Drops Sports to Turn Focus on Fitness," *New York Times* (November 2, 2012), A15.
3. Algebra Blessett, *Recovery*, Entertainment One, 2014.
4. Here I invoke the title of the late Barbara Christian's essay "The Race for Theory," wherein she responds to the focus on theory within literary studies with the assertion that Black women have always been a "race" for theory because of the "pithy" way they have used language to unmask power relations. She suggests that Black women have always been concerned with matters of well-being.

Bibliography

Ahmed, Sara. *The Promise of Happiness.* Durham, NC: Duke University Press, 2010.
Alexander, Jonathan and Jacqueline Rhodes. "Flattening Effects: Composition's Multicultural Imperative and the Problem of Narrative Coherence." *College Composition and Communication* 65.3 (February 2014): 430–53.
Ali, Shahrazad. *The Blackman's Guide to Understanding the Blackwoman.* Philadelphia, PA: Civilized Publications, 1989.
Allison, Dorothy. *Two or Three Things I Know For Sure.* New York: Plume, 1995.
Anderson, James. *The Education of Blacks in the South, 1860–1935.* Chapel Hill, NC: University of North Carolina Press, 1988.
Angry Black Bitch. "But We Can Do Worse With Tyler Perry." September 9, 2009. http://angryblackbitch.blogspot.com/2009/09/but-we-can-do-worse-with-tyler-perry.html.
Arendt, Hannah. *The Human Condition* (1958). Chicago, IL: University of Chicago Press, 1998.
Asante, Molefi. *Rhetoric of Black Revolution.* Boston, MA: Allyn & Bacon, 1969.
———, *The Afrocentric Idea.* Revised and Expanded edition. Philadelphia, PA: Temple University Press, 1998.
Askehave, Inger. "If Language Is a Game—These are the Rules: A Search into the Rhetoric of the Spiritual Self-Help Book." *Discourse and Society* 15.1 (2004): 5–31.
Bambara, Toni Cade, ed. *The Black Woman: An Anthology.* New York: Washington Square Press, 1970.
———, *The Salt Eaters.* New York: Vintage, 1981.
Banks, Adam. *Digital Griots: African American Rhetorics in a Multimedia Age.* Carbondale, IL: Southern Illinois University Press, 2011.
———, *Race, Rhetoric, and Technology: Searching for Higher Ground.* Mahwah, NJ: Erlbaum, 2005.
Bastard Out of Carolina. Directed by Anjelica Houston. New York: Showtime, 1996.

Bawarshi, Anis. *Genre and the Invention of the Writer: Reconsidering the Place of Invention in Composition.* Logan, UT: Utah State University Press, 2003.

Being Mary Jane. Directed by Mara Brock Akil. Los Angeles, CA: BET, 2015.

Bitzer, Lloyd. "The Rhetorical Situation." In *Contemporary Rhetorical Theory: A Reader,* edited by John Louis Lucaites, Celeste Michelle Condit, and Sally Caudill. New York: The Guilford Press, 1999.

"Black Theatre Festival Disses Tyler Perry." YouTube. August 9, 2006. http://www.youtube.com/watch?y=KIMWM6XSn17Y.

Blessett, Algebra. "Writer's Block." *Recovery.* Entertainment One, 2014. MP3.

Bobo, Jacqueline. *Black Women as Cultural Readers.* New York: Columbia University Press, 1995.

Booker, Bobbie. "Vanzant Comes Home to Work." *Philadelphia Tribune.* March 23, 2007, vol. 123, 1D.

Bourdieu, Pierre. *La Distinction: Critique Sociale du Jugement.* Paris: Minuit, 1979.

Brandt, Deborah. *Literacy as Involvement: The Acts of Writers, Readers, and Texts.* Carbondale, IL: Southern Illinois University Press, 1990.

———, *Literacy in American Lives.* New York: Cambridge University Press, 2001.

Brown, Kimberly Nichele. *Writing the Revolutionary Black Diva: Women's Subjectivity and the Decolonizing Text.* Bloomington, IN: University of Indiana Press, 2010.

Browne, Kevin. *Tropic Tendencies: Rhetoric, Popular Culture, and the Anglophone Caribbean.* Pittsburgh, PA: University of Pittsburgh Press, 2013.

Burke, Kenneth. *A Grammar of Motives.* Berkeley, CA: University of California Press, 1969.

———, *A Rhetoric of Motives.* Berkeley, CA: University of California Press, 1969.

———, *Language as Symbolic Action: Essays on Life, Literature, and Method.* Berkeley, CA: University of California Press, 1978.

Bynum, Juanita. *No More Sheets: The Truth About Sex.* Lanham, MD: Pneuma Life Publishing, 2008.

———, "No More Sheets." YouTube. August 3, 2010, https://www.youtube.com/watch?v=A4VpzfsEjN4.

Cannon, Katie. *Katie's Canon: Womanism and the Soul of the Black Community.* New York: Continuum, 1996.

Carby, Hazel. *Reconstructing Womanhood: The Emergence of the Afro-American Woman Novelist.* New York: Oxford University Press, 1987.

Chang, Jeff. *Can't Stop Won't Stop: A History of the Hip-Hop Generation.* New York: St. Martin's Press, 2005.

Christian, Barbara. "The Race for Theory." In *The Black Feminist Reader,* edited by Joy James and T. Denean Sharpley-Whiting, 11–23. London: Blackwell Publishers, 2000.

Cintron, Ralph. *Angels Town: Chero Ways, Gang Life, and the Rhetorics of Everyday.* Boston, MA: Beacon Press, 1998.

Clarke, Cheryl. "Lesbianism: An Act of Resistance." In *Words of Fire: An Anthology of African-American Feminist Thought*, edited by Beverly Guy-Sheftall. New York: New Press, 242–251. 1995.

Cloud, Dana. *Control and Consolation in American Culture and Politics: Rhetoric of Therapy*. New York: Routledge, 1998.

Collier-Thomas, Bettye. *Daughters of Thunder: Black Women Preachers and Their Sermons, 1850–1979*. San Francisco: Jossey-Bass, 1998.

Collins, Patricia Hill. *Black Feminist Thought: Knowledge, Consciousness, and the Politics of Empowerment*. 2nd ed. New York: Routledge, 2000.

———, *Black Sexual Politics: African Americans, Gender, and the New Racism*. New York: Routledge, 2004.

———, *Fighting Words: Black Women and the Search for Justice*. Minneapolis, MN: University of Minnesota Press, 1998.

———, "The Social Construction of Black Feminist Thought." *Signs: Journal of Women in Culture and Society* 14.41 (Summer 1989): 745–73.

"Come Ye Disconsolate." *Timeless Truths Free Online Library*. June 2013.

Cone, James. *The Spirituals and the Blues: An Interpretation*. Maryknoll, NY: Orbis Books, 2003.

Cooper, Anna Julia. *A Voice From the South*. October 2003. http://docsouth.unc.edu/church/cooper/cooper.html 11/1/2005.

Copage, Eric V. *Black Pearls: Daily Meditations, Affirmations, and Inspirations for African Americans*. New York: Amistad, 1993.

Courageous. Director Alex Kendrick. Albany, GA: Sherwood Pictures, 2011.

Cushman, Ellen. "The Rhetorician as an Agent of Social Change." *College Composition and Communication* 47.1 (1996): 7–28.

Daniell, Beth. *A Communion of Friendship: Literacy, Spiritual Practice, and Women in Recovery*. Carbondale, IL: Southern Illinois University Press, 2003.

Diary of a Mad Black Woman. Directed by Darren Grant. Santa Monica, CA: Lions Gate, 2005.

Dolby, Sandra. *Self-Help Books: Why Americans Keep Reading Them*. Urbana, IL: University of Illinois Press, 2005.

Du Bois, W.E.B. *The Souls of Black Folk*. New York: Dover Thrift, 1994.

Enoch, Jessica. *Refiguring Rhetorical Education: Women Teaching African American, Native American, and Chicano/a Students, 1865–1911*. Urbana, IL: Southern Illinois University Press, 2008.

Facing the Giants. Directed by Alex Kendrick. Albany, GA: Sherwood Pictures, 2006.

Five East. "Open Letter to Iyanla Vanzant." http://fiveeast.tumblr.com/post/36029709439/open-letter-to-iyanla-vanzant.

Fireproof. Directed by Alex Kendrick. Albany, GA: Sherwood Pictures, 2008.

Fraser, Nancy. "Rethinking the Public Sphere: A Contribution to the Critique of Actually Existing Democracy." *Social Text* 25/26 (1990): 56–80.

Frazier, E. Franklin. *The Negro Church in America*. New York: Shocken Books, 1974.

Frederick, Marla. *Between Sundays: Black Women and Everyday Struggles of Faith.* Berkeley, CA: University of California Press, 2003.
Ford, Thembi. "An Open Letter to Tyler Perry." September 6, 2009. http://www.thebeautifulstruggler.com/2009/09/open-letter-to-tyler-perry-part-1.html.
Gee, James Paul. *Social Linguistics and Literacies: Ideology in Discourses.* London: Taylor & Francis, 1996.
———, "The New Literacy Studies and the 'Social Turn.'" Eric Database 442 118. February 10, 2010. http://www.schools.ash.org.au/litweb/page300.html.
Gere, Ann. "Kitchen Tables and Rented Rooms: The Extracurriculum of Composition." *College Composition and Communication* 45.1 (1994): 75–92.
Giddings, Paula. *When and Where I Enter: The Impact of Black Women on Race and Sex in America.* New York: Morrow, 1984.
Gilyard, Keith. "A Legacy of Healing: Words, African Americans, and Power." In *Let's Flip the Script: An African American Discourse on Language, Literature and Learning.* Detroit, MI: Wayne State University Press, 1996.
———, *Voices of the Self: A Study of Language Competence.* Detroit, MI: Wayne State University Press, 1991.
Giroux, Henry. "Breaking into Movies: Pedagogy and the Politics of Film." *JAC* 21:3 (Summer 2001): 583–98.
Glaude, Eddie. "The Black Church Is Dead." *Huffington Post,* April 2010. http://www.huffingtonpost.com/eddie-glaude-jr-phd/the-black-church-is-dead_b_473815.html.
Goltz, Dustin Bradley. *Queer Temporalities in Gay Male Representation: Tragedy, Normativity, and Futurity.* New York: Routledge, 2013.
Gornick, Vivian. *The Situation and the Story: The Art of the Personal Narrative.* New York: Farrar, Straus, and Giroux, 2001.
Guy-Sheftall, Beverly. *Words of Fire: An Anthology of African-American Feminist Thought.* New York: New Press, 1992.
Habermas, Jürgen. *The Structural Transformation of the Public Sphere: An Inquiry into a Category of Bourgeois Society.* Edited by Thomas Burger. Cambridge, MA: MIT Press, 1989.
Hall, Mark. "The 'Oprahfication' of Literacy: Reading Oprah's Book Club." *College English,* 65, no. 6 (July 2003): 646–67.
Hamilton, C.V. *The Black Preacher in America.* New York: William Morrow and Company, 1972.
Harris, Duchess. *Black Feminist Politics From Kennedy to Obama.* New York: Palgrave Macmillan, 2011.
Harris, E. Lynn. *I Say a Little Prayer.* New York: Anchor Books, 2006.
Harris-Perry, Melissa. *Sister Citizen: Shame, Stereotypes, and Black Women in America.* New Haven, CT: Yale University Press, 2011.
Harvey, Steve. *Act Like a Lady, Think Like a Man: What Men Really Think About Love, Relationships, Intimacy, and Commitment.* New York: HarperCollins, 2009.

BIBLIOGRAPHY

———, *Straight Talk, No Chaser: How to Find, Keep, and Understand a Man.* New York: Amistad Books, 2012.

Heath, Shirley Brice. *Ways With Words: Language, Life, and Work in Communities and Classrooms.* Cambridge, MA: Cambridge University Press, 1983.

Hernandez, Lee. "Evelyn Lozada, 'Basketball Wives' Star, Writes a Letter to Her 7-Year-Old Self: 'I Will Try to Be Better.'" *Huffington Post.* June 5, 2012.

Higginbotham, Evelyn Brooks. *Righteous Discontent: The Women's Movement in the Black Baptist Church*, 1880–1920. Cambridge, MA: Harvard University Press, 1993.

Hill, Lauryn and Tejmold Nelson. "The Miseducation of Lauryn Hill." *The Miseducation of Lauryn Hill.* Ruffhouse/Columbia, 1998.

Holloway, Karla. *Codes of Conduct: Race, Ethics, and the Color of Our Character.* New Brunswick, NJ: Rutgers University Press, 1995.

Holmes, David. *Revisiting Racialized Voice: African American Ethos in Language and Literature.* Carbondale, IL: Southern Illinois University Press, 2007.

hooks, bell. *Sisters of the Yam: Black Women and Self-Recovery.* Boston, MA: South End Press, 1993.

———, *Talking Back: Thinking Feminist, Thinking Black.* Boston, MA: South End Press, 1989.

———, *Yearning: Race, Gender, and Cultural Politics.* Boston, MA: South End Press, 1990.

Howard-Pitney, David. *The African American Jeremiad: Appeals for Justice in America.* Philadelphia, PA: Temple University Press, 2009.

Hull, Gloria T., Patricia Bell-Scott, and Barbara Smith, eds. *All the Women Are White, All the Blacks Are Men, But Some of Us Are Brave: Black Women's Studies.* Old Westbury, NY: The Feminist Press, 1982.

Hurston, Zora Neale. *Mules and Men.* New York: Harper Perennial Modern Classics, 2008.

I Can Do Bad All By Myself. Directed by Tyler Perry. Santa Monica, CA: Lions Gate Entertainment, 2008.

I Will Follow. Directed by Ava DuVernay. Sherman Oaks, CA: Kandoo Films, 2011.

Illouz, Eva. *Oprah Winfrey and the Glamour of Misery: An Essay on Popular Culture.* New York: Columbia University Press, 2003.

Jackson, Jesse. "Keep Hope Alive." In *Let Nobody Turn Us Around: An African American Anthology,* edited by Manning Marable and Leith Mullings, 535–38. Lanham, MD: Rowman & Littlefield, 2009.

Jakes, T.D. *Daddy Loves His Girls.* Lake Mary, FL: Charisma House, 1996.

———, *God's Leading Lady: Out of the Shadows and into the Light.* New York: Berkley Books, 2002.

———, *Loose That Man and Let Him Go!* Bloomington, MN: Bethany House Publishers, 1996.

———, *The Lady, Her Lover, and Her Lord.* New York: Berkley Books, 1998.

———, *Sacred Love Songs.* INgrooves Fontana/Island, 1999.

———, *Woman, Thou Art Loosed!: Healing the Wounds of the Past*. Minneapolis, MN: Bethany House, 1996.

———, *Woman, Thou Art Loosed: The Novel*. New York: Berkley Books, 2004.

———, *Woman, Thou Art Loosed! Workbook*. Shippensburg, PA: Destiny Image Publishers, 1994.

Jakes, T.D. *Woman, Thou Art Loosed!* Google Books. http://www.msn.com/ http://books.google.com/books?id=FkMYQt8SAQAC&dq=Woman+thou+art+loosed&source=gbs_summary_s&cad=0.

Jakes, T.D. *Woman! Thou Art Loosed: Healing the Wounds of the Past*. August 2010. Google Books.

James, Joy. *Shadowboxing: Representations of Black Feminist Politics*. New York: Palgrave, 1999.

Johnson, Nan. *Gender and Rhetorical Space in American Life, 1866–1910*. Carbondale, IL: Southern Illinois University Press, 2002.

Jones, Vanessa. "T.D. Jakes Lets Loose with His Film About Child Sexual Abuse." *Boston Globe*. October 21, 2004, D1.

Jordan, June. "Poem About My Rights." *Directed by Desire: The Collected Poems of June Jordan*. Port Townsend, WA: Cooper Canyon Press, 2005.

King, Debra. *African Americans and the Culture of Pain*. Charlottesville, VA: University of Virginia Press, 2008.

King, Jamilah and Noelle de la Paz. "Three Feminists Talk About the Media's Obsession With Unwed Black Women." *Colorlines*. October 31, 2011. http://www.colorlines.com/articles/three-feminists-talk-about-medias-obsession-unwed-black-women.

Kynard, Carmen. "'I Want to Be African': In Search of a Black Radical Tradition/African-American Vernacularized Paradigm for 'Students' Right to Their Own Language,' Critical Literacy, and 'Class Politics.'" *College English* 69.4 (March 2007): 360–90.

———, *Vernacular Insurrections: Race, Black Protest, and the New Century in Composition-Literacies Studies*. Albany, NY: SUNY Press, 2013.

La Ferla, Ruth. "Sometimes Piety Isn't Squeaky Clean." *New York Times*. October 14, 2007, late edition.

Lanehart, Sonja. *Sista Speak: Black Women Kinfolk Talk About Language and Literacy*. Austin, TX: University of Texas Press, 2002.

Lathan, Rhea Estelle. "Crusader: Ethel Azalea Johnson's Use of the Written Word as a Weapon of Liberation." In *Women and Literacy: Local and Global Inquiries for a New Century*, edited by Beth Daniell and Peter Mortensen, 59–71. Mahwah, NJ: NCTE, 2007.

———, *Freedom Writing: African American Civil Rights Literacy Activism, 1955–1967*. Urbana, IL: NCTE, 2015.

Lee, Shayne. *T.D. Jakes: America's New Preacher*. New York: New York University Press, 2005.

"Life Lessons—Interview with Tyler Perry." *Beliefnet.com*. September 2008. http://www.beliefnet.com/Entertainment/Celebrities/2008/09/Interview-withTyler-Perry.aspx?p=7.

Lincoln, C. Eric, *The Black Experience in Religion*. Garden City, NJ: Doubleday, 1974.

Lincoln, C. Eric and Lawrence H. Mamiya. *The Black Church in the African American Experience*. Durham, NC: Duke University Press, 1990.

Lofton, Kathryn. "Practicing Oprah, or, the Prescriptive Compulsion of a Spiritual Capitalism." *The Journal of Popular Culture* 39, no. 4 (2006): 599–621.

Logan, Shirley Wilson. *Liberating Language: Sites of Rhetorical Education in Nineteenth Century Black America*. Carbondale, IL: Southern Illinois University Press, 2008.

———, *We Are Coming: The Persuasive Discourse of Nineteenth-Century Black Women*. Carbondale, IL: Southern Illinois University Press, 1999.

Lomax-Reese, Sara. "Inspirational Books Offer Words of Wisdom for African-Americans." *Health Quest*. Chalfont (April 31, 1994): 71–72.

Lorde, Audre. *Sister Outsider: Essays and Speeches*. Trumansburg, NY: Crossing Press, 1984.

Lyle. Timothy. "Check With Yo' Man First; Check With Yo' Man: Tyler Perry Appropriates Drag as a Tool to Recirculate Patriarchal Ideology." *Callaloo* 34, no.3 (2011): 943–58.

Lyons, Julie. "A bishop's book becomes a powerful movie about hypocrisy and salvation." *San Francisco Weekly*. October 20, 2004, 23.8.

Madea's Family Reunion. Directed by Tyler Perry. Lions Gate Pictures, 2006.

Madhubuti, Haki R. *Confusion by Any Other Name: Essays Exploring the Negative Impact of the Blackman's Guide to Understanding the Blackwoman*. Chicago IL: Third World Press, 1992.

Manigault-Bryant, LeRhonda, Tamura Lomax, and Carol B. Duncan. *Womanist and Feminist Responses to Tyler Perry's Productions*. New York: Palgrave Macmillan, 2014.

Mao, LuMing. *Representations: Doing Asian American Rhetoric*. Logan, UT: University of Utah Press, 2008.

McDowell, Deborah. *The Changing Same: Black Women's Literature, Criticism, and Theory*. Bloomington, IL: Indiana University Press, 1995.

McGee, Micki. *Self-Help Inc.: Makeover Culture in American Life*. New York: Oxford University Press, 2005.

Middle of Nowhere. Directed by Ava DuVernay. Sherman Oaks, CA: Kandoo, 2012.

Miller, Carolyn. "Genre as Social Action." *Quarterly Journal of Speech* 70 (1984): 151–67.

Miller, Thomas. "Lest We Go the Way of the Classics: Toward a Rhetorical Future for English Departments." In *Rhetorical Education in America*, edited by Cheryl Glenn, Margaret M. Lyday, and Wendy B. Sharer, 18–35. Tuscaloosa, AL: University of Alabama Press, 2004.

Millner, Denene. "You're All I Need to Get By." *Essence* 40, no. 8 (December 2009): 120–27. *Academic Search Complete*. EBSCO*host* (accessed June 16, 2014).

Morrison, Toni. *The Bluest Eye*. New York: Vintage Books, 2007.

Moss, Beverly J. *A Community Text Arises: A Literate Text and A Literate Tradition in African-American Churches.* Cresskill, NJ: Hampton Press, 2003.

Mountford, Roxanne. *The Gendered Pulpit: Preaching in American Protestant Spaces.* Carbondale, IL: Southern Illinois University Press, 2003.

Moynihan, Daniel Patrick. *The Negro Family: The Case for National Action.* Washington, DC: Department of Labor, Office of Policy, Planning, and Research, 1965.

Neal, Mark Anthony. *New Black Man.* New York: Routledge, 2005.

———, "Why Tyler Perry Matters . . . And Why We Should Be Concerned." *NewBlackMan.* November 9, 2009. http://newblackman.blogspot.com/2009/09/why-tyler-perry-mattersand-why-we.html.

New King James Bible. Grand Rapids, MI: Zondervan. 1992.

Niles, Lyndrey. "Rhetorical Characteristics of Traditional Black Preaching." *Journal of Black Studies* 15, no. 1 (1984): 41–52.

Nunley, Vorris. "From the Harbor to Da Academic Hood: Hush Harbors and an African American Rhetorical Tradition." In *African American Rhetoric(s): Interdisciplinary Perspectives,* edited by Elaine B. Richardson and Ronald L. Jackson, II, 221–241. Carbondale, IL: Southern Illinois Press, 2004.

———, *Keepin' It Hushed: The Barbershop and African American Hush Harbor Rhetoric.* Detroit, MI: Wayne State University Press, 2011.

Olade, Yeye Akilimali Funua Olade. "'Shahrazad Ali Points Finger at Black Women . . . 'For Helping to Destroy Our Black Men!—Sisters This Truth is Bitter But We Must Stop Acting Like Imitation White Girls and Disrespecting Our Black Men.'" *Seattle Times.* December 3, 1990.

Ono, K.A., and J.M. Sloop. "The Critique of Vernacular Discourse." *Communication Monographs* 62 (1995): 19–46.

"Oprah's Lifeclass: Lesson 8: When You Know Better." *Oprah.com.* http://www.oprah.com/oprahs-lifeclass/Lesson-8-When-You-Know-Better-Video.

"Oprah's Lifeclass on The Oprah Winfrey Network." Youtube. July 2016. https://www.youtube.com/playlist?list=PLFAF0HGlvTj4gAh3WqikVaY1bPZOte6iU.

Pariah. Directed by Dee Rees. Universal City, CA: Focus Features, 2011.

Patterson, Robert. "'Woman Thou Art Bound': Critical Spectatorship, Black Masculine Gazes, and Gender Problems in Tyler Perry's Movies." *Black Camera, An International Film Journal* 3.1 (Winter 2011): 9–30.

Peck, Janice. "The Secret of Her Success: Oprah Winfrey and the Seductions of Self-Transformation." *Journal of Communication Inquiry* 34, no. 7 (2010): 7–14.

Pennebaker, James. *Opening Up: The Healing Power of Expressing Emotions.* New York: Guilfold Publication, 1997.

Perez-Pena, Richard. "Spelman Drops Sports to Turn Focus on Fitness." *New York Times.* November 2, 2012. (Web November 16, 2012).

Perry, Tyler. *Don't Make A Black Woman Take Off Her Earrings: Madea's Uninhibited Commentaries on Love and Life.* New York: Riverhead Books, 2006.
———, "We're All Precious in His Sight." *Tyler Perry.Com.* October 3, 2009. http://www.tylerperry.com/messages/were-all-precious-his-sight/.
Perryman-Clark, Staci. "African American Language, Rhetoric, and Students' Writing: New Directions for SRTOL. *College Composition and Communication* 64, no. 3 (February 2013): 469–495.
Peterson, Latoya. "Is Tyler Perry the Right Man to Tell Black Women's Stories?" September 4, 2009. http://jezebel.com/5352723/is-tyler-perry-the-right-man-to-tell-black-womens-stories.
Petry, Ann. *The Street.* New York: Mariner Books, 2011.
Pinckney, Darryl. "Black Victims, Black Villains." *New York Review of Books.* (January 29, 1987): 81.
Pough, Gwendolyn. *Check It While I Wreck It: Black Womanhood, Hip-Hop Culture, and the Public Sphere.* Boston: Northeastern University Press, 2004.
———, "It's Bigger than Comp/Rhet: Contested and Undisciplined." *College Composition and Communication* 63, no. 2 (December 2011): 301–22.
Powell, Malea. "Down by the River, or How Susan La Flesche Picotte Can Teach Us About Alliance as a Practice of Survivance." *College English* 67 (2004): 38–60.
Pritchard, Eric Darnell. "A Litany For Survival: Black Queer Literacies." Order No. 3314337, University of Wisconsin-Madison, 2008.
———, "'Like Signposts on the Road': The Function of Literacy in Constructing Black Queer Ancestors." *Literacy in Composition Studies* 2, no. 1 (2014): 29–53.
The Public Sphere Collective. *The Black Public Sphere: A Public Culture Book.* Chicago, IL: University of Chicago Press, 1995.
Rand, Erin. *Reclaiming Queer: Activist and Academic Rhetorics of Resistance.* Tuscaloosa, AL: University of Alabama Press, 2014.
Ratcliffe, Krista. *Rhetorical Listening: Identification, Gender, Whiteness.* Carbondale, IL: Southern Illinois University Press, 2005.
Richardson, Elaine. *African American Literacies.* New York: Routledge, 2002.
———, *PHD to Ph.D.: How Education Saved My Life.* Philadelphia, PA: New City Community Press, 2013.
Richardson, Elaine and Ronald L. Jackson. *African American Rhetoric(s): Interdisciplinary Perspectives.* Carbondale, IL: Southern Illinois University Press, 2004.
Rowland, Michael. "African Americans and the Self-Help Revolution: A Missing Link in Adult Education." Adult Education Research Conference, July 2001. 1.
Royster, Jacqueline Jones. *Traces of a Stream: Literacy and Social Change Among African American Women.* Pittsburgh, PA: University of Pittsburgh Press, 2000.

Scarry, Elaine. *The Body in Pain: The Making and Unmaking of the World.* Oxford, UK: Oxford University Press, 1987.
"Shahrazad Ali on Donahue (1990)." YouTube. November 20, 2009. http://www.youtube.com/watch? v=Oqt2BcV5xbA&feature=channel.
"Shahrazad Ali on Geraldo (1990)." YouTube. May 19, 2009. http://www.youtube.com/watch?v=6tCJbAs0TrY&feature=channel_page.
"Shahrazad Ali on Sally Jesse Raphael (1990)." YouTube. April 16, 2008. http://www.youtube.com/watch?v=jzXR8rTjnEo.
Shange, Ntozake. *For Colored Girls Who Have Considered Suicide When the Rainbow is Enuf.* New York: Scribner, 1995.
———, *Sassafrass, Cypress, & Indigo: A Novel.* New York: Picador, 1982.
Silverman, Sue. *Fearless Confessions: A Writer's Guide to Memoir.* Athens, GA: University of Georgia Press, 2009.
Simmons, Martha. "Trends in the African American Church." *The African American Pulpit* 10, no. 2 (Spring 2007): 9–13.
Smitherman, Geneva. *Talkin and Testifyin: The Language of Black America.* Detroit, MI: Wayne State University Press, 1977.
Springer, Kimberly. "Divas, Evil Black Bitches, and Bitter Black Women: African American Women in Postfeminist and Post-Civil-Rights Popular Culture." In *Interrogating Postfeminism: Gender and the Politics of Popular Culture*, edited by Yvonne Tasker and Diane Negra, 249–75. Durham, NC: Duke University Press, 2007.
Staples, Robert. "The Myth of Black Macho: A Response to Angry Black Feminists." *Black Scholar* (March–April 1979): 26–27.
Strauss, Bob. "The Many Faces of Tyler Perry." *San Bernadino County Sun.* February 19, 2009.
Street, Brian. *Cross-Cultural Approaches to Literacy.* Cambridge, UK: University of Cambridge Press, 1993.
Stop the Violence Movement. "Self-Destruction." Jive, 1989.
Stubbs, Monya Aletha. "Be Healed: A Black Woman's Sermon on Healing through Touch." In *My Soul is a Witness: African-American Women's Spirituality*, edited by Gloria Wade Gayles, 305–13. Boston, MA: Beacon Press, 2002.
Svetkey, Benjamin. Margeaux Watson, and Alynda Wheat. "'Madea': Bad for black America?: Tyler Perry: The Controversy Over His Hit Movies." *Entertainment Weekly.* March 19, 2009. http://www.ew.com/ew/article/0,,20266223,00.html?print.
Tavris, Carol. *The Mismeasure of a Woman.* New York: Touchstone, 1992.
Taylor, LaTonya. "Jakes on the Loose." *Christianity Today.* September 28, 2004. http://www.christianitytoday.com/movies/interviews/tdjakes.html.
Taylor, Susan. *In the Spirit.* New York: Amistad, 1993.
———, *Lessons in Living.* New York: Double Day, 1995.
The Black Public Sphere Collective. *The Black Public Sphere: A Public Culture Book.* Chicago, IL: University of Chicago Press, 1995.

BIBLIOGRAPHY

Temptation: Confession of a Marriage Counselor. Directed by Tyler Perry. Santa Monica, CA: Lions Gate Entertainment, 2013.

The Family That Preys. Directed by Tyler Perry. Santa Monica, CA: Lions Gate Entertainment, 2008.

The Game. Directed by Mara Brock Akil. Los Angeles, CA: Akil Productions, 2013.

"The Year of the Black Author." *Black Enterprise.* (February 1995):116.

Thrash, Rodney. "Playing to their crowd." *St. Petersburg Times.* November 6, 2004, D2.

"Thousands of Women Set to Gather For a Life Changing Experience: Bishop T.D. Jakes Announces the 2011 'Woman Thou Art Loosed!' Conference." *Culvert Chronicles.* September 2011, 15.

Tucker-Worgs, Tamelyn. *The Black Megachurch: Theology, Gender, and the Politics of Public Engagement.* Waco, TX: Baylor University Press, 2011.

12 Years a Slave. Directed by Steve McQueen. Century City, CA: Fox Searchlight Pictures. 2013.

"Tyler Perry Transforms: From Madea to Family Man." *Fresh Air.* National Public Radio. October 2012. http://www.npr.org/2012/10/15/162936803/tyler-perry-transforms-from-madea-to-family-man.

Van Biema, David. "America's best: Spirit raiser—preacher." *Time* 158:11. September 17, 2001, 52–55.

Vanzant, Iyanla. "Fighting Words: 'The Blackman's Guide to Understanding the Black Woman." *Essence.* September 1990, 55.

———, *In the Meantime: Finding Yourself and the Love You Want.* New York: Simon & Schuster, 1999.

———, *Interiors: A Black Woman's Healing in Progress.* New York: Harlem River Press, 1995.

———, *One Day My Soul Just Opened Up: 40 Days and 40 Nights Toward Spiritual Strength and Personal Growth.* New York: Touchstone, 1998.

———, *Tapping the Power Within: A Path to Self-Empowerment for Women.* New York: Harlem River Press, 1992.

———, *The Spirit of Man: A Vision of Transformation for Black Men and the Women Who Love Them.* San Francisco, CA: HarperCollins, 1996.

———, *The Value in the Valley: A Black Woman's Guide Through Life's Dilemmas.* New York: Simon & Schuster, 1995.

———, *Up From Here: Reclaiming the Male Spirit: A Guide to Transforming Emotions into Power and Freedom.* New York: HarperCollins, 2002.

Van Biema, David. "America's best: Spirit raiser—preacher." *Time* 158:11. September 17, 2001, 52–55.

"ABC's Nightline Tackles Issue of Single Black Women," *Eurweb.com.* http://www.eurweb.com/2010/04/video-abcs-nightline-tackles-issue-of-single-black-women/.

Villanueva, Victor. "Colonial Memory and the Crime of Rhetoric: Pedro Albizu Campos." *College English* 71, no. 6 (July 2009): 630–39.

Vrettos, Athena. "Curative Domains: Women, Healing and History in Black Women's Narratives." *Women's Studies* 16 (1989): 455–73.

Walker, Alice. "Everyday Use." *In Love and Trouble.* Orlando, FL: Harcourt Brace, 2003.

———, *In Search of Our Mothers' Gardens: Womanist Prose.* New York: Harcourt Brace, 1983.

———, *The Color Purple.* San Diego, CA: Harcourt Brace Jovanovich, 1982.

Wallace, Michelle. *Black Macho and the Myth of the Superwoman.* New York: Verso Classics, 1990.

Walton, Jonathan. *Watch This: The Ethics and Aesthetics of Black Televangelism.* New York: New York University Press, 2009.

Watkins, Mel. *On the Real Side: Laughing, Lying, and Signifying—the Underground Tradition of African-American Humor that Transformed American Culture, from Slavery to Richard Pryor.* Chicago, IL: Lawrence Hill Books, 1995.

———, "Sexism, Racism, and Black Women Writers." *New York Times Book Review* 35 (June 15, 1986): 1.

Wanzo, Rebecca. *The Suffering Will Not Be Televised: African American Women and Sentimental Political Storytelling.* Albany, NY: SUNY Press, 2009.

Warner, Michael. *Publics and Counterpublics.* New York: Zone Books, 2005.

Wilentz, Gay. *Healing Narratives: Women Writers Curing Cultural Dis-ease.* Piscataway, NJ: Rutgers University Press, 2000.

Williams, Delores. "*Womanist* Theology: Black Women's Voices." *Christianity and Crisis* (March 2, 1987).

Williams, Heather Andrea. *Self-Taught: African American Education in Slavery and Freedom.* Chapel Hill, NC: University of North Carolina Press, 2007.

Williams, Terrie. *Black Pain: It Just Looks Like We're Not Hurting.* New York: Simon & Schuster, 2008.

Woman Thou Art Loosed. Directed by Michael Schultz. Dallas, TX: Magnolia Pictures, 2004.

Woman Thou Art Loosed: On the 7th Day. Directed by Neema Barnett. Dallas, TX: TDJ Enterprises, 2012.

Woodson, Carter. *The Mis-Education of the Negro.* Chicago, IL: African American Images, 2000.

Young, Courtney. "Tyler Perry's Gender Problem." *Nation.* August 13, 2009.

Young, Morris. *Minor Re/Visions: Asian American Literacy Narratives as a Rhetoric of Citizenship.* Carbondale, IL: Southern Illinois University Press, 2004.

Index

abolitionists, 36, 88, 89
abortion, 153, 158, 162
abuse and trauma: Black pain, concept of, 22–23, 170n26; Black women's healing as cure for, 46–47; literacy and writing, therapeutic aspects of, 3–4, 7–9, 21, 71–73, 113, 152; oppression as cause of, 18–19; social struggles, blaming Black women for, 66–67, 90–91; women's behavior as cause of, 105–109
acceptance and affirmation: benefits of emphasis on, 6, 74–75, 139; men's vs. women's affirmation, 139–140; positive opportunities, recognizing and seizing, 138–140; self-esteem and self-acceptance, 25, 27–28, 84, 98–101
accountability and responsibility: gender and responsibility, encoded messages about, 149–150; nationalist discourses on, 56–58; public shaming of women's behavior, 68, 72–73; resilience of Black women and silencing pain, 137–138; self-determination and individual accountability, 67–68; self-education and, 54; self-healing and feelings of, 109; social struggles, blaming Black women for, 66–67, 90–91; writing processes supporting, 104
action taking: essay writing as call for, 26–27; individual action and societal miseducation, 63–64, 66; literacies as resource for, 7, 41, 146–148; positive opportunities, recognizing and seizing, 138–140; rhetorical competence and, 46; self-action, emphasis on, 67–69; wellness campaigns as resource for, 148; writer's task, concept of, 46, 162

Act Like a Lady, Think Like a Man: What Men Really Think about Love, Relationships, Intimacy (Harvey), 143–144, 146, 152

Acts of Faith: Meditations for People of Color (Vanzant), 61

affirmation. *See* acceptance and affirmation

affirmation language, 74
Afrafemme worldview, 15–16, 44
African American habitus, concept of, 4–5, 169n5

African American Literacies (Richardson), 6, 34

African American rhetorical traditions. *See also* Black vernacular culture and spaces: Black preaching, 4, 13, 79, 82–86, 88, 90, 96, 97, 100; counterlinguistic strategies, 19, 34, 51; hush habor rhetoric, 37; jeremiad, 63, 122, 179, 199; relanguaging strategies, 19, 34, 51; signifyin', 42, 129, 206

African American Rhetorics: Interdisciplinary Perspectives (Richardson and Jackson), 10

195

African Americans and the Culture of Pain (King), 22, 170n26
African Methodist Episcopal (AME), 88
African traditions: healing conjurers and restorative agency, 17–20; spirituality and church traditions, 84; traditional languages, alienation from, 19–20, 170n19
African worldview, 34
Afrocentricity (Asante), 56
"Age, Race, Class, and Sex: Women Redefining Difference" (Lorde), 176n30
agency: of Black female protagonists in film, 119–120; Black women's *vs.* community needs, 65–66; choosing wellness solutions and, 11, 24, 27, 29, 44, 147; essay writing as call to action for, 26–27, 41; expressive agency and language, 19–20; healing conjurers and restorative agency, 18–20; individual agency, 20, 46–47, 66; intellectual resistance and agency, 12, 53–57, 120; literacy as sociopolitical action, 40–43; sexual and social agency, narratives of, 50–51, 120–121; of writers, 46–47; writer's choice and problem solving, 46–47; writing as self-empowerment, 17, 25, 181n14
Ahmed, Sara, 8
Akil, Mara Brock, 166–167
Al-Anon, 29, 72
Alexander, Elizabeth, 172n19
Alexander, Jonathan, 150
Ali, Shahrazad, 58–61, 65, 69, 95
Allen, Richard, 84, 88
Allen, William Francis, 31
Allison, Dorothy, 153, 156–157, 159, 164
ambition and opportunity, emphasis on, 112–113, 123–124
American dream, 22, 53
American Horror Story: Coven (TV show), 18
Amnon (biblical character), 106, 178n74

analytical processes. *See also* teaching models for healing: context in worldviews and interpretation, 33–35; rhetorical healing, approach to, 6–7
Anderson, James, 53
anti-apartheid efforts, 57
anti-male discourses, 21–22, 25–26, 29
Arendt, Hannah, 36, 172n13
Are You Still a Slave? (Ali), 58
Arie, India, 166
Asante, Molefi Kete, 10, 56
Askehave, Inger, 102
audience construction: assumptions on audiences, 151–152; biblical scriptures for, 67–68, 94–95, 110; in Black Women's Literary Renaissance, 22; homogenization and audience identification, 51–52, 75, 150–151; personal testimonies for, 67–68
autonomy: antifeminist thoughts on, 58; of Black female protagonists in film, 119–120; choosing wellness campaigns and, 11, 24, 27, 29, 44, 147; education and literacy fostering, 53–54; individual action and societal miseducation, 63–64, 66; literacy and self-writing for, 25, 181n14

Baby Suggs (fictional character), 20
Badu, Erykah, 166
Baker, Houston A., 172n19
Bambara, Toni Cade, 19, 29, 43–44, 64, 71–72, 146
Banks, Adam, 9, 10, 38–39
Basketball Wives (TV show), 48
Bastard Out of Carolina (Allison), 156–157
Bawarshi, Anis, 32, 41
behavior policing, 35, 38
"Be Healed: A Black Woman's Sermon on Healing through Touch" (Stubbs), 98
Being Mary Jane (TV show), 167
Beloved (Morrison), 19–20
Bernal, Martin, 56
BET Networks, 166–167
biblical scriptures: connecting to audiences, tool for, 67–68, 94–95,

INDEX 197

110; as justification for slavery, 88–89; as restriction for women's roles, 88–91

bibliotherapy and reading cures, 3–4, 9, 21, 152

Birth of a Nation (film), 21

Bitzer, Lloyd, 98

"Black Academic Woman's Self-Care Manifesto, A" (Williams), 165

Black church: as collective community, 84; communalistic and privatistic orientations of, 85–86; community literacy and identity, focus on, 84–85; cultural and social influence of, 36, 38–39, 83–86, 110; feminist and womanist scholarship on, 86, 87–88; function of, history of changes in, 81–86; homosexuality, negative views on, 39, 97, 177n51; patriarchal emphasis in, 80–81, 87–91, 96–98; publications by preachers, rise in, 83; religious realignment, concept of, 82–83, 102, 110; sermons, change from "Christocentric" to "me-centric," 83–86; sexism in, 80–81, 89–91; women's subordinated roles in, 76, 87–91

"Black Church Is Dead, The" (Glaude), 81

Black Feminist Politics from Kennedy to Obama (Harris), 25

"Black Feminist Statement, A" (Combahee River Collective), 44

Black feminist thought. *See also* Black Women's Literary Renaissance; feminist movements and literacies: Black women's *vs.* community's needs, 65–66; dissemblance, concept of, 38–39; habitus, concept of, 4–5, 169n5; intersectionality, 151; male power *vs.*, literacies on, 58–61; on oppression, 44–45, 72–73; on pain, redressing, 147; social change and, 43–45, 44–45, 147

Black Feminist Thought: Knowledge, Consciousness, and the Politics of Empowerment (Collins), 17, 44

Black liberation movements, 15, 32, 43, 53–57, 90–91

Black Liberation Theology, 90

Black literacies, forms of. *See* literacy

Black Lives Matter movement, 150, 181n11

Black Macho and the Myth of Superwoman (Wallace), 21

Blackman's Guide to Understanding the Blackwoman (Ali), 58–61

Black Megachurch: Theology, Gender, and the Politics of Public Engagement, The (Tucker-Worgs), 89

Black men: anti-male discourses in literary renaissance, 21–22, 25–26, 29; Black church, patriarchal emphasis in, 80–81, 87–91, 96–98; "Black pain," experience of, 22–23, 170n26; encoded gender responsibility messages and, 149–150; fathers, family roles of, 98–101, 121, 123, 144–145; gendered messages on responsibility for, 149–150; "good" Christian men, images of, 139–140; Harvey on understanding men, 143–147, 152; male power, criticism of literacies on, 59–61; men's views, societal emphasis on, 147; men's *vs.* women's affirmation, 139–140; as normative center in Black churches, 96–97

Black pain, concept of, 22–23, 170n26

Black Pain: It Just Looks Like We're Not Hurting (Williams), 138

Black Pearls: Daily Meditations, Affirmations, and Inspirations for African-Americans (Copage), 50

Black preaching, 4, 13, 79, 82–86, 88, 90, 96, 97, 100

Black Pride movements, 56–57

Black Public Sphere: A Public Culture Book, The (Baker, Alexander and Dawson), 172n19

Black Public Sphere Collective, 36, 38, 172n19

"Black Rhetorical Condition," 6, 34, 42

Black Urban Theatre, 116–118

Black vernacular culture and spaces, 32, 33–36, 38; Black Urban Theatre, 116–118; hush harbors, 37, 84

Black Woman: An Anthology, The (Bambara), 15, 43, 64, 71–72
"Black Woman as Woman, The" (Lindsey), 43
Black womanhood: "Black pain" and, 22–23; cult of true womanhood, 119; emotional expression, freedom of, 115; narrow conceptions of, 113, 126–130, 141–142, 152–153; self-knowledge and self-definition of, 22–26; universal womanhood, effect on, 43–44; white *vs.* Black women, construction of, 119
"Black Women and the Church" (Grant), 87
Black women's intellectual traditions: agency and intellectual resistance, 12, 53–57, 120; discourse as a learning cure, 29–30; essay writing as a call to action, 26–27, 41; voice as a resource, 22–24; wellness campaigns, rise due to, 5, 29, 115, 120; womanish, concept of, 25–26, 171n35
Black Women's Literary Renaissance: anti-male and anti-family discourses in, 21–22, 25–26, 29, 126; audience construction in, 22; "Black pain," narratives on, 22–23, 170n26; criticisms of, 22, 26; discourse as a learning cure, 29–30; essay writing as call to action, 26–27, 41; intellectual resistance and agency, 12, 53–57, 120; positive images of Blacks *vs.* real experiences, 21–22; social impact of works in, 21, 29–30; voice as resource of, 22–24; wellness campaigns, rise of due to, 5, 29, 115, 120
Black Women's Wellness Day, 165, 182n1
Blessett, Algebra, 166
Bluest Eye, The (Morrison), 16, 51
Boogie Down Productions, 57
boundaries of Blackness, concept of, 36, 37
Bourdieu, Pierre, 5, 169n5
Boyz n the Hood, 125
Brandt, Deborah, 9, 40

Brooks-Tatum, Shanesha, 165
Brown, Kimberly Nicole, 16, 26, 29
Brown, Michael, 77
Browne, Kevin, 10
Burger, Thomas, 172n13
Burke, Kenneth, 95–96, 127, 174n36, 177n47
"But Enough About Me: What Does the Popularity of Memoirs Tell Us About Ourselves?" (Mendelsohn), 156
Bynum, Juanita, 81, 86
Byrne, Rhonda, 8

calls to action. *See* action taking
Campbell, Bebe Moore, 49
Campbell, Maia, 49–50
Cannon, Katie, 83, 90, 96–98
Carby, Hazel, 119
Carnegie, Andrew, 53
Celie (fictional character), 24–25, 29–30, 120–121, 125
character development: appropriation used for, 115–116; subjectivity in, 117–121
Check It While I Wreck It: Black Women, Hip-Hop Culture, and the Public Sphere (Pough), 38
"chitlin circuit" shows, 117–118
Christian, Barbara, 167, 182n4
Christianity. *See* biblical scriptures; Black church; Perry, curriculum of return; spirituality
Christianity Today, 81
Christ-like wisdom, concept of, 102
Church of God in Christ (COGIC), 89
Cintron, Ralph, 40
civil rights movements, 53, 57
Clarke, Cheryl, 26
Clarke, John Henrik, 56
classism, 7, 8, 21, 36
Cloud, Dana L., 7–8
codes of conduct: behavior policing and, 35, 38; male power, emphasis on, 58–61; public shaming of women's behavior, 68, 72–73; social struggles, addressing *vs.*, 21–22; spirituality and self-censure, 76; women's

INDEX

assertive behavior as cause for intervention, 130–131
collective groups: genre frameworks, examining to understand, 33–35; identities of, ensuring, 35–39; survival of, emphasis on, 31–39, 41–45, 66–67, 90–91, 140–141, 177n51
College of Life or Practical Self-Education: A Manual of Self-Improvement for the Colored Race (Northrop, Gay, and Penn), 55
Collins, Patricia Hill, 17, 24, 44, 52, 66–67, 75, 143
colorism, negative impact of, 70, 72, 157
Color Lines magazine, 146
Color Purple, The (Walker), 21–22, 24–26, 29–30, 121, 126
Combahee River Collective, 44
"Come Ye Disconsolate" (hymn), 78, 79
commercialization of healing, 5, 120–121, 147–148
Communion of Friendship: Literacy, Spiritual Practice, and Women in Recovery (Daniell), 29–30
community building, writing processes for, 104
community reputations, protection of, 35
Community Text Arises: A Literate Text and an African American Literacy Tradition (Moss), 85
Cone, James, 31, 90
Confusion by Any Other Name: Essays Exploring the Negative Impact of the Blackman's Guide to the Black Woman (Madhubuti), 59
conjurers, healing, 17–20
consciousness as Black feminist thought: critical consciousness, 52, 75–76, 96, 122–123, 134, 137, 157; duality of identity, Black women, 34; self-consciousness, 35, 38; womanist consciousness-raising processes, 17
consubstantial space, 41, 95, 174nn36–37
context in worldviews and interpretation, 33–35

Control and Consolation in American Culture and Politics: Rhetoric of Therapy (Cloud), 7–8
Cooper, Anna Julia, 50–51, 56
Copage, Eric V., 50
counterlinguistic strategies, 19, 34, 51
counterpublic spaces, 36–38, 84, 115, 118
counterstory, concept of, 20
Courageous (film), 79, 176n3
critical pedagogy: critical consciousness, 52, 75–76, 96, 122–123, 134, 137, 157; critical empathy, 160–162; critical thinking, need for, 148; critical thought, criteria for examining, 155–164; discomfort, classroom resistance to, 153, 155–161; listening pedagogically, 159–160, 182n21
"Critique of Vernacular Discourse, The" (Ono and Sloop), 11
crooked room metaphor, 67, 175n50
culture of lack, 12, 62, 64–65, 67, 89–90, 97, 121, 146–147, 149, 152
"Curative Domains: Women, Healing and History in Black Women's Narratives" (Vrettos), 17
Cushman, Ellen, 46

Daddy Loves His Girls (Jakes), 13, 81, 83, 91, 99–102, 106–107
Daddy's Little Girls (film), 123
Daniell, Beth, 29, 52, 72
David (biblical character), 106, 178n74
Davis, Angela, 22
Dawson, Michael C., 172n19
determination: self-determination and individual accountability, 67–68; self-education and, 54
diaries. *See also* writing: journal writing, 1, 70–73, 113, 126; memoirs as learning cures, 27–28, 154–155; as narrative tool, 116, 120–122, 125–128, 132, 136, 151
Diary of a Mad Black Woman (film), 116, 120–122, 125, 128, 132, 136, 151
Digital Griots: African American Rhetorics in a Multimedia Age (Banks), 38–39

Diop, Cheikh Anta, 56
discomfort, classroom resistance to, 153, 155–161
discourse communities, 5, 30, 37
disidentification, concept of, 22, 60–61
dissemblance, concept of, 38–39
distancing techniques, 95–96, 98
Dolby, Sandra, 54, 56, 62, 89–90, 93, 97
Dollar, Creflo, 81
Don't Make a Black Woman Take Off Her Earrings: Madea's Uninhibited Commentaries on Love and Life (Perry), 115, 123
double consciousness, concept of, 34
Du Bois, W. E. B., 34, 56
DuVernay, Ava, 119–120

education. *See also* self-education: afrocentricity, concept of, 56; critical thinking and, 148; critical thought, criteria for examining, 155–164; importance of, 27, 153, 154, 157, 159, 161–163; "knowledge is power" adage, 12, 54; learning as liberation from pain, 32; literacy education, historical importance of, 53–54; miseducation *vs.*, 61–69, 76–77; rhetorical education, 5, 6, 9, 55, 77, 88, 148, 164; societal benefits of, 181n13
Education of Blacks in the South, 1860–1935, The (Anderson), 53
Elise, Kimberly, 79–80
Elliot, George, 156
empathy, critical development of, 160–162
empowerment. *See also* agency; resistance, acts of: critical consciousness for, 52, 75–76, 96, 122–123, 134, 137, 157; learning cures for, 27–28; self-discovery and, 15–17; self-knowledge and depictions of, 22–26; subjectivity in assessing, 46
Enoch, Jessica, 147, 181n8
epistolary novels, 24–25, 99
essay writing: as call to action and resistance, 26–27, 41; intellectualism and expression in, 26–28; as self-empowerment, 17
Essence magazine, 37, 50, 59–61, 144–146
"Everyday Use" (Walker), 146
"Eye to Eye: Black Women, Hatred, and Anger" (Lorde), 27, 28

Facing the Giants (film), 79, 176n3
faith. *See* Black church; spirituality
family, emphasis on, 113, 115–118, 121–124, 140–141
family relationships. *See also* mothers: ambition and opportunity, emphasis on *vs.*, 112–113, 123–124; anti-male and anti-family discourses in, 21–22, 25–26, 29, 126; divorce and, 103; fathers, family roles of, 98–101, 121, 123, 144–145; marriage, 16, 105–109, 116, 124–132, 136–144; restoration of centrality of, emphasis on, 132–136; self-knowledge and healing in, 24–26
Family That Preys, The (film), 123–124, 141
fathers: family roles of, 98–101, 121, 123, 144–145; father-daughter relationships, 98–101, 121
Fearless Confessions: A Writer's Guide to Memoir (Silverman), 155, 160–161
feminist movements and literacies: on Black church, 86; Black feminist thought and social change, 43–45, 44–45, 147; conscientiousness-raising in, 55–56; on racism and sexism, 21, 44–45; universal womanhood, problems with, 43–44
Feminist Wire, The, 165
Fern, Fanny, 156
Fighting Words: Black Women and the Quest for Social Justice (Collins), 66
"Fighting Words" (Vanzant), 59–62
film. *See also* Perry, Tyler: "bitter Black woman" and relationships in, 127; Black people, representations in, 113–115, 125; perceptions of reality, as tool for, 119; persuasive and instructional power of, 114–115

INDEX

Fireproof (film), 79, 176n3
Five East, 50, 66
Fix My Life (TV show). *See Iyanla: Fix My Life* (TV show)
For Colored Girls Who Have Considered Suicide When the Rainbow is Enuf (Shange), 12, 21, 23–24, 26
forgiveness: distancing from past and, 103, 110; in families as healing, 133; internal disease and unforgiveness, 73–75; survival and, 68–69; transformation and, 81–82; unforgiveness *vs.*, 74; wellness by forgiving, 39–40, 125, 137, 140–141, 178n1
"Forgiveness Diet" writing exercises, 74
Frankie (fictional character), 116, 139
Franklin, Benjamin, 53
Fraser, Nancy, 36
Frazier, E. Franklin, 84
Freedmen's Bureau, 88
freedom, literacy as form of, 25
Freedom Writing: African American Civil Rights Activism, 1995–1967 (Lathan), 151–152

Game, The (TV show), 166
Gates, Bill, 53
Gause, Louisa, 53–54
Gee, James Paul, 40
gendered oppression: as barrier to wellness, 23; historical roles in Black churches, 88
Gendered Pulpit, Preaching in American Protestant Spaces, The (Mountford), 88
"Genre as Social Action" (Miller), 33
genre frameworks for rhetorical actions, 33–35
Gere, Ann Ruggles, 145, 180n6
Giddings, Paula, 176n24
Gilyard, Keith, 10, 12–13, 19, 20, 51, 76
Giroux, Henry, 114
Glaude, Eddie, 81, 83, 84
Goltz, Dustin Bradley, 10
Gornick, Vivian, 155–156, 160–161, 181n18
gospel literacies, 151–152

gospel music, 6, 34
gospel stage plays, 80, 113, 116–118
Grant, Jacqueline, 82, 87–88
gritball, 133–134, 135
Gross, Terry, 114

Habermas, Jürgen, 36, 172n13
habitus, concept of, 4–5, 169n5
Hall, Mark, 9
Hamlin, Larry, 116–118
happiness, promises of, 8
Harlem Renaissance, 117
Harper, Frances Ellen Watkins, 43
Harper, Hill, 12, 144
Harper Collins, 143
Harris, Duchess, 25
Harris, E. Lynn, 177n51
Harris-Perry, Melissa, 67, 175n50
Harvey, Marjorie, 144
Harvey, Steve, 143–147, 152
healers, traditional, 17–20
healing and wellness campaigns. *See also* Jakes, curriculum of transformation; Perry, curriculum of return; teaching models for healing; Vanzant, curriculum of revision: audiences of, assumptions about, 151–152; Black church, influence of, 36; Black feminist thought and social change, 44–45; Black women as subjects *vs.* agents of, 46–47; commercialization and commodification of, 5, 120–121, 147–148; conferences for, growth of, 165–166; contemporary projects in, growth of, 165–168; healing, subjectivity of, 46; literacy and writing, therapeutic aspects of, 3–4, 7–9, 21, 71–73, 113, 152; normalcy, concept of in, 7–8; public confessions for, 3; templates for construction and tracking of, 149–151; usefulness of, need for research on, 151–153
heartbreak, portrayals of, 116, 124–132, 136–140
Heath, Shirley Brice, 40
Henry, Velma (fictional character), 16
Higginbotham, Evelyn Brooks, 84, 87
Hill, Lauryn, 63–64

hip-hop music, 57, 63
historical memory and healing, 19–20
Holloway, Karla, 129–130
Holmes, David, 10
home place, emphasis on, 113, 115–118, 121–124, 140–141
homogenization, concept of, 51–52, 75, 150–151
homosexuality: bibliotherapy in LGBT communities, 152; in Black church, negative views on, 39, 97, 177n51; lesbianism, narratives on, 25–26, 119, 120–121
hooks, bell, 7, 16, 17, 52, 74–75, 122, 126, 134, 157
Howard-Pitney, David, 63
How Not to Eat Pork, or Life Without the Pig (Ali), 58
How Stella Got Her Groove Back (film), 120, 128
Huffington Post, 48
Human Condition, The (Arendt), 172n13
humanity, assumptions on, 150, 181n11
Hurston, Zora Neale, 18, 20
hush harbor spaces, 37, 84

I Can Do Bad All by Myself (film), 113
identification: Black identity and collective survival, 31; homogenization and audience identification, 51–52, 75, 150–151; infirmity as form of, 110–111; self-identification and worldview, 34
I Know I've Been Changed (play), 113
Illouz, Eva, 4–5, 9
individualism: resilience and independence, 136–138; self-discovery, importance of, 15–16; self-education and, 54–55; sermons, change from "Christocentric to "me-centric," 83–86; social self, concept of, 54–55, 61–62, 89–90
"I Need You to Survive" (song), 33
inferiority, feelings of, 27–28
infidelity, 16, 112, 124–125, 127, 141–142
"infirm woman," concept of, 93–98
innovation, as rhetorical competence, 46

In Search of Our Mother's Gardens: Womanist Essays and Prose (Walker), 171n36
inspirational literature, 131–132
intellectualism: agency and intellectual resistance, 12, 53–57, 120; Black feminist thought and social change, 21–22, 44–45; language and expression in essays, 26–28; men's views, emphasis on, 147; social self, concept of, 54–55, 61–62, 89–90
Interiors: A Black Woman's Healing in Progress (Vanzant), 13, 50, 52, 55, 67–70
interpretation, effect of worldviews on, 33–35
In the House (TV show), 49
In the Meantime: Finding Yourself and the Love You Want (Vanzant), 52
In the Spirit (Taylor), 50
introspection, 70–73
invention, writers, 32, 33, 35–39
I Say a Little Prayer (Harris), 177n51
isolation syndrome, concept of, 107–109
"It's Bigger than Comp/Rhet: Contested and Undisciplined" (Pough), 148
I Will Follow (film), 119
Iyanla: Fix My Life (TV show), 13, 48–50, 66, 71, 73, 77
Izrael, Jimi, 144

Jackson, Jesse, 57–58
Jackson, Ronald L., 10
Jakes, curriculum of transformation: abuse and trauma, intervention for, 85–86; audience construction, context mandates in, 93–94, 104; biblical scriptures for audience construction, 94–95, 110; Black church, changes in and works of, 81–86, 91; communalistic and privatistic orientations of, 85–86; crisis-driven themes, emphasis on, 92–93; derogatory images and stereotypes, portrayal of, 96–97, 114, 119, 172n19; distancing techniques and language used by, 95–96, 98; on enemy's plan, rejecting, 103–105;

INDEX 203

father-daughter relationships and spirituality, 98–101; forgiveness, emphasis on, 103, 110; function of, Jakes on changes in, 81–82; gendered constructions in, 103–109, 113–114, 116; infirmity, transformation as cure for, 93–98, 110–111; instructional approach to, 101–102; media franchise of, 79–80; ministry-based media franchise of, 79–81; pain, women's behavior as cause of, 105–109; personal testimonies as teaching tools, 125; relationship interventions in writings of, 101; religious realignment, application of, 82–83, 102, 110; renewing the mind, 94, 102–105; self-esteem, compassion and acceptance for, 98–101; sentimentalizing discourse, use of, 105–107; sexism in Black church, 81; sexual abuse victims, influence of, 91–92; "sin-sickness," emphasis on, 96–97; spirituality and relationships with God, 105–106; Sunday School curriculum of, 82–83, 92–94, 102; touch, written forms of, 98, 100; transformation as curriculum, 101–109; women's relationships as object to heal, 98–101
Jakes, Serita, 81
Jakes, T.D.: *Daddy Loves His Girls,* 13, 81, 83, 91, 99–102, 106–107; *Lady, Her Lover, and Her Lord, The,* 101; popularity and success of, 81–83; *Sacred Love Songs,* 101; *Woman Thou Art Loosed: Healing the Wounds of the Past* (Jakes), 80–81, 91–94, 97, 102, 105; *Woman Thou Art Loosed!* (film), 78–82, 109–110; *Women Thou Art Loosed: On the 7th Day,* 81
James, Joy, 45
Jarrett, Vernon, 21
jeremiad, 63, 122, 179, 199
Johnson, Chad Ochocinco, 48
Johnson, Lutie (fictional character), 22–23, 24
Johnson, Nan, 10–11
Jones, Noel, 81

Jordan, June, 22, 67, 174n49
journal writing, 1, 70–73, 113, 126
Judith (fictional character), 112, 142

Keepin' It Hushed: The Barbershop and African American Hush Harbor Rhetoric (Nunley), 37
King, Debra Walker, 22, 23, 170n26
King, Jamilah, 146
Kingston, Maxine Hong, 153
Kynard, Carmen, 10

Lady, Her Lover, and Her Lord, The (Jakes), 101
Lanehart, Sonja, 151, 181n14
language and expression: affirmation language, 74; alteration and articulation for self-concept, 73–75; Black vernacular culture and spaces, 32, 33–36, 38; counterlinguistic strategies, 19, 34, 51; critical empathy and discomfort, 160–162; disidentification, concept of, 22, 60–61; intellectualism in essay writing, 26–28; multicultural approaches to literacy, 40; nomenclature and perceptions of reality, 177n47; restorative agency and language, 19–20; talking cures, 3, 4, 9
Language as Symbolic Action (Burke), 177n47
"Latent Rapists" (Shange), 23
Lathan, Rhea Estelle, 10, 151–152
Laveau, Marie, 18
learning cures: Black women's discourse as, 29–30; for empowerment, 27–28; self-hatred, reeducation for self-love, 26–28; Winfrey's emphasis on, 146
Lee, Jarena, 88
Lee, Shayne, 82
"Legacy of Healing: Words, African Americans, and Power, A" (Gilyard), 12, 19
lesbianism, 25–26, 119, 120–121
"Lesbianism as an Act of Resistance" (Clarke), 26
Lessons in Living (Taylor), 50

Let Nobody Turn Us Around (Marable and Mullings), 33
Letters to a Young Sister: DeFINE Your Destiny (Harper), 12, 144
Liberating Language: Sites of Rhetorical Education in Nineteenth Century Black America (Logan), 6
Lifeclass. See Oprah's Lifeclass (TV show)
Lincoln, Abbey, 64–65
Lincoln, C. Eric, 85
Lindsey, Kay, 43
Lisa (fictional character), 116, 131, 133–136, 138–139
listening pedagogically, 159–160, 182n21
"Litany For Survival: Black Queer Literacies, A" (Pritchard), 174n34
literacy: Black literacies, forms of, 42, 174n34; community-forming function of, 30; cultural mandates and protection of, 40, 174n34; discourse communities, 5, 30, 37; essay writing, 17, 26–28, 41; as freedom and empowerment, 25; gospel literacies, 151–152; journal writing, 1, 70–73, 113, 126; literacy sponsors, concept of, 9; motives and decision making, integrating, 160–163; multicultural approaches to, 40; narrow concepts of, mainstream society, 39–40; reading, civic nature of, 10–11; rhetorical listening, concept of, 159–160, 182n21; for self-examination and interpretation, 70–73, 104; social turn, concept of, 40; societal benefits of, 181n13; as sociopolitical action, 40–43; therapeutic aspects of, 3–4, 7–9, 21, 71–73, 113, 152; transformative aspects of books and healing, 16–17
literary renaissance. *See* Black Women's Literary Renaissance
Locke, Alain, 117
Lofton, Kathryn, 3–4
Logan, Shirley Wilson, 6, 9–10, 55, 75, 77
Long, Eddie, 81

Lorde, Audre, 27–28, 77, 146, 153, 176n30
Love and Basketball (film), 120
Love and Hip Hop (TV show), 48
Lozada, Evelyn, 48, 71
Lyle, Timothy, 113–114
Lyons, Julie, 80–81

Mack, Tasha, 166
Madea's Family Reunion (film), 14, 116, 121, 133, 135, 139–141, 168
Madhubuti, Haki R., 59
Mama Day (fictional character), 19
Mama Day (Naylor), 19
Mamiya, Lawrence H., 85
Manpower conventions, 79
Mao, LuMing, 10
Marable, Manning, 33, 36, 37
marriage. *See also* family relationships: "crisis" of Black women's marriageability, 144; heartbreak, portrayals of, 116, 124–132, 136–140; infidelity, 16, 112, 127, 141–142; women's relationships as object to heal, 105–109, 124–125, 140
Marshall, Paule, 16
Martin, Trayvon, 181n11
McCarter, Helen (fictional character), 116, 124–132, 136–140
McGee, Micki, 52, 53, 74–75, 104
McMillan, Terry, 1, 120, 128
Meet the Browns (film), 113
Megafest conventions, 79, 110
memoirs as learning cures, 27–28, 154–155. *See also* writing
men. *See* Black men
Menace II Society, 125
Mendelsohn, Daniel, 156
metaphysical dilemma, concept of, 162
Michelle (fictional character), 79–80, 109–110
Middle of Nowhere (film), 119
Miller, Carolyn, 33
Miller, Thomas, 5, 29
mind cures, 3, 4, 9
miseducation: revision, overcoming with, 61–69, 76–77; social progress,

INDEX   205

Black women as hurting, 66–67; sociopolitical history of, 63
"Miseducation of Lauryn Hill, The" (musical album), 63
Mis-Education of the Negro, The (Woodson), 63
Mismeasure of Woman, The (Tavris), 7
modulation, concept of, 155–157, 162–163. *See also* rhetorical criticism concepts
Morrison, Toni, 16, 19–20, 51, 170n19
Moss, Beverly J., 10, 40, 85, 93, 95, 104, 111
mothers: family and home place, emphasis on, 113, 115–118, 121–124, 140–141; family healing as responsibility of/, 116, 118, 121–124; generational wisdom gained from, 27–28, 154; mother-daughter relationships, 98–101; patriarchal representation of in film, 113, 133–136; representations of Black mothers, 66, 90, 119, 123, 136, 179n27; as welfare mothers, disparaging images of, 66, 90, 119, 123, 136, 179n27
Mountford, Roxanne, 88
Moynihan, Daniel Patrick, 123, 136, 179n27
Mules and Men (Hurston), 18
Mullings, Leith, 33, 36, 37
music: Black music traditions, misconceptions of, 31; gospel music, 6, 34; healing themes in contemporary songs, 166; on miseducation, overcoming, 63–64; *Sacred Love Songs* (Jakes), 101; Stop the Violence Movement, 57
Myrtle (fictional character), 121–123, 132, 136–137, 140–141

National Association of Colored Women, 176n24
National Baptist Convention, 89
National Black Theatre Festival, 116–117
National Black Women's Life Balance and Wellness Conference, 165

National Public Radio (NPR), 114, 144
nation within a nation, concept of, 84–85, 87
Naylor, Gloria, 19
Neal, Mark Anthony, 177n51
neo-soul music, 166
New Black Man (Neal), 177n51
New Orleans, 18
Nightline (TV show), 144
Niles, Lyndrey, 100
No More Sheets: The Truth About Sex (Bynum), 86
Nunley, Vorris, 10, 37

Ofori-Atta, Akoto, 175n66
Ono, Kent, 10–11
On the Real Side: Laughing, Lying and Signifying—the Underground Tradition of African-American Humor that Transformed American Culture, from Slavery to Richard Prior (Watkins), 117
oppositional knowledges, 17, 24, 28, 29, 75, 104, 146. *See also* Black women's intellectual traditions; literacy
oppression: Black feminist thought on, 44–45, 72–73; gendered oppression, 23, 88; racialized oppression as barrier to wellness, 23; silencing of women's pain, 38–39, 137–138; trauma caused by, 18–19
"Oprahfication of Literacy, The" (Hall), 9
Oprah's Lifeclass (TV show), 1–5, 7, 39, 110
Oprah Winfrey and the Glamour of Misery (Illouz), 4
Oprah Winfrey Show, The, 5, 8–9, 39–40, 113, 144, 145
oral folk culture genres, 93
Orlando (fictional character), 116, 126, 128–130, 139–140
OWN (the Oprah Winfrey Network), 1, 2, 48, 71, 77, 145

pain, Black women's: "Black pain," experience of, 22–23, 170n26; commercialization and

pain, Black women's: (*continued*) commodification of, 5, 120–121, 147–148; mainstream media, emphasis on, 1–7, 15–16, 166–168; self-knowledge and healing, 22–26; wounding and pain, naming forms of, 15–17
Pariah (film), 119
Paul, Mary Jane (fictional character), 167
Paul D (fictional character), 19–20
Peck, Janice, 3, 8, 169n3
Pennebaker, James, 72
Perry, curriculum of return: angry Black women, perpetuation of images of, 125–128; appropriation, use of, 115–116, 120–121, 124–127; bitter Black women, need for healing, 127–131; Black Urban Theatre and, 116–118; Black womanhood, narrow conception of, 113, 126–130, 141–142, 152–153; character development, subjectivity in, 117–121; collective survival, affirmative messages of, 140–141; criticism of, 113–114; faith, restoring centrality of, 131–132; family, restoring centrality of, 121–124, 132–136; forgiveness and restoration, emphasis on, 125, 178n1; gendered constructions in films of, 113–114, 116; home place, emphasis on, 113, 115–118, 121–124, 140–141; journaling, 113, 126; moral messages in films of, 113, 125; opportunity and ambition as harmful, 112–113, 123–124; patriarchal family representations, 133–135, 137, 139; persuasive and instructional power of, 114–115; popularity and success of, 113, 116, 119, 120; positive opportunities, recognizing and seizing, 138–140; racial implications in gospel plays of, 116–118; resilience, resolving to exercise, 136–138; therapeutic goals in films of, 114; women's assertive behavior as cause for intervention, 130–131; women's relationships as object to heal, 105–109, 124–125, 140
Perry, Tyler: *Daddy's Little Girls* (film), 123; *Diary of a Mad Black Woman* (film), 116, 120–122, 125, 128, 132, 136, 151; *Don't Make A Black Woman Take Off Her Earrings*, 115, 123; *Family That Preys, The* (film), 123–124, 141; *I Can Do Bad All by Myself* (film), 113; *I Know I've Been Changed* (play), 113; *Madea's Family Reunion*, 14, 116, 121, 133, 135, 139–141, 168; *Meet the Browns* (film), 113; *Temptation: Confessions of a Marriage Counselor*, 112–113, 142; *Why Did I Get Married?* (Perry), 118
Perryman-Clark, Staci, 10
personal testimonies, 61–62, 65, 67–68, 86, 95, 125
Petry, Ann, 22–23, 24
Peyton-Caire, Lisa, 165
PHD to Ph.D.: How Education Saved My Life (Richardson), 27, 153, 154, 157, 159, 161–163
Pinckney, Darryl, 22, 25, 29
plays and theatre, 116–118
"Poem about My Rights" (Jordan), 67, 174n49
poetry, 21, 23, 26–27, 67, 137, 174n49
police violence, 77, 181n11
positive opportunities, recognizing and seizing, 138–140
positive thinking, emphasis on, 3, 8
post-civil-war-conduct books, 9–10
Pough, Gwendolyn, 10, 37, 38, 148, 153, 164, 172n19
Powell, Malea, 10
Praisesong for the Widow (Marshall), 16
preachers. See Black church; Jakes, T.D.
Pritchard, Eric Darnell, 10, 152, 174n34
privilege: multicultural teaching methods, need for, 150–151; social change, effect of, 46
"promise of happiness," concept of, 8
public confessions for healing, 3
Public Enemy (musical band), 57
Publics and Counterpublics (Warner), 36
public sphere: Black theatre and themes of nation building, 118; Black

INDEX 207

women's poverty and, 67; concept of, 36–38, 172n13, 172n19; resistance strategies and, 38

queer communities. *See* homosexuality

"Race for Theory, The" (Christian), 156, 182n4
racism: homogenization and, 51–52; racialized oppression as barrier to wellness, 23; systematic racism and self-worth, 34–35; in women's liberation movement, 15
Rand, Erin, 10
Ransom, Minnie (fictional character), 15, 16, 19, 165
Ratcliffe, Krista, 159–160, 163, 182n21
R&B Divas (TV show), 49
reading cures, 3–4, 9, 21, 152
Real Housewives of Atlanta, The (TV show), 48
realignment, concept of, 82–83, 102, 110
reality-based TV series, 35, 48
Reckless Eyeballing (Reed), 22
Reconstructing Womanhood: The Emergence of the Afro-American Woman Novelist (Carby), 119
Recovery (musical album), 166
re-creation, process of, 33–35
Reed, Ishmael, 22
reeducation and relearning: self-hatred to self-love, 26–28; social change and, 56–57
Rees, Dee, 119–120
Reggie (fictional character), 79, 109
Reid, Jacque, 144
reinvention, emphasis on, 12, 53–57, 82. *See also* Jakes, curriculum of transformation
relanguaging strategies, 19, 34, 51
relationships. *See also* family relationships; mothers: heartbreak, portrayals of, 116, 124–132, 136–140; positive opportunities, recognizing and seizing, 138–140; women's relationships as object to heal, 98–101

religion. *See* biblical scriptures; Black church; spirituality
religious institutions, establishment of, 35–36
religious realignment, concept of, 82–83, 102, 110
representations of Black men, 21–22, 25–26, 29, 126
representations of Black women: as angry Black women, 125–128; as gold-diggers, 114–115, 141; harmful effect of, 90–91; as Jezebels, 114–115, 119; as mammies, 114–115, 119; as Sapphires, 90, 119; as welfare mothers, 66, 90, 119, 123, 136, 179n27
resilience: Black women's resilience and silencing pain, 137–138; self-determination, 67–68; self-education and, 54
resistance, acts of: African American vernacular culture and need for, 34–35; asserting authority, challenge of, 65–66; Black feminist thought and social change, 43–45; essay writing as, 26–27; expressive agency during slavery, 19–20; healing as, 40–43; healing conjurers as resource for, 18–19; intellectual resistance and agency, 12, 53–57, 120; literacy as sociopolitical action, 40–43; public sphere, concept of, 36–38, 172n13, 172n19; self-education and self-improvement for, 53–57
return, curriculum of. *See* Perry, curriculum of return
revision. *See* Vanzant, healing curriculum of revision
rhetoric. *See also* African American rhetorical traditions: disidentification, concept of, 22, 60–61; distancing techniques, 95–96, 98; ethos, 9, 37, 61, 64, 65, 68, 86, 95, 125, 126, 162, 174n37; "Genre as Social Action" (Miller), 33; personal testimonies, 61–62, 65, 67–68, 86, 95, 125

"Rhetorical Characteristics of Traditional Black Preaching" (Niles), 100
rhetorical criticism concepts: genre frameworks for rhetorical actions, 33–35; rhetorical competence, 41, 46, 161; rhetorical consequences, 46–47, 75, 127
rhetorical education: critical thinking and, 148; critical thought, criteria for examining, 155–164; defined, 147, 181n8; independent rhetorical education, 88; literacy campaigns and, 5, 6, 77; nineteenth-century African American literacies, 55; positive social change and, 164; talking cures and, 9
rhetorical listening, concept of, 159–160, 182n21
Rhetorical Listening (Ratcliffe), 159–160, 182n21
rhetorical tropes: biblical scriptures for connecting to audiences, 67–68, 94–95, 110; diary writing as narrative tool, 116, 120–122, 125–128, 132, 136, 151; "infirm woman," concept of, 93–98; miseducation, 61–69, 76–77
Rhetoric of Motives, A (Burke), 174n36
Rhodes, Jacqueline, 150
Rich, Adrienne, 156
Richardson, Elaine, 6, 10, 28, 34–35, 40, 42–43, 52, 76–77, 81, 134, 153–154, 157–164
Room of One's Own, A (Woolf), 156
Rowland, Michael, 57
Royster, Jacqueline Jones, 6, 10, 26–27, 40–42, 47, 60, 61, 94, 162, 174n37
Russ, Joanna, 156

sacred and secular spaces, 34, 35
Sacred Love Songs (musical project), 101
Salt Eaters, The (Bambara), 15, 16–17, 29
Sassafrass, Cypress and Indigo (Shange), 16
Save Our Sons (TV show), 149
Scarry, Elaine, 22, 170n26
Seattle Times, 59
Secret, The (Byrne), 8

self-actualization, 56, 121
self-affirmation exercises, 74–75
self-censure, spirituality and, 76
self-consciousness, 35, 38
self-deliberation, 75
"Self-Destruction" (Stop the Violence Movement), 57
self-determination, 67–68
self-education: empowerment and, 9–10, 154–155; intellectual resistance and reinvention, 12, 53–57; social self, concept of, 54–55, 61–62, 89–90
self-empowerment. *See* empowerment
self-empowerment literature, 52, 81. *See also* Vanzant, Iyanla
self-esteem: infirmity, effect of idea of, 98–101; internal shame, overcoming, 25, 27–28, 84, 98–101; protection of, need for, 27–28, 155; self-hatred, reeducation for self-love, 26–28; systematic racism and self-worth, 34–35
self-examination: Afrafemme worldview, 15–16, 44; interpreting the past and healing, 70–73; literacy and writing, therapeutic aspects of, 71–73, 104; for reflection and self-improvement, 44, 48–50, 70–73, 104; self-discovery, importance of, 15–16
self-hatred, reeducation for self-love, 26–28
Self-Help Books: Why Americans Keep Reading Them (Dolby), 54
self-help genre: Afrocentric philosophies and education, 56–57; commercialization and commodification in, 5; forgiveness as healing in, 137; gendered dynamics of, 57; improvement and change as goals of, 48–50, 55–56; invention and reinvention, emphasis on, 12, 53–54; mainstream society, goals of conforming to, 55–56; *Oprah's Lifeclass* and, 1–5, 7, 39, 110; oral folk culture *vs.*, 93; popularity of, 53; reeducation themes in, 77; therapeutic aspects of, 3–4, 7–9, 21, 71–73, 113, 152

INDEX 209

Self-Help Inc.: Makeover Culture in America (McGee), 53
self-improvement: "do the work," emphasis on, 13, 16, 49–50, 52, 70; literacy and writing, therapeutic aspects of, 3–4, 9, 104; self-knowledge and self-examination for, 48–50; writing processes and, 104
self-invention, concept of, 53
self-knowledge: importance of acquiring, 11; oppositional knowledges, 17, 24, 28, 29, 75, 104, 146; positive opportunities, recognizing and seizing, 138–140
self-realization, 120–121, 125
self-writing. *See* writing
sensus communis, concept of, 37
sermons as genre, 38–39, 86
Sethe (fictional character), 19–20, 170n19
Set It Off (film), 120
sexism: Black church, patriarchal emphasis in, 80–81, 87–91, 96–98; in Black church, 80–81, 89–91; in Black communities, 21; in Black liberation movements, 15, 90–91; homogenization and, 51–52; male power, literacies on, 58–61; pain, women's behavior as cause of, 105–109
Shadowboxing: Representations of Black Feminist Politics (James), 45
shame, feelings of: discomfort, classroom resistance to, 159–160; internal shame and self-esteem, overcoming, 25, 27–28, 84, 98–101; public shaming and blame, 68, 72–73; self-consciousness and, 35, 38; self-definition and, 24; Sunday School curriculum and transformation, 92–94
Shange, Ntozake, 5, 12, 16, 21–24, 27, 30, 162
Sherpherd, Sherri, 144
Sherwood Baptist Church, 176n3
Sherwood Pictures, 79, 176n3
Shug (fictional character), 25, 120–121
silencing of women's pain, 38–39, 137–138

silent mobility, concept of, 23
Silverman, Sue, 155, 160–161
Simmons, Martha, 82–83, 86
Sista, Speak!: Black Women Kinfolk Talk about Language and Literacy (Lanehart), 151, 181n14
Sister Citizen: Shame, Stereotypes, and Black Women in America (Harris-Perry), 67, 175n50
Sister Outsider (Lorde), 27
Sisters of the Yam: Black Women and Self-Recovery (hooks), 7, 16
situated ethos, concept of, 61, 174n37
Sixo (fictional character), 20
slavery: biblical scripture to justify, 88–89; brutality and repression, 19–20, 170n19; healing conjurers roles during, 17–18; literacy education, historical importance of, 53–54; self-education during and after, 9–10
Slave Songs of the United States (Allen), 31
Sloop, John, 10–11
Smitherman, Geneva, 10, 34
social change: Black women's healing as catalyst for, 46–47, 50–51; civil rights movements, 53, 57; codes of conduct, breaking for, 21–22; healing and wellness, scholarship of social function of, 7–14; literacy as action for healing, 40–43; rhetorics of healing as means for, 39–43; subjectivity in assessing, 46
social conditioning, 157–158
social imaginary, concept of, 114, 119, 172n19
social self, concept of, 54–55, 61–62, 89–90
social turn, concept of, 40
sociocognitive ability, 41
socioeconomic institutions, establishment of, 35–36
socioeconomic oppression: as barrier to wellness, 23; narratives of, 24–25; social struggles, blaming Black women for, 66–67, 90–91
Souls of Black Folk, The (Du Bois), 34
Souls of Black Girls, The (film), 157

spaces and spatiality. *See also* public sphere: Black church as community space, 38, 84–85; Black interior spaces, 37; Black Urban Theatre, 118; Black vernacular culture and spaces, 32, 33–36, 38; boundaries of Blackness, concept of, 36, 37; consubstantial space, 41, 95, 174nn36–37; counterpublic spaces, 36–38, 84, 115, 118; hush harbor spaces, 37, 84; interior Black world, 36–37; rhetorical dynamics of, 36–37; sacred and secular spaces, 34, 35
spatial politics, 34, 37, 44–45
Spelman wellness initiative, 165–166
Spielberg, Steven, 120
spiritual capitalism, concept of, 4
spirituality: African worldview and, 34; alteration and articulation in language and, 73–75; Christian influence on wellness campaigns, 38; Christ-like wisdom, concept of, 102; faith, restoring centrality of, 131–132; healing conjurers, 17–20; religious realignment, concept of, 82–83, 102, 110; sermons as genre, 38–39, 86; touch, written forms of, 98, 100; Yoruban spirituality, 61, 63
Spirituals and the Blues, The (Cone), 31
Springer, Kimberly, 113, 129
Stamp Paid (fictional character), 20
stereotypes. *See* representations of Black men; representations of Black women
Stewart, Maria W., 43, 89
Stop the Violence Movement, 57
Straight Talk, No Chaser: How to Find, Keep, and Understand a Man (Harvey), 145, 146
Street, Brian, 40
Street, The (Petry), 22–23
Structural Transformation of the Public Sphere (Habermas), 172n13
Stubbs, Monya Aletha, 98–100
subjectivity: in character development, 117–121; empowerment, assessing, 46; healing, term of, 46; in writing as racialized or gendered "other," 34

"Subversive Self-Care: Centering Black Women's Wellness" (Brooks-Tatum), 165
suffering as universal, 51–52, 75, 150–151
Suffering Will Not Be Televised: African American Women and Sentimental Political Storytelling, The (Wanzo), 51
suicide, 16
survival: Black women's accountability for, 66–67, 90–91; collective survival, emphasis on, 31–39, 41–45, 66–67, 90–91, 140–141, 177n51; forgiveness and, 68–69; healing conjurers during slavery, 17–18; individual self-preservation and, 43–45

Talkin and Testifyin: The Language of Black America (Smitherman), 34
talking cures, 3, 4, 9
talk shows. *See Iyanla: Fix My Life* (TV show); self-help genre; Winfrey, Oprah
Tamar (biblical character), 106, 178n74
Tapping the Power Within: A Path to Self-Empowerment for Women (Vanzant), 13, 52, 62–66, 70, 74, 76, 150
Tatum, Beverly, 165–166
Tavris, Carol, 7
Taylor, Susan, 50
T. D. Jakes: America's New Preacher (Lee), 82
teaching models for healing: critical empathy in, 160–162; critical thinking, need for, 148; on ideologies, vision and interrogation, use of, 151–153; literacies on pain, addressing discomfort about, 153, 155–159; social change and action, critical thinking on, 149–151; voice modulation and empathy, use of, 153–163
Temptation: Confessions of a Marriage Counselor (film), 112–113, 142
Terrell, Mary Church, 176n24
theatre and plays, 116–118

"Three Feminists Talk About the Media's Obsession with Unwed Black Women" (King), 146
Tims, Riva, 11–12
touch, written forms of, 98, 100
"To Whom Will She Cry Rape" (Lincoln), 64
Traces of a Stream: Literacy as Social Change Among African American Women (Royster), 6, 40, 46
transformation. *See* Jakes, curriculum of transformation
Trinity Broadcast Network, 79
Truth, Sojourner, 43, 147
Tucker-Worgs, Tamelyn, 89
Turner, John, 54–55
turning it out, concept of, 129–130
12 Years a Slave (film), 157
Two or Three Things I Know For Sure (Allison), 153, 156–157

unforgivness, concept of, 74
Up From Here: Reclaiming the Male Spirit (Vanzant), 74

Value in the Valley: A Black Woman's Guide Through Life's Dilemmas (Vanzant), 13, 48–49, 52, 76, 150
Van Biema, David, 99
Vanessa (fictional character), 116, 131, 133–136, 138–139
Vanzant, curriculum of revision: action and evolution for resuming life path, 76; Afrocentric philosophies and social change, 56–57; alteration and articulation for self-concept, 70, 73–75; critical consciousness, empowerment through, 52; critical vision of oppression, lack of, 72–73, 77; criticism of, 72–73, 77; culture of lack and injustice, addressing, 62–64; disidentification, use of, 22, 60–61; "do the work," emphasis on, 13, 16, 49–50, 52, 70; ethos and audience cultivation, 64–65; forgiveness and survival, 68–69; "Forgiveness Diet" writing exercises, 74; homogenization, use of, 51–52; internal disease and unforgiveness, 73–74; journal writing and voice, 70–73; male power, criticism of literacies on, 59–61; miseducation as call for healing, 61–69, 76–77; misinformation, crisis of, 57–61; narratives and textbooks as teaching action, 51–52; on pain, defining, 3–4; personal testimonies, use of, 61–62, 65, 67–68, 125; public shaming, criticism of, 73; reeducation to understand crisis, 51, 77; relanguaging strategies, 19, 34, 51; revision as essential, 69–70, 76–77; self-action, emphasis on, 67–69; self-affirmation, 74–75; self-education and intellectual resistance, 53–57; self-examination and interpretation, 48–50, 70–73, 104; self-knowledge and self-improvement, emphasis on, 48–50; social struggles, blaming Black women for, 50–51, 66–69; spirituality as self-empowerment, 62–63, 65, 94; teaching techniques, 13, 48–50, 104; vision as spiritual and social resource, 69, 71, 94
Vanzant, Iyanla: *Acts of Faith,* 61; "Fighting Words," 59–62; *Interiors,* 13, 50, 52, 55, 67–70; *Iyanla: Fix My Life,* 13, 48–50, 66, 71, 73, 77; *In the Meantime,* 52; personal life and background of, 2, 61–62; popularity of, 2–3, 150; *Tapping the Power Within,* 13, 52, 62–66, 70, 74, 76, 150; *Up From Here,* 74; *Value in the Valley,* 13, 48–49, 52, 76, 150
vernacular culture and spaces, 32, 33–36, 38
Villanueva, Victor, 10
voice: Black female protagonists in film, 119–120; in Black women's literary renaissance, 22–24; concept of, 161; diary form in films for, 125–126; diary writing for self-discovery, 25; journal writing for, 1, 70–73, 113, 126
voice of experience, 160–161
voice of innocence, concept of, 160

voodoo, 18
Vrettos, Athena, 17, 19
vulnerability as strength, 166

Waiting to Exhale (film), 120, 128
Walker, Alice, 5, 22, 24–26, 30, 120–121, 125–126, 146, 156, 171nn36–37
Wallace, Michelle, 21
Wanzo, Rebecca, 3, 51, 150
Warner, Michael, 36
Warner Brothers, 120
Watkins, Mel, 21–22, 117
Well, Ida B., 43
wellness campaigns. *See* healing and wellness campaigns
When and Where I Enter: The Impact of Black Women on Race and Sex in America (Giddings), 176n24
When It All Falls Apart: Finding Healing, Joy, and Victory through the Pain (Tims), 11–12
Why Did I Get Married? (Perry), 118
Wilentz, Gay, 18
Williams, Erica Lorraine, 165
Williams, Heather Andrea, 53–54
Williams, James (Chancellor Williams), 56
Williams, Terrie M., 138
Winfrey, Oprah: on *Color Purple, The* (Walker), 30; communication style of, 3–4; on forgiveness, 39–40; homogenization, use of, 51–52; learning cures, investment in, 146; *Oprah's Lifeclass* (TV show), 1–5, 7, 39, 110; *Oprah Winfrey Show, The*, 5, 8–9, 39–40, 113, 144, 145; OWN (the Oprah Winfrey Network), 1, 2, 48, 71, 77, 145; popularity and success of, 4; positive thinking, emphasis on, 3, 8; reading for self-improvement, 9
womanish, concept of, 25–26, 171n35
Woman Thou Art Loosed: Healing the Wounds of the Past (Jakes), 80–81, 91–94, 97, 102, 105

Woman Thou Art Loosed! (film), 78–82, 109–110
Woman Warrior (Kingston), 153
women's liberation movements, 15, 32, 53, 96, 176n30
Women Thou Art Loosed: On the 7th Day (Jakes), 81
Woodson, Carter G., 63
Woolf, Virginia, 156
worldviews: Afrafemme worldview, 15–16, 44; African worldview, 34; Black interior spaces and, 37; faith as tool to support, 131–132; interpretation influenced by, 33–35; privilege, effect on, 46
wounded self, concept of, 62, 89–90, 97, 125
"Writer's Block" (song), 166
writer's choice, concept of, 46–47
writer's task, concept of, 46, 162
writing: agency of writers, 46–47; community building, writing processes for, 104; journal writing, 1, 70–73, 113, 126; memoirs as learning cures, 27–28, 154–155; as narrative tool, 116, 120–122, 125–128, 132, 136, 151; as self-discovery, 113, 124–126; as self-empowerment, 17, 25; as self-improvement, 104; as social action, 26–27, 41; as therapy, 3–4, 7–9, 21, 71–73, 113, 152; writer's invention, 32, 33, 35–39
Writing the Black Revolutionary Diva: Women's Subjectivity and the Decolonizing Text (Brown), 171n37

X Clan (musical band), 57

Yoruban spirituality, 61, 63
Young, Courtney, 113
Young, Morris, 10

Zami: A New Spelling of My Name (Lorde), 153

Metropolitan College of NY
Library - 7th Floor
60 West Street
New York, NY 10006